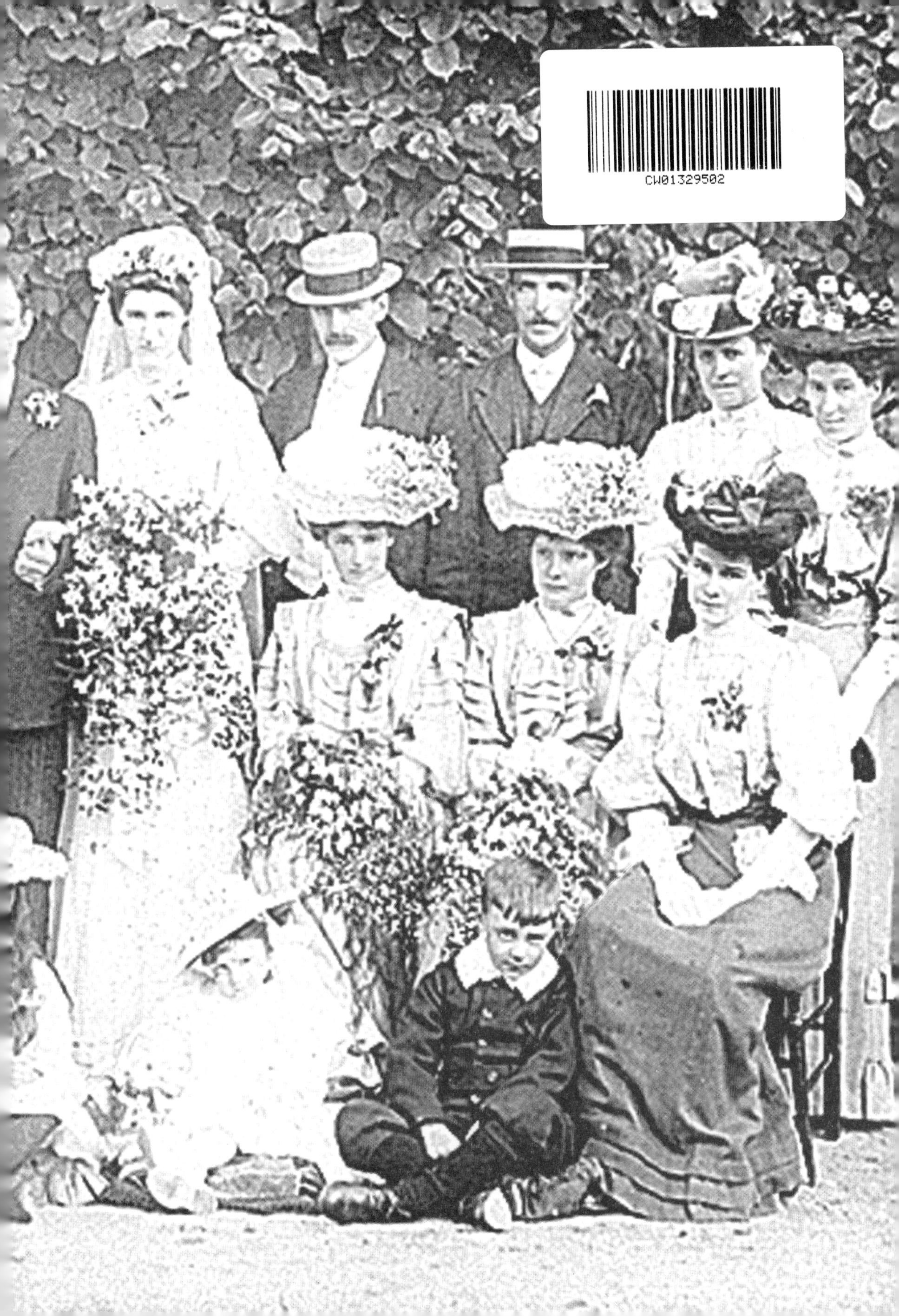

# LUST, DUST AND COBBLESTONES

## by Sue Fisher

A personal look at Hitchin and the surrounding area from 1900 until 1913, through the pages of the Hertfordshire Express newspaper. History, as it was lived at the time

**One child in eight died in Hitchin before their first birthday**

*Dr Day, medical officer of health, 1908*

# Contents

| | |
|---|---|
| Page 5 | Foreword by Victoria Glendinning |
| Page 6 | Acknowledgements |
| Page 7 | The Spell of our Cobblestone Past |
| Page 8 | With Hine-sight |
| Page 9 | The Very Best Little Town in the World |
| Page 13 | The Day Annie Killed her Baby |
| Page 19 | Favourite Express-ions 1901 |
| Page 21 | All's Well, Love to All – Boer War |
| Page 29 | Favourite Express-ions 1902 |
| Page 32 | The Curate's Wife who Took to Drink |
| Page 38 | Favourite Express-ions 1903 |
| Page 42 | The Coronation that Proved a Riot |
| Page 47 | Dying with Panache |
| Page 52 | Favourite Express-ions 1904 |
| Page 55 | The 30-Year Vigil in one Room |
| Page 60 | How to be Faux Pass free at a Coronation |
| Page 68 | Favourite Express-ions 1905 |
| Page 72 | The Convict's Fortune and his Heir |
| Page 74 | Dirt and Grime Behind the Gipsy Myth |
| Page 75 | An Adventure with Dr Livingstone |
| Page 78 | Favourite Express-ions 1906 |
| Page 80 | The Schoolboy who Killed his Mother |
| Page 84 | Favourite Express-ions 1907 |
| Page 86 | Dr Williams' Pink Pills Save Another Life |
| Page 91 | The Cabbage Patch Baby |
| Page 98 | Favourite Express-ions 1908 |
| Page 101 | The New-Born Baby Dying in the Garden |
| Page 103 | The Long Arm of the Law |
| Page 107 | Leisure and Pleasure |
| Page 113 | Favourite Express-ions 1909 |
| Page 118 | The Day Emily Pankhurst Came to Town |
| Page 135 | Favourite Express-ions 1910 |
| Page 138 | Bigamy and Two Claimants to a Will |
| Page 142 | The Angry Vicar who Followed Christ |
| Page 148 | It was Christmas Day at the Workhouse |
| Page 156 | Favourite Express-ions 1911 |
| Page 158 | The Plane that Dropped Like a Bird |
| Page 163 | The Sherlock Holmes Detectives |
| Page 165 | Favourite Express-ions 1912 |
| Page 168 | The Battered Boy Left for Dead |
| Page 170 | The Neighbour from Hell |
| Page 175 | How to get a Drink in a Teetotal Town |
| Page 178 | Favourite Express-ions 1913 |
| Page 182 | God Punishes Man with Titanic Disaster |
| Page 184 | The Patient No-one Cared About |
| Page 186 | Dates and details to decode the Edwardian Age |
| Page 187 | Countdown to Women Winning the Vote |
| Page 188 | Remember the Bulldozers, Dirt and Hurt |
| Page 189 | Index |

# To Mike Sadler: *In loving memory of a dear friend.*

## Pictures
Cover: Designed by Gwennyth Capon
Front endpapers: An Edwardian wedding
Title page: Churchyard, Hitchin, pictured between 1878 and 1902
Frontispiece: Portmill Lane, Hitchin, looking towards Queen Street, at the end of the 19th Century
Back Endpapers: Old houses in Churchgate, Hitchin, 1878 – 1902

*A North Herts country scene between 1915 and 1920*

Copyright Sue Fisher 1999

To the best of my knowledge and endeavour, the information in this book is correct. I apologise if there are any errors and would be interested to hear new information about people or events mentioned. The text is based on a personal interpretation of newspapers at the time and was never intended as a reference book but to bring an age to life as it was lived then. *Sue Fisher*

ISBN 0 9535740 0 8

Printed in England by Streets Printers, Royston Road, Baldock, Herts SG7 6DB
Published by Sue Fisher

All rights reserved. No part of this book may be reproduced or transmitted in any form or by any means, electronic of mechanical, including photocopying, recording or by any information storage or retrieval system without permission in writing from the author.

# Foreword

Hitchin, surrounded by gentle hills, once thickly wooded, has been fortunate in its recorded history. There were people living here on the Hiz even before the Romans came; William the Conqueror kept the little town as royal possession, and it remained a royal manor into modern times.

In spite of numbers of poor and deprived people – who once huddled in courts and alleys between the church and Queen Street, where the market now is – Hitchin has always enjoyed a comfortable sort of prosperity. It is still very much a community and a country town, in spite of modern encroachments and the nearness to London.

The town has been fortunate, too, in her local historians, from Sir William Chauncey to Reginald Hine and on into our own day. A collection of 'Hertfordshire books,' in which Hitchin and its environs always plays a star role, fills a very long shelf.

It's not history and geography, however, that bring the past to life and link it with the present, but stories about local people and what happened to them.

This is why this book makes such a lively contribution to what we know about Hitchin, and about the towns and villages that cluster around it, in the years before World War 1. The Hertfordshire Express has proved to be a treasure house, not only of evocative old photographs but of anecdotes and scandals, celebrations, disasters, feuds, farces and tragedies, which have made up the ordinary and extraordinary experience of local heroes, villains, grandees and unfortunates.

Reading their stories, brought back to vivid life by Sue Fisher, we can almost hear their voices.

**Victoria Glendinning**
*Biographer, novelist and a member of Hitchin's prestigious Seebohm family*

## ACKNOWLEDGEMENTS

Many individuals and organisations have given generous help with this book. I would like to thank them for making it possible. They include:
Joanne Benson and all the staff at Hitchin Museum for endless help, advice and the use of many of the photographs reproduced
Robert Lancaster and Elizabeth Cummings at First Garden City Museum, Letchworth
Alan Fleck, Arts and Museums Officer, North Herts District Council
Bedford Public Records Office
Knebworth House Collection
Stevenage Museum
Luton Museum Service
Hythe Civic Society
The Comet Newspaper and its long-suffering staff, especially Phil Morey, Richard Thomson and Andy Wallis
Paul Fletcher, for valuable early advice and Jane Fletcher for endless encouragement
Alan Candy, Janice Parker and Pauline Minnis for proof reading
Alan Millard, Mike Sadler, Mike Howarth and John Fisher for photographs
John Mahoney for advice
Scilla Douglas and Pauline Humphries of Hitchin Historical Society for valuable advice, warm support and proof reading

Also thank you to all the people who showed interest and encouraged me during this long project. Like everything in Hitchin, it has been largely a community effort. Thank you all.

*The Bancroft Hygienic Bakery, Hitchin, pictured in about 1900*

# The spell of our cobblestone past

*To research this book I worked in a small room at Hitchin Museum, sandwiched between exhibits and administration. There was silence and heat, chill and slow tedium. A Victorian tape played in the next room and I read to the sound of horses' hooves, to the chatter of people calling in, to piercing police sirens and footsteps in the corridor. I sat in the world of now, immersed in a world of long ago.*

*Others will go there, reread, repeat, reiterate and, wondering, rewrite. They in turn will pore over the decaying copies of the Hertfordshire Express, peering through the dust of death into an alien and yet familiar world. I know all the people featured, each and every one. I seem to meet them now; making the same points, jeering, jabbing, generous, fixed in age-old grooves.*

*The sheets of the newspapers disintegrate as you touch them; when you rise you leave a flurry of dandruff at your feet. Every name you read is the name of someone dead and yet the link from those long-gone lives still holds us firm. Every crisis that they faced, every depression and fret and frenzy, each petty feeling and meaningless squabble, each aspiration and benevolent thought, is part of now.*

*When I left the small museum room sometimes I would sit in the Market Place, the sun warm on the cobbles. Here they all came, the famous and the tawdry. They held their meetings, rallied their troops, proclaimed their kings. They marched and they strolled, they processed and they squabbled and they did it here. And here I am now, my shadow faint across the ground, leaving my reed-thin mark on a town worthy to be loved.*

*Sue Fisher*

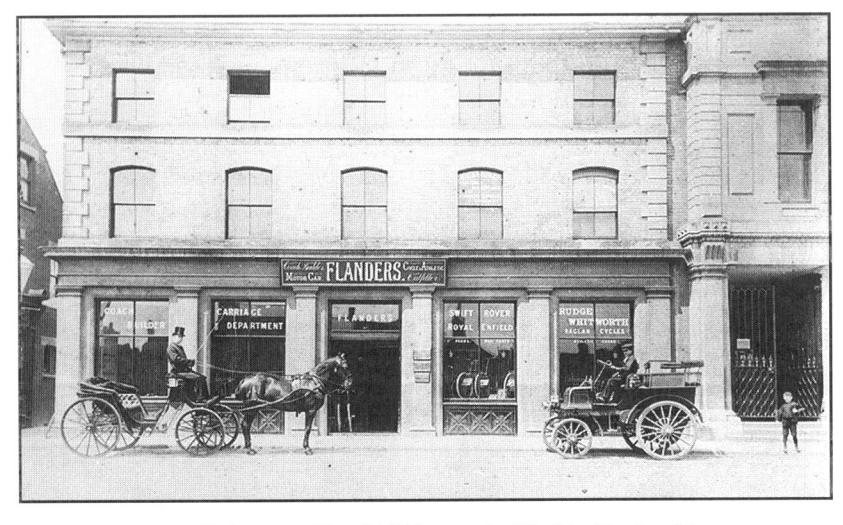

*The colliding worlds of 1902 meet in Hitchin Market Place*

# With Hine-sight

Here is a town – one of the few fortunate ones left in England – to which people
still love to come for the antique grace and delightfulness of its trades and
habitations. Why should we be such fools as to strip ourselves of our chief,
if not only, attraction? I dread to think that some day our children
will rise up and call us accursed. Will they not be right?
We slept on – and the Philistines came and filched our inheritance away.
*Reginald Hine, Historian and writer, March 1922.*

Are we to go on with this petty, parochial idea that this place is our own to do as
we please with? Or shall we recognise at last that it's not so much
'this parish of Hitchin' as 'This piece of England' – a precious inheritance
of the nation at large to be looked on by us in whose temporary custody it is,
in the nature of a trust, and handed on unimpaired?
All those who love this place – and there are thousands of them dispersed
through England – are in a sense its citizens as well as we are.
If we choose to block our own traffic and obstruct our market stalls
and waste our substance in extravagant schemes, that is our own affair;
but when we commit a breach of trust and desecrate
"whatever things are fair and venerable and of good report"
then the whole neighbourhood, and in a measure,
the whole nation, are concerned. – *Reginald Hine, 1925*

# The very best little town in the world

*Hitchin Market Place as is appeared in 1910*

SLEEPY Hollow was the nickname given to Hitchin at the turn of the century. It both annoyed residents and secretly pleased them – a quiet life was just what they really wanted.

They could recall the glorious days of the past, when Elizabeth I was said to have slighted Spanish vineyards, telling a nobleman:

*"My Hitchin grapes surpass them or those of any other country."*

In the 18th Century the town was, reported the Hertfordshire Express, in 1903:

*"Second in the county for the number of streets, houses and inhabitants but second to none for its markets for corn, especially wheat, both in quality and quantity, while its malt was highly prized even beyond the neighbouring counties."*

By then the town had swelled to 10,000 residents. It was still based on ancient streets skirting a central market place. There on Tuesdays and Saturdays townsfolk and villagers gathered from miles around, as they had done for generations. With a shop for every 40 residents, Hitchin needed the regular influx of customers to keep it prosperous.

Cattle were still herded through the unpaved streets, lit inadequately by gas, while horses pulling traps were a regular cause of accidents. On market day cattle were allowed to roam freely, sometimes escaping into buildings or butting passers-by.

Despite the beauty of many buildings, the town had its black side with slums, poverty and disease. The semi-anonymous FBW, writing in the town's prestigious newspaper The Hertfordshire Express in 1904, said:

*"Side by side with a few undoubtedly quaint and old world streets there were some dismal and dreary slums where the poor huddled together in dingy, small and unhealthy dwellings."*

He went on to mention narrow tortuous lanes and alleys irradiated by flickering gas lamps that merely served to make the darkness visible.

Some hovels had no lighting at all and their ashes and rubbish were kept in boxes or piled into heaps until they were collected by the dustmen.

In 1904 the Express reported that one house, where the floor was 18 inches below the level of the ground and green growth covered the walls, had seen the death of seven out of 10 children.

The Queen Street slums were roundly condemned in a letter to the newspaper from Alexander Part of Radlett, written in August 1907. "I do not think that the inhabitants of Hitchin can be fully alive to the fact that there exists in this part of the town slums which would put to shame any in London," he said.

Up to 5,000 people were crammed into 20 acres, he went on, and the area was regarded as unsafe by many residents, especially at night.

On one evening, 11 separate fights had taken place in Queen Street, watched by idle loiterers who patronised one of the eight or nine pubs. It would be better, commented Mr Part, for the children to literally be put on the streets.

*"Hitchin is in many respects a charming town, and this fearful blot ought surely to be removed."*

Two years later another article described conditions in the curious collection of yards off Queen Street and St Andrews Street "with old properties in decaying condition."

The "tiny cottages in cramped positions have not sufficient air, light and space for healthy occupation." Many were back to back with small windows. In 1903 Hitchin Rural District councillors heard of 13 people sleeping in two rooms, one measuring 11.5ft by 11ft and the other 8.5ft by 7ft. Both were only seven feet high.

Hundreds of homes had no toilet or water, using shared non-flush privies and a tap in the yard.

To have a bath most people had to carry water in and heat it in large cauldrons over an open fire.

Bad as these cottages were, they at least provided shelter for a family. Many had none, a problem that worried medical officer of health, Dr Day. He told councillors in 1903:

"Many parts of the district contain much wretched cottage property which must soon be dealt with.

"There is a great dearth of cottages for a man earning 12 to 15 shillings a week, especially if he has a large family." He highlighted over-crowding as a great evil and great danger to the health of the rising generation.

Even the rich were affected by poor conditions – the streets were often filthy and deep with mud while rats were such a problem that at one stage the police offered a halfpenny for a tail.

The poor would buy coal in a pail and bring their own cups or basins to the shop for jam and pickles, dispensed from seven-pound jars.

*Hitchin's disgrace – Chapman's Yard off Queen Street in 1910 in the heart of the slum area*

Groceries such as sugar and rice were sold in thick paper bags, while sweets were put into twists of paper. Garratt and Cannon, which made its own confectionery in Bancroft, sold lucky bags of broken bits – considered extra lucky if they contained a toy or charm.

Children played in the streets, vying for space with muffin men, who rang bells, the scissor grinders and packmen with household goods. Bakers would deliver to the door as late as midnight and most shops stayed open until 7pm or 8pm at night, and on Sundays.

In contrast with the widespread and often overwhelming poverty, a few wealthy residents owned most of the town. Income tax was very low (one shilling in the pound or five per cent) and only the well off paid anything at all – just one in 33 people were eligible.

*Hitchin High Street, with the Cock Hotel, pictured in about 1900*

The richer folk put great emphasis on food, starting the day with a cooked breakfast and having an ample lunch, tea and a large dinner. It was not unusual for upper and middle class families to have four, five or even six-course meals.

Whatever your class, the Edwardian resident was affected by the state of the streets.

In May 1909, the Express published a letter on the dust nuisance and the dilemma of "having to choose between keeping even the bedroom windows tightly closed or finding the whole house quite smothered in dust.

*"The quantity of water used is absurdly inadequate, one water cart in particular leaving a sort of striped appearance behind. If streets were thoroughly saturated once or twice in the morning it would have a lasting effect."*

In June 1907 Arthur Halsey, who ran a grocer's shop in Churchyard, wrote to the council about the dust problem. "I should be glad if you could arrange to have the Market Place more frequently watered on those days on which there is no rain.

*"The nuisance of the fine granite dust has been intolerable during the past few days and seriously damages the goods displayed for sale on our counters."*

Although many streets smelt very foul indeed, there was also the strong odour of lavender and the flowers and herbs distilled by Ransom's in Bancroft to provide a small consolation. In 1904 the Express reported: "The lavender harvest is said to be the most abundant on record in Hitchin."

It was a time of tremendous change, with a growing number of cars running side by side with the traditional horse and carriage system. The first motor mail van was used in 1904, coming from Northampton, to help cater for the 21,000 letters delivered each day in Hitchin alone.

An unpredictable electricity supply arrived in 1906 and by 1911 three telephonists took care of 70 telephone subscribers.

The town became a location in a book in 1906, but the Express reviewer, who thought little of the work of fiction, refused to name it. Instead he just quoted the local passages, such as: "Hitchin's a jolly little country place, stocked with quaint corners."

The hero promises the heroine a visit to what sounds like the Cock Hotel, although the Express thought it might be the Sun.

"There's a fine old-fashioned inn in the High Street, about 300 years old, with a regular coaching courtyard – that's where we will have tea," he tells her. The heroine walks round the market as dusk falls.

*"The entire picture of the numerous sweet stalls with their loads of brightly coloured sweets, the vegetable stalls with their borders of brilliant greens and glaring reds that picked out daubs of colour with no outline and no shapes, offered such an effect as a Whistler might have produced."*

The lamplighter was at work. "One by one, as he passed down the street, a little beacon was kindled in its brazier and sought out its reflection in a puddle that made murky mirrors in the road." At last the heroine gets her tea.

*"He brought her back to the hotel, and there in the coffee room, before a blazing fire, where big logs of wood were burning with an aromatic scent, they had their tea served.*

*"Well, what do you think of Hitchin?" he asked. "'Tis a nice place,' she said."*

Many would have agreed with her and gone even further. Opening the first purpose-built fire station, in August 1904, the urban district council clerk, Mr W O Times, said the town was prosperous, in pleasant surroundings and very nice indeed.

But Cllr W B Moss declared simply, to applause: "Hitchin is the very best little town in the world."

*Hitchin Market Place full of hustle and bustle, as it appeared shortly before the end of the 19th Century*

# The day Annie killed her baby

*Charlton, where Annie Tomlin drowned her small daughter Margaret in 1909*

It rained the day Annie Tomlin killed her baby. The skies opened and great gobbets of water lashed the earth. They pounded against young Annie as she struggled along the road, trying to shelter the baby in her arms, frantic to arrive in safety and terrified to reach the end of her road.

Annie walked for almost nine miles, across the steep hills from Luton to Hitchin, through the storm. At Offley her sister Alice passed her in a trap but she did not stop. She did not even acknowledge that she had seen Annie, although she knew full well where she was going, holding Margaret tight to her breast, her bonnet over her forehead in a feeble attempt to keep the water from her eyes.

At Charlton Annie turned aside from the main road and walked into the village. There, the rain running in rivulets through the street, the dust churned into mud, Annie knelt by the pond and held her baby under the water. The bemused, panicky struggle soon ceased. Finally, almost composed and numb to her core, Annie finished her long walk and stumbled to her father's house.

"I have drowned my child," she said. Her father scarcely looked up. "You had best go to the police then," he said and never moved.

The following day, a Friday in May, 1909, Annie appeared at her daughter's inquest. She could scarcely stand. Totally distraught, she fainted and cried by turns, wringing pity from almost everyone who saw her.

The surgeon William Grellett, who had declared Margaret dead the day before, now attended the pitiful mother.

The courtroom was packed, the case already a cause celebre. The circumstances were outlined and reported in the Hertfordshire Express, under the heading: "A Hitchin tragedy, illegitimate child drowns, mother confesses her guilt."

A sympathetic jury returned a verdict of manslaughter committed in a fit of desperation and recommended Annie for every consideration at the hands of the law. As a rider they thought her father should be censured for his unkind and callous treatment.

A few days later Annie appeared in court again and was committed to trial at Hertford Assizes. The compassionate plea of the inquest jury was disregarded: Annie was accused of murder. If convicted she might forfeit her life.

She stood in the dock with the matron of the hospital on one side and the Rev H E Jones, vicar of St Mary's Church, on the other. The Express reported: "Although far from in the collapsed state she was in on Friday, the girl still looked ill. It was only by repeated efforts on the part of those around her, including W P Grellett, that she was kept from fainting."

The evidence given at Margaret's inquest shocked middle-class Hitchin. Here was an impoverished woman of 21, burdened with a small child and no husband to support her.

Worse, she was disgraced, forced to keep her baby secret from her employer and spurned by her family.

Struggle as she might, she could not earn enough to keep the child. Even the workhouse, her last desperate resort, had failed her.

*Mr Moulden in his organist's robes*

The jury at the inquest was appalled. The foreman, Mr Henry George Moulden, wrote to the local paper afterwards.

Mr Moulden was a respected man in Hitchin, a freemason, a member of the Board of Guardians, which administered the workhouse, and a fellow of the Royal College of Organists. His letter was immediately published.

"It is evident that the poor girl had been in terrible suffering since the birth of her child and when once a man or woman is down in the world everything seems to combine to keep him there," he wrote.

"Apparently this girl was thrown from pillar to post – her immediate relations rather giving her the cold shoulder. It's the way of the world.

"One can't help feeling for the poor girl who, in a fit of desperation, got rid of her child. Surely the person to blame is the man responsible for her trouble not the girl who is now suffering for her sin. I consider it a very hard case."

So did Mary J King, who also wrote a letter to the Express. "Surely if they had known of her plight some of the Christian ladies of our town, who do keep an oversight of such, would have befriended her in her sad plight?

"The innocent little life is no doubt safe in another world and has thus escaped any repetition of her poor mother's sins and troubles, but has not the distracted young woman already suffered enough in her lonely struggle and fears? Now after acknowledging the extent of her sin she stands charged (quite lawfully) with wilful murder.

"While fatherhood is kept secret might not the partial cost of such poor innocent children be borne by the state for some years?

*"If a little more responsibility were thrown onto the general public and less on the weaker and more helpless parents, it might have good effect."*

Annie's trial took place at Hertford Assizes in early June. In a faint voice she pleaded not guilty to the charge of murder.

Her prosecutor, the man who could send her to the gallows, was Mr G H B Renwick. He briefly outlined the case.

Twelve men heard the old story; the disgraceful birth, the family's rejection, the parceling of poor Margaret from a nurse to the workhouse and then back to Annie because she could not pay the fees.

They learned of the brief golden months in Margaret's life when she was fostered, free of charge, by Mr and Mrs Jones at Stopsley.

And finally they were told of the desperate day that Mr Jones, a labourer, lost his job and the couple could no longer afford to keep the child. Mrs Sarah Jones took Margaret herself and went down to the house in Luton where Annie was a servant, working with people who had no idea she was the mother of a bastard child.

"The prisoner," Mr Renwick told judge and jury, "was in a terrible dilemma. "She was in an honourable and respectable position of employment in domestic service and with the child on her hands she had in some way to disclose its existence, while her family would not assist her in providing for it. The prisoner was unable to find any means of securing the support of the child and deliberately took its life.

*"If that were so, however much you might reprobate the prisoner's family for leaving her without assistance at such an important time, you must find her guilty. There is no room for a verdict of manslaughter."*

Mr Murphy, speaking for the defence, agreed with the last sentence. It was not a manslaughter verdict he wanted, but exoneration. He set about demolishing the character of Annie's father and sister.

They had already appalled everyone at the inquest. Now they left a new audience chilled.

The last hours of Margaret's life unfolded yet again. Mrs Jones told the court how she had cared for the baby for 13 months, until the very day before her death, when she had told Annie she could not keep Margaret any longer.

Annie had begged Mrs Jones to take Margaret to the workhouse in Hitchin and, kind heartedly, she agreed.

For the first time during those terrible final two days Margaret was taken along the road from Luton to Hitchin. It was a wasted journey – the relieving officer at the workhouse refused to admit the child.

Mrs Jones turned to the police station but they were even more reluctant to accept an 18-month-old baby into their hands. Mrs Jones decided there was nothing to do but take the baby to Annie's family.

There she met Alice Tomlin, Annie's younger sister, who greeted her like a messenger of doom.

Finally, with infinite reluctance, she took poor Margaret in her arms and flounced inside, declaring that she would not look after her sister's bastard.

She got the response she wanted from her father, who agreed it was impossible and the baby would not stay longer than one night under his roof.

The next morning Alice and Margaret took a cart to Luton and called on Annie.

> 'She came to the house and said she had drowned the baby'

> 'Did you allow that wretched girl to go alone to the police?'

Confronted by the angry Alice, Annie managed to beg some time off work and came out to take Margaret into her arms.

She said she was coming back to their father's house and asked for a lift back to Hitchin. A furious Alice snapped that there was no room for her in the cart. Later she passed Annie on the road near Offley with the baby in her arms.

It was this evidence that so angered Mr Moulden at Margaret's inquest, when the coroner Francis Shillitoe had asked incredulously: "Did you speak to her?"

"No sir," replied Alice without contrition. "Nor she to me. She came to the house at 7pm and said she had drowned the baby."

A juror had cried out in shock: "Didn't you think you could have given your sister a lift? It would have been more sisterly." Alice replied stolidly: "There was no room."

Her father James Tomlin was no kinder at Annie's trial. He had told the jury that Annie arrived about 7pm and said she had drowned the baby. "She was only crying," he declared. "I have seen her do it before. At first I thought it was just some of her bogey."

Mr Murphy asked harshly: "Did you allow that wretched girl to go alone to the police station." There was a pause before Mr Tomlin said stiffly: "She went alone."

"Did you offer to go with her?" barked Mr Murphy. Another pause and a grudging: "No, I didn't." Mr Murphy went on relentlessly. He talked of Annie's illness at Christmas, when she was admitted to hospital with an internal disease. Then he asked: "With the single exception of having been seduced by some man, has this girl always been a good girl?"

"She has been a good girl," replied Mr Tomlin reluctantly.

"She went to work at 13 and kept herself except for the period after the birth?"

It was so.

Mr Murphy railed at Mr Tomlin, accusing him of making life thoroughly uncomfortable for Annie and refusing to have "her little bastard" at home. At last he drew a denial.

Mr Murphy went on: "When the baby was brought in by Alice you told her to take it to her sister to see what she would do with it. But your daughter Alice said she would not be troubled with the brat." Mr Tomlin was nonplussed and muttered: "I don't think so."

Remorselessly Mr Murphy continued: "Do you think it would have made much difference to have had that little child at home?" A miserable Mr Tomlin replied: "Yes, sir, I think it would."

Mr Murphy was not giving up now. He asked Mr Tomlin where Annie had been in service but her own father did not know.

Mumbling, he told the court he thought she went to her grandmother's in Luton and perhaps was working in one of the factories. He had not been to visit her since her arrest.

The final blow was as neatly delivered as the rest. Quietly Mr Murphy asked: "Has she at times complained of pains in her head?" "Yes, sir."

"And did she go on working even though she had pains in her head?" "Yes, sir."

Mr Tomlin left the witness box and Alice took his place. She was only 19 but already a hard and ruthless girl, seemingly quite unmoved by the tragedy which had engulfed her sister.

Mr Murphy challenged her at once. Had she told her aunt:

*"I am not going to look after a child and father won't have the bastard at home."*

"I didn't want it," Alice agreed.

*The Rev Canon H Jones*

Mr Murphy talked about Margaret's last hours, about the trip from Luton to Hitchin with Mrs Jones on the Tuesday, the ride back in the cart with Alice on Wednesday and, finally, the dreadful walk Annie made in the rain as evening fell.

"The Lilley road from Luton to Hitchin is nine miles," Mr Murphy told Alice. "Why didn't you take the baby in the cart?" He paused, then added: "Did you say 'Take your child back, I won't touch it'."

"No," cried an indignant Alice.

"You passed her in that weather, you riding along and she walking with the baby in her arms in the rain?"

"Yes, sir."

"It was a four-wheel cart."

"But it was full of things."

"Was she crying when she came home, distressed?" Alice was silent.

The relentless pressure of that afternoon drummed on the jury's ears. The information piled up in the close courtroom as the evidence unfolded.

Annie's Aunt Lily explained how Annie came to her with Margaret that last afternoon. "Annie was crying and seemed strange," Mrs Woodley told the court. "She didn't know what to do with the baby."

Annie got no support from her grandmother, Mrs Watson, who lived with Mrs Woodley. Mrs Watson testified: "I told Annie I could not have the child. I told her to go to Hitchin and see her father."

At this point Annie fainted and had to be taken downstairs, out of the court. It was a telling interruption as the next witness was Mr Grellett, who testified to her appalling condition at the magistrates' committal.

"She was in a most pitiable condition," he declared.

*"She repeatedly fainted, was hysterical and collapsed and to my mind was not in a condition to understand the charges brought against her."*

Afterwards she had to be taken to hospital.

Through the eyes of Sergeant Knight the jury saw Annie as she arrived at Hitchin Police Station after killing Margaret and leaving her cold father. Twisting her baby's hat in her trembling hands, she had told him: "I want to give myself up for drowning my baby."

She was, Sgt Knight told the court: "Calm, cool and collected."

She was also drenched to the skin. "She had been out in heavy rains, she said she had kept the child dry and got wet herself doing it," testified Sgt Knight.

*Tilehouse Street, west of the Highlander by Grays Lane, pictured at the turn of the century*

When police arrived at the pond in Charlton they found Margaret's body floating on the top of the water, wearing a frilly dress. Only her bonnet was missing.

There was no doubt where the sympathy of the courtroom lay as Annie stood, frail and white in the dock. Prosecutor Mr Renwick made an effort to get control of the situation again.

"The attitude of the prisoner's family, however callous or brutal, is not relevant," he said. Then he softened and conceded:

*"The prisoner was placed in a terrible dilemma and must have the sympathy of everyone in the court."*

Defender Mr Murphy scented victory and went in for the kill. The crux of his argument was that Annie had become unhinged on the long, despairing, torrential walk.

Had she not been passed by her cruel sister? Had she not struggled through "a fearful storm which raged and drenched her though she kept her baby quite dry?" Where was she to go when she arrived? Who would care for the baby, how would she get money to pay them, where could she sleep?

"She lost her mental balance sometime on the walk back from Luton – a time when human nature could not hold itself together any longer," he declaimed.

"Was it surprising that this girl, feeling herself to be the object of scorn and ignominy, became so upset that her mental balance began to give way?

*"When they knew that the girl had been traipsing up and down hills in the rain, carrying the child until she was exhausted, could they wonder that anything terrible did happen?"*

They could not. There was intense silence in the courtroom as the jury returned at 5pm. Annie was brought up from the cells, once more composed, and looked at the jury in a self possessed and calm manner.

The verdict was announced. As the words 'not guilty' were spoken there was sensation in the courtroom, quickly silenced as the judge asked: "Do you find that she committed the act but was insane at the time?"

Into the stillness the foreman replied: "That is our verdict." A ripple of applause broke out at the back of the court, immediately hushed by the judge.

He drew himself up, surveyed the courtroom, glanced at the jury and settled his eyes on young Annie, a wraith of a girl scarcely able to stand. Firmly he told her she would be detained as a criminal lunatic until his Majesty's pleasure was known.

Accompanied by the Rev and Mrs Jones, Annie was taken by train to St Albans prison, stepping onto the platform at Hertford just 45 minutes after the jury delivered its verdict.

*Left: the poverty of Hitchin was apparent at Thorpe's Yard, Queen Street, even in the 1920s*

*James Tomlin and Alice lived at Russell's Slip, Hitchin. Annie became pregnant while working for Mrs Pass in Baldock in 1907 and left because of her condition. She had the baby while employed at a house in Tilehouse Street, Hitchin.*

*The baby, Margaret Irene, was first nursed by Miss Castle, of Union Path, Hitchin, before going to Hitchin Workhouse in Chalkdell. Both refused to keep the child because Annie fell behind with the fees.*

*Margaret was then taken in by Mr and Mrs Jones of Stopsley while Annie worked for Edward Verity, a draper, in Luton who said 'she was always satisfactory.'*

# Favourite Express-ions – 1901

★ A New Year rabbiting expedition at Guilden Morden went sadly wrong for 46-year-old labourer Isaac Thompson of Royston. He was shot in the foot when Herbert Westrope's gun 'went off quite unexpectedly.' Poor Herbert, who was only 12, was not held to blame by the coroner, called in because Isaac died of tetanus after having his foot amputated.

★ The new century started for Victorians on January 1, 1901 and they celebrated Watch Night or New Year's Eve with gusto. In Hitchin the town band played Auld Lang Syne followed by dance music in the Market Place but, contrary to many other towns, the church bells were not rung – an omission which was "remarked upon."

★ Mr Fordham, the respected North London magistrate who lived at Ashwell, heard a rather sad and curious case in January. A "respectable-looking woman, wearing gold-rimmed spectacles," told the court she was being bothered by some persons, who wanted her to marry them. "There are so many of them and they pester me so much," she explained to Mr Fordham, adding that she heard voices and that people were always pretending to be friends with her. "Take no notice of them," advised Mr Fordham. "Kill them with silence and they won't pester you with attentions."

★ Queen Victoria, who had ruled much of the world for more than 60 years, died in January. The news reached Hitchin by telegraph, with a bell tolling from St Mary's Church and from Holy Saviour at 9am. By midday the shops had draped their windows in black and many residents were wearing mourning. A few days later her son Edward VII was proclaimed King in the Market Place.

★ New measures had recently been introduced to deal with inebriates, dividing drunks into two categories – those who broke the law while under the influence and habitual drunkards with repeated convictions for being drunk and disorderly. One strategy for curing alcoholics involved getting them out of the habit of drinking anything at all.

"The inebriate becomes a thirsty soul and if he during his reformation is allowed to drink indiscriminately, even of non-alcoholic fluids, he is much more exposed to danger of relapse than if before discharge he is broken of what one may call the habit of thirst."

★ Hitchin's post office was condemned as the worst in the country in February. Its air was so polluted that the centre of London on a foggy day was more pleasant, reported the Express in February.

"Imagine about 30 employees crowded into the place with many gas burners alight and no proper vent," the reporter went on.

"If the window is open the draught is unbearable. If the office were a private place of business it would be condemned as unfit for use, day or night, by the medical officer." On top of the appalling atmosphere, there were no toilets in the building.

*Queen Victoria, who died after a reign of 63 years*

★ Cyclists weren't too impressed with Baldock, where there were no signposts to help them take the right road.

The situation was not going to improve either, as urban district councillors decided in February that they would not pay for direction signs to Hitchin, London, Biggleswade and Royston.

The chairman couldn't understand why signs would be necessary to London as: "Cyclists are intelligent as a rule and they would only have to follow the telegraph posts if they desired to get to London. They can always ask the way and if they do go a little bit wrong it would not be much trouble for them to turn back."

★ Women were exhorted not to wear feathers from sea birds such as osprey by the Hitchin Auxiliary of the RSPCA in March because "it involves great cruelty"

★ In March Pirton School had to be closed for six weeks because of scarlet fever. The disease had got a grip "because of the gross carelessness of many parents," reported the Express. "It was only by threats of legal action that obedience to directions could be enforced."

★ A master at St Mary's School in Hitchin was fined for hitting a three-year-old boy. He gave him a black eye and knocked out one of his teeth.

★ The editor of the Express was obviously much amused by a story from Austria, for he included it in the Express in June, despite its lack of local interest. It concerned a wedding in Austria, after the bridegroom started a correspondence with a girl he had never met.

She sent him a picture of herself and pleasing letters, he proposed and they met for the first time at the altar. Imagine his horror when the bride lifted her veil and he saw, not the beauty in his photograph, but her elderly spinster sister "of scant charms." He was busy getting the marriage annulled.

★ The average Hitchin bike rider was more concerned about the danger from dogs running loose through the streets and children playing with hoops. "The cyclists lot is not enviable," reported the Express.

★ Mr and Mrs Steggles of Dacre Road celebrated their golden wedding in February. Mrs Steggles could remember Victoria, when a Princess, coming to Hitchin with her mother and getting out at the Sun Hotel.

★ Henry Wildman was well named. Although only 10 years old, he already had an alias (McKay) and was a hardened criminal. He appeared in court in June, charged with stealing a bike, and was sentenced to five strokes of the birch. It was unlikely to do much good – he had been whipped only two weeks earlier for wilful damage.

A six-year-old appeared at the same court accused, along with three older boys, of stealing wood. He was discharged because of his age.

Two other lads were the subject of a report in the Express in September, after one produced a small pistol, declared it was not loaded, and proceeded to fire a live bullet at his friend. The boy was in danger of losing his hand. "It is strange that more strict supervision is not exercised over their sale and use," commented the Express on the gun issue.

★ News came through in November that cyclist bugler J S Hunt, son of J T Hunt of Hitchin, was sailing to New Zealand. Mr Hunt junior had served in South Africa in the cyclist section of the Hitchin Volunteer Company.

*Hitchin Hill, as it appeared in the early years of the 20th Century*

# 'All's well, love to all' – the Boer War

The letter from Tommy Goodwin arrived as the new century broke, crossing thousands of miles to reach his parents in Arlesey. Thrilled, proud, anxious and over wrought, they sent it immediately to the Hertfordshire Express, so everyone could see how their Grenadier son fared in the Boer War, raging in South Africa.

He had written the letter only hours after taking part in a battle at Belmont in November, 1899. "Dear Mother, I can tell you I am very lucky," he wrote and continued with equal understatement.

*"We were right in the midst of very heavy firing for over two hours. Bullets were flying all around us all of the time before we made the charge and it was the Lord's mercy that we didn't all get cut up; but I was one of the lucky ones to come out alive and I hope, praise the Lord, I may always do so.*

*"The fight lasted seven hours and it was very hard. We were all knocked up and could hardly walk back."*

Battle resumed the next day for another eight hours.

About the same time Mrs Hugget of Sandy received a letter from her husband, written on December 5, 1899:

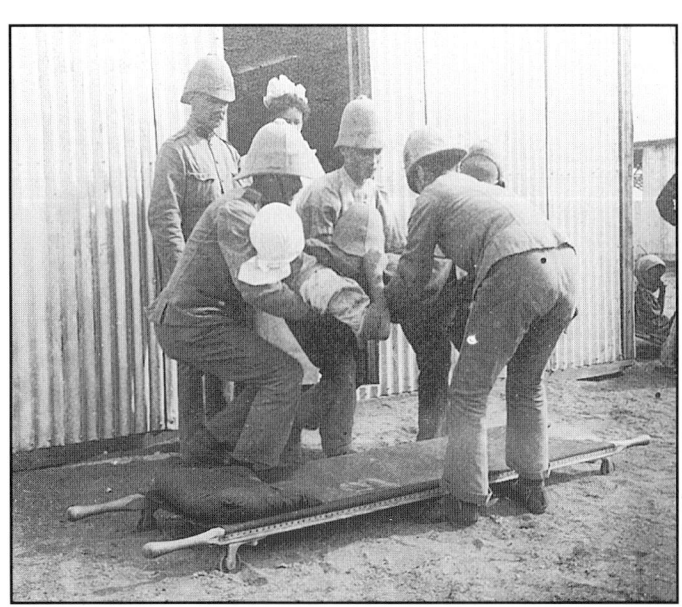

"The Boers' losses were terrible. We have dragged over 130 bodies out of the river where the Boers tied stones around their necks to make them sink so that the British would not know how many were lost. We are drinking the same water which doesn't seem quite the thing, but there is no other.

"We are off tomorrow for another big fight. They expect this war to be over now very soon and I hope it will be. You should have a look at this village where we are now; it is all smashed to atoms. It does seem a shame – such nice houses broken down as they were. We lost a lot at this battle. There were some terrible sights to see – heads and limbs blown off. Well, you must partly guess what a battle field is like, not a pretty sight, I can tell you."

One soldier described marching 15 miles a day:

*"And lucky to get one meal in 24 hours consisting of biscuits and corned beef. We have suffered most from want of water, going from one stage to another without a drink in the broiling hot sun – much hotter than the hottest day we get in England in July or August."*

Another soldier wrote to a friend in Stevenage about a 14-hour battle at Belmont in November:

"When we had dressed our wounded we were called to go further on and we had not had anything to eat. It was just 10'o'clock in the night and we marched till 12'o'clock the next day.

"We had only hard biscuits and water. It was not because we had not got anything, we had plenty of beef and mutton, also bread, but we dare not light a fire to show the enemy where we were."

The same man wrote again on December 1, reporting a very narrow escape – a bullet had gone through his water bottle.

"You can tell how stiff we have had it, we have not had our clothes off since we came from the ship, only as we came across some water, and that is thick as mud at

*A sick man is taken into the Orange River Hospital in South Africa in 1900*

times. We could only get a pint of water a day for three days and that was for breakfast and tea, but there is plenty where we are now. The weather is not like Christmas here, the heat is terrible."

Sometimes the letters are not so grim. One soldier wrote to his parents in Clifton.

*"Our duty here is to guard the railway line. We are stationed close to an ostrich farm and it is no unusual thing to pick up a splendid ostrich feather. The ostrich will come close up to us, feed from our hands and we sometimes pluck a few feathers. If I live to return I will bring one home."*

Private James Monk told his mother in Hitchin: *"The Boers' wives are fighting with them. It is a great shame to see the little children cut up but it can't be helped."*

A note from Express editor was printed under this letter, saying Pte Monk must be mistaken:

*"For it's hardly likely they would be allowed to remain anywhere in the neighbourhood of the battle ground, besides which, the enemy is fighting on British territory, away from their homes."*

Private S Brown wrote to his mother in Dunstable, describing his Christmas Day. It sounded very bleak.

*"We have only coffee and bread to eat and my only comfort was my good old pipe. As we lay in the trenches the bullets came over us like hail storm and the shrieks of the shells sounded like the wind in the telegraph wires on a rough night.*

The heat during the daytime is unbearable and as we lay in the trenches and looked towards the hills from where the Boers were firing I thought that if mother could see me now she would hardly enjoy her Christmas.

"But we enjoyed ourselves as well as we could in the circumstances.

*"On Christmas Day we lay in the trenches and sang songs, one of the favourite songs being 'A soldier and a man whatever my fate.' May I be a soldier and a man."*

Private Brown went on: "I am not in the best of health; I think it is through drinking the dirty water from the Modder and the hot country.

*"The dust gets down our throats and makes us drink heavily of the river water. And then we are short of food. "If I live to come home the first thing I will enjoy is a good feed and I can tell you I am looking forward to it."*

Gunner William Silsby of Hitchin wrote of fighting in the heat of battle.

*"We have lost all our officers who were all shot down and also our sergeant major was shot right through the head. It was an awful sight; I shall never forget it as long as I live."*

He describes bullets "flying in thousands around us" and goes on:

*"I was standing at my gun, the bullets falling all around me. I was loading as quickly as I could and my fingers were bleeding with pulling out the pins. The sun was burning hot, my neck was skinned with the sun and my water bottle and haversack skinned my neck too and my number one was shot and was lying at my feet.*

*"The poor fellows were falling all over the place and at this time our ammo had expired. I had just loaded the last shell I had left and then we had an order to leave.*

*"I don't know what sort of Christmas you had at home but I do not want another like ours. I had just a drink of water out of my bottle which had been in for two days. Our Christmas dinner was a bit of fat which we had to throw away. I wish I was a good reader and writer, I would show up those who have put in the papers that we get good and plenty."*

The letter sent to Mrs Purser of Biggleswade may have been the shortest reported in the Express, but it was the most poignant of all. Her son was in the beleaguered town of Ladysmith, besieged by the Boers for four months over the summer of 1899/1900.

His message was sent by a runner to Estcourt on December 31 and telegraphed to friends at Durban, who sent it on to Mrs Purser.

It said simply: *"All's well. Love to all."*

The soldiers' families were left struggling to survive while their men fought in South Africa. The public were asked to donate money and goods such as flannel cloth and tobacco to the Soldiers and Sailors Families Association, while women knitted comforts to send out to the men.

The Express reported in February:

*"As an outcome of the wave of patriotic feeling that has swept over the country in connection with the war, a movement has been set up in Stevenage to form a rifle club to encourage young men of all classes to take up the practice of rifle shooting."*

The newspaper had good news for the soldiers: *"The proprietor of Beecham's Pills desires us to state that he will be pleased to send gratis a box of Beecham's Pills, postage paid, to any individual soldier now on active service in South Africa. He adopts this course having received so many letters complaining that Beecham's Pills cannot at present be obtained at the front."*

John Dickinson and Co, the Hertfordshire paper manufacturers, were even more generous. For the New Year they supplied a gift of stationery to every soldier.

One hundred thousand large envelopes were specially manufactured and inside were six court shape envelopes, six sheets of ruled notepaper and a sheet of blotting paper.

Even Olive, the frivolous lady columnist of the Express, became preoccupied with the war. "The patriotic spirit is manifesting itself in many ways now, some of which are very curious," she wrote.

A woman who could not pay a tradesman's bill was taken to court. When she explained that she had no money because her husband was at the front:

*"The plaintiff then and there made the defendant a present of the amount together with his best wishes for her husband's safe return."*

Olive also had good news for war widows. She wrote in March, 1900:

*"Widow's caps are especially becoming just now with pretty little Marie Stuart coifs, with long ends at the back.*

*"This decorative little item is somewhat different to the hideous arrangement deemed correct a decade or so ago. The then widows' caps almost covered the head and resembled nothing more than the cumbersome night cap beloved of our great grandmothers. A widow need no longer make herself hideous to behold, her garments are now as light and pretty as sable trappings will permit."*

Jet, she added, was also becoming fashionable again for mourning. By May 1901 she had moved onto more general fashion.

*"Military fever is evident in many of the dresses prepared for this season. Khaki is, of course, out of favour. But soft shades of it known as dun, fawn, mushroom and biscuit remain with us and in this modified form are decidedly pretty and becoming. Military scarlet is adopted by but few wearers who will soon, it is to be hoped, discard their unbecoming tint."*

*A cow is slaughtered for food on Christmas Day 1900, by the Modder River*

Olive announced in the spring of 1900 that a virulent influenza outbreak could be blamed on the war in South Africa.

*"No one can deny that the serious aspect of affairs in South Africa is causing a good deal of public anxiety and a good deal of individual worrying amongst those who have friends and relatives at the front.*

*"Now undue worrying undoubtedly leads to those conditions of depressed vitality which are the starting point of most colds and chills etc.*

*"It is therefore not improbable that the war has had something to do with the prevalence of sickness and influenza, which is responsible for the present alarmingly high death rate all over the country."*

Olive was a mine of information. She condemned the Boers sternly on March 10, declaring:

*"The Boers around Mafeking seem to have no scruples whatever in firing upon women. Colonel Baden-Powell has complained of it again and again. The Boer women appear to be more brutalised than the men."*

Apparently they cheered as English women, cowering in a shelter, were bombarded by shells.

A writer in the Express had a word of sympathy for the men forced to stay at home.

*"Heavy responsibilities, usually in the form of a wife and children, have alone restrained many men from offering themselves for service in South Africa, and thousands are fuming over the thought that they are not doing their share as Britons."*

In February 1900, Ladysmith was finally relieved. Joy gripped the nation. "The news gives much satisfaction in Hitchin and the neighbourhood," recorded the Express of March 3. The good news reached Hitchin via a telegram at 10.30am.

*"Flags began to appear in windows, and by one'o'clock the town was gay. Church bells were set ringing and pealed at intervals during the day. A bill appeared saying a torchlit procession would take place in the evening."*

A committee was formed to organise everything and Mr Flanders rushed up to London to buy torches and fireworks. By 8.30 that night a surging crowd of thousands had gathered in the Market Place.

*"Through this throng the procession went, at first rather straggling but it tidied up again towards the end and by the time the Market Place was again reached it had attained a respectable form. Its progress round the streets was punctuated by the discharge of cannon crackers and coloured lights as well as torches."*

The evening finished with two bands playing while the torch bearers marched round and round.

In Stevenage the fire brigade led a parade accompanied by martial music and fireworks. At Arlesey staff hoisted a Union Jack over the Three Counties Asylum while their band played *God Save the Queen*. Flags 'gaily decorated' Codicote High Street while children sang patriotic airs. Everywhere church bells mingled with laughter and joy.

The patriotic spirit was heightened. At the end of March, Olive reported that parents were giving their children 'war' names, with mixed results. She rather liked Pretoria but thought Bloemfontein 'not so desirable.'

"Ladysmith is already a favourite, so is Kimberley," she wrote. Other selections included Glencoe, Tugela, Colenso, Frere and Modder River. "Some of the selections are most ill chosen and inappropriate," she added, citing as examples poor babies known forever as Modderina Belmonina Methuena Jones and James Spion Kop Skinner. The catalogue of disaster rolled on.

*"Many fond parents fasten upon the names of distinguished generals such as Roberts, Kitchener, Redvers, Buller, Baden-Powell, French, White, Symons, and from these make all sorts of selections and combinations with no doubt the best and most patriotic of intentions but what is not always the best of taste and effect."*

At the end of May 1900 came even better war news – Mafeking was relieved. Once again the news reached Hitchin by telegram, at about 10.30pm – but Royston had to wait for the morning papers to arrive next day, whereupon: "The wildest excitement prevailed and towards evening was unparalleled in the history of the town."

In Hitchin joyful residents had already met up the night before, singing Rule Brittania in the Market Place. "A procession was hastily arranged and headed by torches and flags and a small cannon. Several hundreds of people marched round the town while at intervals fireworks were let off and the cannon was discharged."

*Celebrations in Bucklersbury, Hitchin, after the relief of Mafeking in 1900*

This was only a rehearsal for what was to come the next day. The streets were decorated with bunting and "almost every house was adorned."

Shopkeepers agreed to close at 8pm and the rejoicing started at three in the afternoon, with another procession featuring a mounted khaki-clad warrior and people in costume and fancy dress.

By 8pm an immense crowd had gathered, to hear Major Harris tell them of the great practical lesson to be learned from Mafeking:

*"The splendid example of what great things could be accomplished through patience and perseverance."*

Biscuits, ginger beer and other good things were handed out at the Musgrave Arms and the evening finished with a torchlight parade.

Another celebration looked likely in July, when peace seemed so imminent that a subscription was taken up to pay for a victory party. It proved a false alarm, however, and the peace committee had to be disbanded in October.

All the money raised was returned and the expenses of £11 15 shillings were paid by the members.

In 1901, Express readers heard from Corporal W E Tooley of Whitwell.

*"Things look very black in South Africa at the present time. I, with my comrades, spent a most anxious Christmas Day and night."*

They were attacked by Boers on Boxing Day, 1900. *"By jove, we had a warm time of it then, bullets were striking the timbers and corrugated iron, making a most horrible row and tearing through the planks.*

*"In the midst of this fearful fusillade of bullets one of our cooks (a native) came and caught me by the arm and said the Boers were attacking on the other side so I at once rushed to that point and our sergeant (poor dear old Walter) was just in the act of raising his rifle when a Mauser struck him in the very centre of the forehead, making a ghastly wound from which the blood flowed in torrents. He just moaned, never spoke, and fell dead beside me."*

Reinforcements rushed in to help the Boers and their numbers steadily grew. Shells rained around the English soldiers, making 'a horrible row' and they had nothing to reply with. The corporal wrote:
*"We thought it was all up but the boys said they would die but never give in."*
When his officer called for a volunteer to go for assistance, he kept quiet – "It was too d--- hot" – but "having a splendid horse" he was selected. The real drama began to unfold.
*"I crept on my hands and knees or rather wriggled like a snake to the stable, saddled and leapt on his back and reached the Boer gauntlet."*
He stormed through their lines, too fast for them to catch him, and arrived safe and well at Brakpan, four miles away. But bad news awaited him – they had one man killed, one wounded and were in no position to help anybody. The corporal was back on his horse in a moment, riding on to Boksburg.

He covered ten miles in a mere 45 minutes, only to see his haste rendered pointless.
*"Even when they got news of the fearful plight we were in they were awful slow to turn out and our men practically relieved themselves through three of them stealing out of the lines and outflanking the Boers."*
The corporal's efforts were not all in vain though – he was able to report that his conspicuous bravery had been noted.
As the war dragged on the initial fervour faded. Olive reported in early 1901:
*"The new year brings, unfortunately, no slackening in the need for charitable help for the families of those who are still fighting for their country in South Africa. As time goes on the absence of the bread winner means more and more straightened circumstances for those left behind and it is a sorry encouragement for the war-worn soldier to know that his own hardships are not the only sacrifices he is called upon to make."*

*An English drummer boy writes home to mother from South Africa during the Boer War*

Her words fell on stony ground for she was reporting only weeks later:

*"The war has lost a good deal of its fashionable complexion and except what private people are doing for their relatives at the front, there is not a very warm response to Lord Kitchener's appeal for home comforts for the troops. This is partly no doubt due to the uncertainty of gifts reaching the men."*

Knebworth became en-fete to welcome home Lt Cotton when he returned from South Africa in August 1901. A railway carriage was reserved from King's Cross for "the hero of the hour and his party," who arrived to loud cheering from the crowd gathered on Knebworth platform.

Offley, not to be outdone, welcomed its war hero Lt Gosling when he came home to Wellbury House. "At the top of Offley Hill the whole village had turned out to do honour to the returned warrior," reported the Express in September 1902.

The horses were removed from the carriage and their places were taken by nine Offley men who had served in South Africa. The procession was accompanied by Hitchin Church Lads' Brigade playing *See The Conquering Hero Comes* while villagers decorated their bicycles and put bunting up on the green.

But the party the whole nation was waiting for didn't come until June 1, 1902, when the Boers finally capitulated. The news came through to Hitchin by telegraph messages which reached the town's railway and police stations at about 9pm on the Sunday evening.

The Press Association sent a telegram to the Hitchin office of the Hertfordshire Express at 5.55pm but it was not received until 8.05am the next day, much to the editor's fury. He declared:

*"It seems a pity that upon such an important occasion Post Office authorities cannot shake off some of their red tape and act as a common sense establishment would do."*

This telegram may have been at the root of a furious letter published in the Express on June 7, signed "From an inhabitant."

*"May I be allowed to ask how it was the telegram informing our authorities that war was at an end, received at about 5pm, was suppressed from the public until about 9.45pm? I am bound to say this shows a great want of humanity. Do they realise the gnawing anxiety of mothers and relatives during this long and arduous campaign and how much relief from even one hour of uncertainty would have meant to such, they would have put aside all dilatoriness and acted like London's Lady Mayoress and let mothers know the truth at once."*

It would certainly have been amazing to have received such a telegram in Hitchin at 5pm, since that was when Lord Kitchener's victory statement was posted at the War Office.

The Express declared: "There was never any doubt that our armies would bring the war to a successful conclusion" and glossed over the dark days, but honestly summed up the conflict up as "two years of trying and wearisome ordeal, wearing down the Boer commandos."

Rejoicing was the order of the day in every town and village. "Few villages heard the news on Sunday but in those where the tidings reached on the Sabbath evening there was mostly some decoration or other demonstration, while on Monday the world was a mass of flags and a blaze of illuminations.

*"The lonely cottage by the roadside as well as the town house displayed its flags and bunting and old and young caught the infection of happiness.*

*In many places schools were closed. Last Sunday will remain an epoch-making day."*

Hitchin Market Place was soon packed as the news spread and a parade was arranged. Torches were supplied by Mr F Newton and the town band turned up to lead a procession, which wandered through the streets singing patriotic songs, ringing bells and banging on door knockers.

The musical Express reporter complained that "several songs were all going at the same time in diverse keys."

He had more legitimate cause for complaint when rowdy lads formed gangs and caused "discreditable scenes" as they paraded around, arm in arm, singing snatches of hymns and ditties while others "none too sober, celebrated Peace by fighting at street corners."

The next morning householders were at work early decorating their houses and by noon "the town presented a very gay appearance."

A procession was arranged and many of the children taking part wore fantastic garb. At 9pm there was a second, better organised, torchlit parade. But again there was trouble.

"As usual on these occasions it was joined by a large section of the undesirable element who, it is said, were responsible for a deal of mischief. Fireworks were let off all over the town and a few rockets were sent up, while the frequent discharge of guns kept the town centre lively." Numberless flags and illuminations, put up by patriotic residents, were stolen.

On Tuesday free churchmen got together to pray "as they had never prayed before for the Earth to learn the art of war no longer." The rumour that war was over reached Biggleswade in the early hours of Monday morning and Dan Albone ran to the signal box at the station to confirm it. Disregarding the fact it was now 3.15am, Dan rushed to his workshop and got up a head of steam to rouse the townsfolk with the "indescribable notes of his hooter."

His neighbours took the interruption well and by 4am the First Company Volunteer Band was playing in the streets while the church bells rang out. "Few people were in bed by 6am," said the Express in characteristic understatement.

Soon after noon on Monday, 1,400 people gathered in the Market Place and: "There followed what has never before been witnessed – all the ministers in the town sharing in the conduct of a public service of thanksgiving."

Children were given oranges and the day finished with an open air concert and a bonfire at Hick's-pit, lit by Fred See, amid cheering.

Baldock folk were roused from their slumbers earlier than those in Biggleswade – they heard the news when the church bells were rung at 11pm on Sunday. They gathered in the Market Place and "notwithstanding it was Sunday" fireworks were let off and the local volunteers fired a volley. A bonfire was lit in Whitehorse Street at midnight.

In nearby Arlesey, the superintendent at the Three Counties Asylum was anxious that everyone should join in the fun. Only necessary work was done on the Monday and a cricket match was arranged between the patients and attendants. "Great fun was occasioned by one of the cricketers (who had borrowed a pair of shoes) leaving them behind him every time he ran after the ball," reported the Express.

In many ways "the terrible war raging for two years nine months" had shaken the British. But good years lay ahead for the wealthy and the middle classes.

They were moving towards the last days of a seemingly unassailable Empire and they moved with confidence and certainty.

The drums of war would not roll for another 12 years but then they were to thunder out the passing of an age.

*The corner of Hitchin Market Place, pictured in 1902*

# Favourite Express-ions – 1902

✯ A stepfather in Luton told the Board of Guardians he could not contribute towards his mother's care because he had married a widow with nine children. Spectator, the right wing Express columnist, commented: "The old excuse of having married a wife must, it would seem, be allowed in this instance."

✯ Mr R D Innes Taylor of Little Berkhamsted was summoned for keeping a servant without a licence. In his defence he told magistrates he didn't think he needed one as he had got the boy from a home and did not pay him any regular wage. The boy was in delicate health and didn't stay long, he added. He was given a small fine.

✯ Charles Sharpe of Royston was sent to prison for 14 days for stabbing his wife in the head while Hitchin magistrates jailed tramp Walter Shepherd for a week for stealing a jumper.

✯ Women's hats were causing problems at Hitchin Town Hall. A letter writer to the Express declared that action was imperative if the bulk of the audience were to get any view of the stage. At a recent performance, two or three ladies were asked to take off their hats, but they refused.

✯ Mrs Stevens of Clifton applied for a judicial separation from her husband, who was in prison for assaulting a child. She said he ill treated her and she could not live with him again. The magistrates refused, saying: "Perhaps imprisonment would make the man a better husband." Without a separation order, the man could not be forced to give his wife any money for maintenance.

*Hitchin High Street at the turn of the century*

★ There was concern that free libraries, such as the one at Luton, were breeding grounds for betting. Apparently readers were pouring over the newspapers to study form.

Some libraries had resorted to blocking out the betting news but columnist Spectator thought this "a clumsy plan and one sadly out of harmony with national traditions."

Libraries should only supply reference books and classics, he asserted while: "People who want information about betting should be called upon to pay for it."

★ A heat wave in the summer proved unfortunate for eight pigs travelling from Luton to Hitchin. The men transporting them in an open cart thought it would help them keep cool if they covered them with a tarpaulin.

But the cover slipped and smothered the pigs, with two actually dying before the journey's end. The Express headline was "Killed by kindness."

Meanwhile one man died of heat exhaustion at Bedford and two others were struck by lightning.

★ The St Albans coroner dealt with two shooting accidents in July. In one a lad of 16, out to wing wood pigeons, climbed a tree and dropped his gun, firing it into his own body.

In the second an attendant caring for a lunatic, looking after his private patient at home, took two guns into the garden to clean them. He was killed as one gun discharged by mistake.

There was some comment made at the inquest about two guns being available in the home of a lunatic, even if he was not homicidal.

★ In August four nine-year-old girls appeared before Hitchin magistrates charged with stealing apples to the value of 6d (2.5pence). Alice Monk, Minnie Harley, Beatrice Odell and Annie Garley, all of Hitchin Hill, had been caught red handed coming out of a neighbour's garden.

It was the eighth time George Deacon's trees had been raided that summer and his patience was at an end. The girls were each fined half a crown.

★ Housewives were told to keep their servant problems from their husbands. "Most women of the middle class know how terribly tiring these problems are, but it is worse than useless hashing them up at dinner," advised the Express. It would only make the master of the house angry.

★ Should doctors be required to shave their beards off? That was the question posed in the Hertfordshire Express in September. "Beards and moustaches, if bacteriologists are to be believed, form the happy hunting ground of numerous microbes.

"Perfect cleansing of hair is always attended with considerable difficulty," the paper lectured sternly.

In Germany, the reporter added, surgeons must be prepared to signify their thoroughness by sacrificing facial adornment.

*Townsfolk gather in Hitchin Market Place to celebrate the 1902 coronation of King Edward VII, after it was postponed due to his illness*

★ The home coming of Colonel and Mrs Shuttleworth from their honeymoon sent Mid Bedfordshire into a ferment of excitement in August. The happy couple were met by crowds at Biggleswade Railway Station and drove through thronged streets in a horse and pair, with flags flying from every place of business.

At Old Warden the cottages were decorated in the couple's honour, a Union Jack floated from the clock tower and the words 'Welcome Home' had been erected in an arch.

Estate tenants were joined by members of the Bedfordshire Imperial Yeomanry and the band of His Majesty's 13th Hussars, who added a brilliant note in their blue uniforms laced with gold. Bells rang out merrily as the tenants unharnessed the horses and several men took their places to draw the carriage to the house. A Yeomanry detachment carrying lances escorted the couple while the band, leading the procession, played Home Sweet Home.

"The pretty bride looked charming in an exquisite blue and white figured muslin dress," wrote the enthusiastic Express reporter. At the garden gate an elaborate arch had been constructed boasting the words "Long Life and Happiness."

The tenants and guests, numbering almost 800, poured into a huge double marquee erected in the grounds ready for the lunchtime celebration.

★ A telegram delivered to Mr Bellward, a carpenter, while he was at work outside Hitchin brought him terrible news in September. His six-year-old son Fred had been killed in an accident near his school in Queen Street when he ran out into the road as two horses and vans passed by. Fred was kicked by a foreleg and then fell under a carriage wheel. The family lived in Wymondley Road, Hitchin.

★ Two men appeared in court at Hatfield in October, charged with furious cycling on a tandem. Pc Baldock gave evidence that they went past him: "Just like a flash." Alarmed he called after them to steady their pace but they took no notice. The trip ended in tears – roadman William Scott was knocked over and broke his leg and collar bone. Mr Offin, defending the two cyclists from Clerkenwell, said they were respectable men and not like "the ordinary scorcher who was very properly brought before the bench for hard riding." The men were fined nonetheless.

★ E Ripley and Sons advertised that the Pirle finish for clothing was indispensable for the open air girl. "Pirle costume doesn't spot or cockle with rain or sea water."

★ A strange chain of events was set in motion at R H Baker's shop in Bancroft, Hitchin, after a boy broke a window by throwing an apple. The culprit, who had owned up and expressed his penitence, offered to pay for the repair.

But no sooner was the job done than a sharp-eyed burglar, seeing the putty was soft, crept up and pushed the pane out. He reached inside and grabbed six bottles of "seductive spirit." What he didn't realise was that the whisky was not real, but a dummy of coloured water for display.

★ Elephants stampeded through Newmarket in November, only a day after leaving Hitchin. They were part of a programme packed with wild beasts, appearing on Butts Close with Lord George Sanger's Circus. Large crowds watched a special noonday parade in Hitchin but at Newmarket the elephants broke down the gates of their compound one night and ran amok.

★ A butcher was fined by Hitchin magistrates for bringing a loaded revolver into the refreshment room at Hitchin Railway Station. John Clark said he hadn't realised this was in contravention of the bylaws and didn't know it was loaded anyway. He denied pointing it at two ladies, but they certainly thought he had when they rushed out of the room screaming.

★ A sad case came to court at the end of the year. Mary Boddy of Buntingford was charged with unlawfully wounding her husband Thomas by cutting his throat with a razor.

The magistrates heard that she had been complaining that her head hurt for a week and that she was worried about money after the Board of Guardians asked her to contribute to the cost of keeping her father in the workhouse. Scared she would be forced to sell up her home, she had taken to drinking in excess.

After she attacked her husband, not cutting him badly, she begged him to take her to the police. "I meant to kill the old man and then kill myself," she said.

# The curate's wife who took to drink

The headlines were damning. *Curate's Sad Tale of a Wife's Downfall*, blazed one in the Hertfordshire Express newspaper of January 1909. *Baldock labourer as Co-respondent* said another and a third read *Shocking Story – Really Perfectly Shocking. Petitioner Absolutely Ruined.*

And so he was. Enthralled Express readers soon learned how.

The petitioner was the Rev Samuel Reginald Levelis Vosper-Thomas, who was suing for divorce from his wife Mabel on the grounds of her misconduct with four correspondents.

The case was heard before Sir Gorell G Barnes and a jury. The four correspondents were named as Frederick Cole, Peter Fitzjohn, John Wilson and James Terry Hunt.

The Rev Samuel Reginald Levelis Vosper-Thomas married Miss Mabel Marsh in 1903, when he was 26 and she was 23. It seemed a promising union of well matched families. The court heard:

*"She was a young lady of respectable parentage and a good upbringing."*

The Rev Vosper-Thomas, who came from a clerical family, took up a post as curate and the couple moved to their new home. But, despite her early successful pregnancy, things soon started to go wrong. The curate became ill and grew so weak that he had to resign his living after only eight months.

Already his young wife had started to drink heavily. The birth of their son, John Leslie, did nothing to curb her new excesses – indeed she began to behave in a very worrying way:

*"Doing the most extraordinary things whilst intoxicated."*

These included trying to drown poor John in the bath. He was only rescued when her husband broke down the door.

Despite his problems the Rev Vosper-Thomas recovered his health enough to take up a new living in Hampshire – but he wasn't destined to stay there long, especially after an embarrassing incident when his wife locked herself in the house and tried to set it on fire.

*A typical well-to-do Edwardian family – Alfred Ransom pictured with his loved ones in the grounds of their house in the Benslow area of Hitchin*

He struggled to persuade Mabel to stop drinking "but she broke down again and again." Nothing he did could curb her bad behaviour and the situation became so desperate that finally his angry vicar intervened, forcing Mr Vosper-Thomas to resign.

In desperation he moved his family across the country and took a living as a curate in Stowmarket.

But the change of air did his wife no good at all – in fact she got worse and became notorious for her bad behaviour.

She would get so drunk that she fell down in public and eventually the police became involved. "It was one continuous scandal in the parish," reported the Hertfordshire Express.

The poor Rev Vosper-Thomas was driven from his new home and church once again, trailing his baby son and his debauched wife in his wake.

But this time Christian charity prevailed. A kindly vicar in Ipswich, aware of the situation, took pity on the couple and offered them a home with "the idea of reclaiming the lady."

His charity was misplaced; he had no more success than her husband. The Herts Express reported at the divorce hearing:

"At last her conduct became so terrible and so notorious when she was drinking that it became a common headline in the local papers: 'Mrs Vosper-Thomas drunk again'."

To compound her crimes the desperate woman tried to commit suicide once, leaving her open to the risk of prosecution. Her husband was at his wits' end.

He described to the divorce court his frantic efforts to control his wife, who always 'broke out again." "He brought every possible means to bear on her but she even drank methylated spirits when she could not get anything else," he said in evidence.

Ipswich had been their last chance but the situation was more out of control than ever. At last the Bishop of Norwich himself intervened, ordering the curate to resign and warning him that he would never get another living unless he separated from his wife. Seeing no other way out, the curate allowed a deed of separation to be drawn up and was granted custody of his little son. It was the summer of 1907 and the young couple had been married for just four years.

Mabel was to receive an allowance of £1 a week from her husband, but he soon refused to pay as rumours of her debauched lifestyle reached him. Instead he sued for divorce. A court refused to hear Mabel's pleas for financial help until after the divorce case, many months later.

The story of Mabel's decline from drink into adultery emerged at the hearing.

She had taken lodgings with a fishmonger in Colchester, where she took a fancy to the odd job man, Frederick Cole, and was soon "compromised."

But she showed no inclination to stay with him or keep out of her husband's way. Instead she followed the curate to Clothall Rectory, where he was staying with his father and their son, eking out his meagre finances.

The harassment went on as time and again Mabel walked into the village, drunk even if it was early in the day, and demanded money and help.

> 'It was one continuous scandal in the parish as the wife made headlines'

> In despair the family had Mabel admitted to an asylum

*Left: Hunts Temperance Hotel in Bancroft, Hitchin, where Mabel Vosper-Thomas caused a scandal*

She brought one of her lovers, James Hunt, up to the Rectory, where they prowled around, planning to kidnap her son. In despair the family had her admitted to an asylum but the staff could not deal with her.

She was discharged as sane, although diagnosed as a chronic alcoholic. Next the family sent her to a home for inebriates at Ware, but she would not stay.

There seemed to be no solution for poor Samuel. A particularly embarrassing incident took place on Sunday, August 11, 1907, when Mabel arrived in Clothall at about 10.30am, promising she would try to reform and asking for money to get back to the inebriates home in Ware.

The family would not admit her but asked her to wait by the church. The Rector called the police and one of his sons went out to the churchyard to talk to Mabel.

When local bobby Thomas Unwin arrived he agreed to escort her into Baldock, where she could catch a train. He walked behind her out of the village, keeping her in view all the way along the dusty, hot road.

But Mabel was wily. She had no intention of going to a home for inebriates – instead she turned aside at the very first pub she came to in Baldock, the Hen and Chickens. Pc Unwin stepped inside too and warned the landlord not to serve her.

Foiled, the lady walked on and soon began chatting to a man standing in his garden with his son. Peter Fitzjohn, a widower, invited her into the house and she accepted.

Peter's son Alfred gave evidence at the divorce hearing. By then he was 16 and a sailor on board the training ship Exmouth. He appeared at court in his smart uniform, with clear memories of the summer day the strange lady called at his home. He said:

*"She asked the way to the station. Then she asked father to take her in and she stayed till Monday morning."*

Peter told his son to go out and when he came back, at about 9pm, he had to sleep downstairs because his father was upstairs with the lady.

The Rev Vosper-Thomas kept trying to help Mabel, who continued to promise to reform if only she could have another chance. The inebriates home having failed, he took her to Hunt's Temperance Hotel in Hitchin on August 3, 1907, where alcohol was strictly forbidden.

Men however were not and within two days her husband heard reports that his wife was going about with a married man.

It soon emerged that Mabel had become very friendly with the hotel's owner, James Terry Hunt – so friendly indeed that his wife moved out of the hotel altogether and fierce rows broke out between Mr Hunt and his son Bruce, who also seemed rather partial to the young guest.

The situation was getting out of hand and Mr Hunt decided to follow his wife to Maidenhead. For a short while Mabel lived with both of them, before moving into lodgings in Stevenage with a couple called Smith. There she continued to drink, imbibing to such an extent that she fell ill and was frequently abusive and violent.

Finally, sick in body and at heart, she asked Mrs Smith to send for her guardian, naming him as James Terry Hunt.

Mabel had thoroughly unsettled the Smith household, threatening members of the family and behaving so badly that when Mr Hunt arrived Mrs Smith was in a lather of anxiety. She actually begged him not to go into Mabel's room because: "She had come to the conclusion that she was a very dangerous woman."

Mr Hunt told her not to worry, that it would be all right, and went straight inside. Mrs Smith was not placated. Indeed she was so concerned that she followed Mr Hunt into the room, waiting to make sure all was well.

She told the divorce court that she clearly heard Mabel cry out: "Oh darling Terry, Terry dear. I must come back to you."

Mrs Smith thought this a strange comment for a ward to make to her guardian and determined to stay during the interview, telling the court later that she didn't want a scandal in her house. Mabel and Mr Hunt were equally determined to be alone and resisted all Mrs Smith's entreaties.

In the end, neither side yielding, the forceful Mabel pushed Mrs Smith out of the door and had her private 'interview' with her 'guardian.' When Mr Hunt finally emerged, a furious Mrs Smith told him to take Mabel away and to never come back. Mr Hunt's sojourn in Maidenhead was over. He returned to run his hotel in Hitchin while helping Mabel move to new lodgings in Stevenage, and the pair continued to meet.

The Rev Vosper-Thomas, hearing of the renewed scandal, decided he wanted an end to the farce of his marriage, which had reduced him to penury, made him unemployable and taken away his future.

*Baldock when the streets were simply mud*

So desperate was he for evidence against Mabel that he hired a private detective who stayed at Hunt's Temperance Hotel for two weeks, trying to get proof that adultery had occurred. The court heard:

*"On one occasion at least there was the most direct evidence that misconduct took place."*

But by now judge Sir Gorell Barnes was sickened by the whole business. He did not want any more details of the Hunt-Mabel liaison and, without hearing a word about any shenanigans with the fourth named co-respondent, John Wilson of Kings Road, Hitchin, who denied adultery, the judge called a halt to the proceedings.

He told the jury he was quite satisfied after hearing the evidence already given that the respondent had degraded herself and two cases had been proved – against Cole and Fitzjohn. The decree nisi was granted.

But what was to happen to Mrs Vosper-Thomas, he asked? He could not get over the case: "It was a shocking story, really perfectly shocking," he told the court.

Her husband was absolutely ruined, not allowed to take even casual duty at his father's church since his wife had taken to arriving at the Rectory in an inebriated state.

Mr Vosper-Thomas, no doubt elated to be legally free of his nightmare spouse, assured the judge that as soon as he managed to get a little money together he would give some to Mabel. But before the year was out his errant wife was back in the news, causing him yet more embarrassment, distress and pain.

This time she appeared before Luton magistrates' court along with a Norwich tramp called Thomas Brown. They were charged with breaking into a house in Stopsley and stealing various items including a silver watch chain and a loaf of bread. A report in the Express said: "The female prisoner, who is a woman of superior education, wore a tailor-made coat, a black hat neatly trimmed and a dark veil.

*"The male prisoner, who looks like a typical tramp and is apparently possessed of little refinement, had to be accommodated with a seat."*

He suffered from heart problems, the court was told.

Mabel's new companion had not improved her behaviour. The court heard they had lurked in a street at 6am, watching until the owner of one house left for work before breaking in.

His wife, cowering in bed, heard voices downstairs but hid under the blankets while the thieves took sugar, butter, cocoa, a loaf, a towel and a silver watch chain.

Oddly enough it was the loaf that proved most distinctive, being home-made and of a special shape.

When Pc Wood, obviously acting on more than random chance, found the tramp at the First and Last public house, with a partly eaten loaf on the table in front of him, he was able to identify it at once.

Mabel arrived soon afterwards and asked the tramp if he was feeling better. She told Pc Wood that he was her husband and he had not been well.

This touching scene of domestic bliss was rather spoiled when the constable noticed a bottle wrapped up in her cloak and, as she took it off, a silver watch chain fell to the floor.

She was also, testified Pc Wood, under the influence of drink.

This evidence infuriated Mabel, who called out in court: "I couldn't have had much – I bought it for this man's benefit, he was having fits."

She turned to the magistrates and made an impassioned plea of innocence.

She declared: "I am not guilty of the charge brought against me.

"In the name of heaven I am not.

## 'I am not guilty, in the name of heaven I am not'

"I was going to an inebriates home and ran away but I was making my way back."

It was all too much for the tramp and he collapsed and had to be assisted out of the court. It was too much for the magistrates too when they heard there was another charge of larceny at Lilley outstanding against the inadequate Bonnie and Clyde. Mabel and the tramp were committed to stand trial at Bedford quarter sessions.

The next mention of Mabel in the Express is at Welwyn Magistrates' Court in Hertfordshire. The headlines read *A Divorced Woman's Escapades* and *Mabel Vosper-Thomas Again Before the Magistrates*.

It was January 28, 1910, and Mabel, who was still only 30 years old, was subject to a lengthy charge, that "she had duly entered into certain recognisances but she did fail to observe the conditions as to abstaining from taking intoxicating liquors and to stay in the same place for three years, until November 1909, and had absconded."

All her promises were broken and her vow to attend an inebriates' home had been hollow.

Her address is given as formerly of Hitchin, but now of no fixed abode. Mabel pleaded guilty and had nothing to say in answer to the charge. In contrast the chairman of the bench, Sir Alfred J Reynolds, had plenty.

They were very sorry to see the defendant before them again, he told her wearily.

She was trying the patience of everyone. He always made it a rule that, if anyone had broken a bond they had entered into, he gave them the maximum penalty. But the defendant, in consequence of what she had done, was making their duty extremely difficult.

As she was willing to go to a certified home again, and Lady Henry Somerset had consented to receive her back in the home (which was against the rules) she would be sent there for two years.

She must believe she was going to Lady Somerset's home in Surrey under quite different circumstances this time and if she broke her bond she would be liable to be arrested as an ordinary criminal and very differently dealt with.

There was a further charge against Mabel – feloniously stealing a loaf of bread, one and a half pounds of cheese, two rashers of bacon, an enamel dish and a neck wrap from Chequers Public House on November 17, 1909, in Welwyn. No evidence was offered.

*Mabel, the court heard, had seven previous convictions dating from December, 1907. The last one was for larceny only days earlier, in Slough, when she had been sentenced to one day's imprisonment.*

The report finished with the comment that the defendant appeared quite willing to go to Lady Somerset's home, from where she had escaped, and Mabel left the court to turn over yet another new leaf.

There was an interesting footnote to this story. In May 1911 Mr James Hunt, son of the late proprietor of the Temperance Hotel in Hitchin, along with his wife and three-month-old baby, were involved in a fearful accident at sea.

The steamer they were travelling on, from Havana to New York, collided with another in dense fog.

In the midst of the panic and confusion Mr Hunt, a mining engineer, assisted in keeping back a number of Mexican firemen who tried to get into the boats.

As he grappled with the men, his wife fainted and her unconscious body was picked up and tossed onto a raft.

The small baby rolled away from her grasp and was left unnoticed on the deck, until finally a sailor took it in his arms.

The family, along with the rest of the passengers, escaped the catastrophe with their lives.

*Church Lane, Stevenage, pictured in about 1905*

# Favourite Express-ions – 1903

★ A cow, being driven down Hitchin Hill, took a great dislike to a five-year-old boy in her path and, catching him between her legs, threw him on her horns. The unfortunate lad broke his thigh.

★ John Trolley had been luckier when he was a boy – he had ridden a bullock round Baldock to celebrate the battle of Waterloo. The Express reported his death early in 1903, commenting that the 94-year-old had only spent about six nights in his entire life outside the town, and never for more than one at a time.

A boot and shoe maker, he had worked until well in his 80s and lit a bonfire in the town to mark the Relief of Mafeking.

★ At Christmas time in 1902 a huge blaze had caused severe damage at Arthur Ransom's farm in Hitchin town centre. The fire brigade had been criticised for being too slow, badly organised and using broken hose.

Captain Edwin Logsdon was furious – he told the Express that some men had to run a quarter of a mile in their fire boots and belts and then "stuck to their work like Britons."

"The present fire station is only 15ft by 18ft and I would like to know if anyone can wash, dry, oil etc 16 lengths of hose, varying in length from 50 to 100 feet, in such a very limited space."

A few months later their colleagues in Stevenage fared better, with a letter in the Express singing their praises and asking for a fire station. "We have the first requisite, a band of volunteers under an efficient captain. We have also some bright helmets and a most imposing alarm bell. What else? A manual fire engine kept in a shed and an old hose that leaks."

★ The weather was so cold in January that a field was flooded in Biggleswade for ice skating.

★ The news that resident Thomas Day had lost £11 to a London pickpocket at a horse sale moved the folk of Stevenage to start a subscription list of donations for him at the end of January.

*Hitchin Station and staff in 1903, in front of the cabmen's shelter now standing in the Market Place. Picture: Courtesy of Betty Fell and Jean Maylin. Inset: Henry Porter, station master from 1890 until 1903.*

✶ Dr Clark spoke to the Church Missionary Society in February, at Hitchin Town Hall. He told his enthralled audience: "It was not civilisation that India wanted but the Gospel. People must not be too hasty and impatient; some people put a penny in a missionary box and expect a convert at the other end, much in the same way as confectionery was obtained from a penny in a slot machine."

A few weeks later the Rev Isidor Gelbflaum gave a lecture on behalf of the Mission to the Jews. His life had not been easy and he had been turned out of his home by his parents in Warsaw when only 19, because he had received Christ as his saviour, he said.

✶ If cleanliness was next to godliness, things looked bad for a housewife cautioned by Mr Blood, the Hitchin inspector of nuisances, in February. Her house was filthy. "Her husband," Mr Blood continued: "said he had done all he could to get her to keep the place cleaner, he had thrashed her but it had done her no good," (laughter) reported the Express. The housewife obviously hadn't followed the dictum of Dr Sworder of Luton, who came up with some ideas to reduce infant mortality, in August. "During her last term at board school every girl should receive specific instruction in the feeding of infants. Directly she leaves school at the age of 13 or so she will probably have to look after the baby brothers and sisters."

✶ In March a picturesque thatched cottage in Walsworth Road burned down in the middle of the morning. A messenger ran for the fire brigade while women and schoolchildren (released for the purpose) removed furniture. After this disaster Mr Franklin gave permission for the telephone at the station warehouse to be available in case of fire. "By using this several minutes would have been saved," reported the Express.

✶ George Malkin, who lived in Queen Street, was one of Hitchin's less savoury characters. In the run-up to the urban district council elections in April, Mr Malkin decided he would back Francis Newton. He put blue on his face and wore a chimney pot hat. "But what at first was perhaps thought amusing seems afterwards to have become a source of annoyance," reported the Express.

"Mr Newton asked him to desist but he didn't and Mr Newton issued handbills saying 'I have asked him several times to stop. His procedure is most annoying'."

Mr Malkin retaliated by walking about wearing a sandwich board saying: "The man Malkin has stopped shouting for the man Newton.

He did his best to get him in two years ago and charged him nothing and was doing his best to get him in again. If this is how Newton treats his friends, turn him out and keep him out altogether."

Mr Malkin's final entreaty went unanswered and Mr Newton was re-elected.

A few weeks later Malkin was a witness in court, after his wife Julia was charged with assaulting him.

He told the magistrates a long story of "domestic unpleasantness.

He said his wife hit him on the head with a small poker or the leg of a chair."

In her defence Julia claimed he came home mad drunk and was a lazy man. She was bound over.

✶ Walking fever gripped the countryside in June, and a large crowd gathered to watch the Rev A C Madden, who said he could walk almost 12 miles from Stevenage to Hatfield in two hours 45 minutes. He was right and strolled home with 31 minutes to spare.

Enthusiasts set themselves a sterner task at Hitchin, setting out from the Three Moorhens to reach High Barnet, 22 miles away. The winner took 4hrs and 14 mins.

*Edwin Logsdon, fire chief*

*Rural life – Pegsdon Hills and a flock of sheep, probably pictured in about 1903 or 1904*

But the man who undertook to walk eight miles in an hour at Stevenage in August failed miserably, watched by hundreds of people as he paced to and fro on a marked course.

★ London children coming to holiday in the countryside often brought disease and an outbreak of measles in Pirton was laid at their door. But nothing could be done, as every child "had to pass a doctor before they came and they were certified to be free from disease," Hitchin Rural District councillors were told. Chairman Mr N J Hine thought the holidays were beneficial for the youngsters: "But at the same time it was very hard for the villages to which they came."

One family in Pirton were "continually having fresh batches of children."

★ A three-year-old child was reunited with his parents after Hitchin police chalked a notice on the pavement outside the post office, stating: "A lost boy is at Hitchin police station." Officers were praised by the Express for their ingenuity.

★ Hitchin became the centre of a national frenzy when the newspaper Tit Bits buried a treasure of 500 sovereigns near the town. Special trains were laid on and cyclists, motorists and pedestrians poured in. It was even possible to buy postcards showing the site.

★ Eight-year old Peter Reynolds of Pirton suffered severe internal injuries when he rolled to the bottom of Pegsdon Hills.

★ A dog bite proved fatal to Ambrose Brown, a 74-year-old Hitchin tailor from Verulam Road. As the blood poisoning took hold Mr Brown muttered: "To think I have got to lose my life through a dog bite." His wife wanted a certificate to prove he had been bitten: "Because people say I tell lies," adding: "People told me it did not matter if he is dead or alive for what good he does me." The doctor William Grellett tried feeding him up, but to no avail.

★ Beautiful postcards were available in Baldock, showing the site of the planned new garden city at Letchworth. Ebenezer Howard explained his revolutionary principles to a meeting at Hitchin Town Hall.

"The inhabitants of the city would have good air, good water and good houses, more trees, ornamental lakes and combine the social benefits of the town with the advantages of country life," he said. There would be low rent and high wages, leading to "a new eve of life."

✷ Taking a single drink to fight off a cold proved fatal for teetotaller Thomas Thornton, a 28-year-old from Bushey, who had survived two years' fighting in South Africa.

He went shopping in Watford, swallowed 6d of gin and then wove his way unsteadily home. On the way he was knocked over by a bike.

The cyclist told the coroner that Thornton just stepped in front of him, staggering about, and he rang his bell furiously.

The unhappy man added: "It will be a long time before I ride a bicycle again."

An Ashwell cyclist, who had been to Dunstable for the day, did not fare much better. Mr Kelley, of Cold Harbour, rode into the shaft of a trap in fog in Bancroft, Hitchin and was badly injured.

✷ Barley was cut in a field in Ickleford in November – so late that the Express said it was unprecedented and then, contradicting itself, that the last time it happened was in the wet season of 1860.

✷ The newspaper looked back at Hitchin's past in a special article published near the end of the year. In about 1790 the town was: "Second in the county for the number of trades, houses and inhabitants but second to none for its market for corn, especially wheat, both in quality and quantity, while its malt was highly prized even beyond the neighbouring counties."

*Bancroft, Hitchin, pictured at the turn of the century*

# The coronation that proved a riot

Never was appendicitis more ill timed. Edward VII's life was in danger, his family distraught, his doctors in turmoil. The country rocked with the blow.

Miles of bunting, millions of cakes, games, festivities and jamborees, all were cancelled or rushed through to stop the food spoiling. It was a disastrous end to months of work and anticipation. Few monarchs, across all nations and chronology, had missed their own coronation.

What was to be done with the Japanese lanterns, the tons of muslin in red, white and blue, the bucket lamps and the fireworks? Who would buy Hitchin's special Coronation book including a necrology of well known townsfolk, published by Paternoster and Hales of Sun Street? Would the new fire station in Paynes Park, planned to honour Edward VII, go ahead if he died hours before the planned ceremony? What of all the china, specially made and bearing the date June 26, 1902?

So much had to be cancelled. Hitchin had planned street decorations of Venetian masts bearing pennons and wands, furnished with wreaths and heraldic shields. Festoons were to garland the Market Place with evergreens interwoven with white ribbon. Other countries would be honoured – Newfoundland and the Colonies and the great dominions of Canada, India, Ceylon and New Zealand would be represented by shields.

It was same everywhere. Villages had saved and planned for months, laying on teas for the children and old folk, bonfires and sports.

At Hexton a cricket match was arranged, along with a show of decorated bikes, a men's barrow-pushing contest, a tug of war and, for the women, a washing and hemming competition. All events were paid for by the Lord of the Manor.

Hitchin had laid its plans for months. In April they had decided to hold a children's tea, an old people's dinner, a carnival, procession and bonfire with fireworks, and a sports day.

The King knew this and of one thousand score similar events to pay him honour. He fought so hard to attend the Coronation that he seriously risked his life. Finally he submitted to an operation on June 23rd and the disbelieving, shocked, worried nation, waited for news.

Edward rallied; relief took the place of anxiety. But a host of practical problems remained. There were riots when festivities were cancelled in many towns, including Stevenage, Luton and Watford.

The "lowest class", full of "bitter resentment," took part in wild talk and rumours galore in Stevenage. They infuriated three tradesmen who were overheard to say "that pigs' troughs were good enough to feed these people in."

'These people' decided to make the tradesmen sit up. "From 8pm until midnight the town was in the possession of a gang of roughs which marched up and down beating tin trays and pans, shouting popular songs and generally making the place insufferable," reported the Express.

Because of another riot in Watford, only two police officers remained in the town and they were powerless to quell the crowd. Their hero was Mr George Ayres, the only Coronation committee member who had voted to go ahead with the dinner. He was cheered repeatedly.

At 9pm "after repeated halts for liquid refreshment" the crowd kicked in a butcher's door and then went from shop to shop causing trouble.

They only halted at the bottom of Orchard Road when the Rev A C Madden harangued them, finally persuading them to go home. The departing crowd gave three cheers for Sgt Brice who, through wisdom or necessity, had left them alone.

Stotfold had a much easier time, although organisers were criticised for selling the children's cake to conserve funds for the real event, rescheduled for August 9.

In July, Express women's writer Olive declared that no colour became the new Queen Alexandra better than heliotrope, which she had worn to the Imperial Coronation bazaar.

In an aside she referred to the tragedy which overtook the event, when a flag rope became dislodged, killing one and injuring several. The poor victim who died was a Miss Strothy who had come over from Canada especially for the Coronation.

Olive was piqued about the timing of the big event. "If only the Coronation could take place in the afternoon or, better still, the evening, had long been the cry of peeresses," she wrote.

"But it was not to be. For once at least in our lives the fortunate recipients of invites to the Abbey had to be up at dawn, admit the coiffeur, and don the regulation white gown and robes, not the most becoming toilette at that hour of the day."

Westminster Abbey may have been the most exciting and glorious place in the world that summer, but Hitchin laid on a splendid pageant.

"The tragic postponement of the events and the circumstances of the King's illness gave it a more solemn significance," reported the Express.

There was no hint of riot now – nothing but perfect accord, everything in the best of taste, and nothing to offend even the most sensitive.

Hitchin's day kicked off with a service at 11am at St Mary's Church, followed by a dinner for old soldiers at the Sun Hotel. From 12.30pm until 1.15pm the town band played in the Market Place, with up to 4,000 people joining in God Save the King.

*Sun Street in 1902, decked out for King Edward VII's coronation*

At 2.30pm the procession started, with great bustle and excitement. Among the marchers were councillors and schoolchildren, but the most cheers were reserved for the volunteer firemen who accompanied both the steam and manual engines.

"One cannot speak too highly of the procession," reported the Express, praising everything as "striking, splendidly conceived and executed with the utmost attention to detail and without regard to the amount of labour involved.

"Hitchin Fire Brigade, with their flashing helmets and their highly polished engines, added greatly to the artistic effect of the pageant."

At the head walked the "gorgeously attired beadle, armed with a rattle and old horn lantern, tokens of his ancient office as firemaster, followed by the fire engine from 1774, escorted by a number of men garbed in the quaint uniform of the period." The procession was brought up at the rear by an Empire car "in accordance with the sentiment of the day."

It featured figures representing John Bull, Paddy, a Scot, a Welshman, a Bengal Lancer, a Zulu, an Australian bushman, a New South Wales lancer, a Canadian Scout, a Maori, a North American Indian, an Egyptian, an Indian maharaja, an admiral and a general.

The Royal standard was hoisted at 4pm and at 5.30pm there was a parade of decorated cycles, followed by a carnival masquerade and torchlit procession at 8.30pm with a firework display and bonfire on Butts Close.

At the workhouse fairy lamps lit the edges of the path in the evening and special rations were issued, including roast beef and plum pudding. A pint of beer or mineral water was issued to everybody and men had a packet of tobacco.

*Hitchin Market Place decorated for the 1902 Coronation*

*Royal celebrations followed thick and fast – in 1897 Queen Victoria held her diamond jubilee. Here townsfolk gather in Hitchin Market Place to sing God Save the Queen at 11am on Thursday, June 23.*

Inmates were allowed to go to church, attend a few of the festivities in the town and "wander about the grounds of the workhouse at will and from this point they could see the fireworks."

The next day Mr Seebohm raised money to pay for 150 brakes – open horse-drawn carriages – which took the inmates through the town to see the decorations and on a trip to Walsworth and Willian.

Every town and village took part in the pageantry. At Stevenage the houses were lavishly decorated and a tea was laid for 820 children in the High Street.

The leftovers were distributed among the poor. Games included obstacle, ginger beer (for boys), bun (for girls) and wheelbarrow races along with a greasy pole to climb with a leg of mutton at the top.

Knebworth did not hold its Coronation celebration until the following January, although the food, already purchased, was given out to villagers in June. When the big day finally came the village was in the grip of a diphtheria outbreak and it was considered unwise to go ahead.

So in January the villagers gathered at Deards End Farm, where a barn was decorated with greenery, plants and flags, while 350 sat down for a special concert.

There had been a 64-year-long wait for the 1902 coronation – Queen Victoria had reigned for longer than any other British monarch. It was a mere nine years before the next celebration, in June 1911, when George V was crowned, but there had been vast changes in technology and in society during that time.

As one small indication, the Pixmore Institute in Letchworth showed a special series of cinematograph pictures depicting in living manner the Royal Coronation Procession in its progress to and from Buckingham Palace and Westminster Abbey.

Thanks to a special scientific process, the films were rendered entirely non-flammable, so this most interesting exhibition could be watched in perfect safety.

Coronation day itself was cold and wet but most festivities went ahead as long planned.

Churches held special services and massed choirs sang in Town Square, Letchworth. There was a procession, sports and teas for the children and old folk, with dancing until 9pm.

Events were even more lively down the road. "As befits a Royal Manor, the display of loyalty at Hitchin was most generous," wrote the Letchworth Citizen newspaper.

"No road, no lane or street was without its lavish display of bunting, decorations, banners, crowns etc and even byways, yards and courts bore tribute to the gaiety of the occasion."

Most thoroughfares were a blaze of colour with garlands, festoons and appropriate drapings of the Royal colours giving the quaint and varied houses and establishments a new and most festive appearance.

Garlands were set on tall poles, topped with shields blazoned with the arms and names of different colonies and countries of the Empire. Everything was ornamented: "Hats, bicycles, coats, costumes, carts and horses were all expressive of the Coronation spirit."

Baldock excelled itself – "no town in England could better show its loyalty to the throne." Nearly every window was decorated with very pleasing results and every child was given a china Coronation mug, a papier mache plate, a bun and a packet of sweets.

Every woman in the country called Mary, May, Maria, Marian, Marion or Marie was asked to contribute to a Coronation gift for Queen Mary. Anything from a penny to a sovereign would be acceptable, they were told.

The appeal raised £12,000 and won a heartfelt 'thank you' from the new Queen, who said: "I thank most warmly all the Marys in the Empire who have been so generous."

She was given an insignia of the garter and a picture of the King and her son, to be handed down as heirlooms.

But not everyone was happy. The Letchworth Citizen carried a letter in June 1911 complaining about the huge sums squandered on the festivities at a time of high unemployment.

The writer, who called it imbecilic, contrasted empty grates with the ostentatious waste of bonfires, fireworks, bunting and flags.

*The proclamation of George V in 1910, in Brand Street, Hitchin*

# Dying with Panache

Annie Woods was 71 when she died, in October 1902. It was not a bad age and Annie still knew how to enjoy herself – she looked forward to a couple of drinks on Saturday nights, when she was paid her small allowance from the parish of Melbourn.

Not everyone in the village approved of the game old widow, who lived with her son Samuel, and several busy bodies had tried to coax her into the workhouse. When Annie said she would not go, they talked about cutting off her allowance to force her into it, whatever she wanted.

She foiled them in the end though. One Saturday night Samuel, a farm labourer, was settled in bed and drifting off to sleep when he noticed a strange smell permeating the cottage.

Thoroughly alarmed he rushed downstairs to investigate and found his mother slumped against the front door with her clothes on fire. Frantically he beat out the flames and tried to help Mrs Woods into her room.

But she was too weak to walk and he had to carry her gently to the bed and lay her down. "I feel easier now," she reassured him. "I'll lie here and rest for a time." Samuel nodded and left the room but, worried about his mother, he returned several times during the night to check on her.

At 7am he decided to consult his sister who, with more common sense than her brother, immediately fetched a doctor.

It was too late. Mrs Woods died the following evening, leaving an insoluble mystery behind her. The inquest could not determine how her clothes had caught alight. Was it from the fire in the living room? If so why was she by the front door? And how had the blaze begun anyway?

Samuel gave evidence that, although his mother generally got tipsy on a Saturday night, she had not drunk much that evening. The coroner recorded a verdict of accidental death and Mrs Woods went to her grave without ever having to set foot in the hated workhouse.

*Sun Street, Hitchin, about 1890*

The funeral of poor Edith Moss caused more consternation and ill feeling than the poor woman had earned in life.

A barmaid of 28, she was found dead in the river after she was sacked from her job at the Castle Hotel in Cambridge for not giving satisfaction. Her boss described her as a "nervous peculiar girl" with a bad memory and a tendency to give the wrong change.

But customers at the Sun Hotel, Hitchin, where she worked for a year, remembered her as refined and well liked.

The inquest jury returned a verdict of found drowned but the vicar officiating at her burial in Wicken decided it was a suicide and refused to conduct a full burial service. Instead the "few sorrowing friends and a sympathetic group of villagers" heard little more than a psalm read. Edith's cousin protested but the vicar said he had no choice, creating "an unfortunate and painful impression," reported the Express.

A moment's inattention on a busy washing day cost little Herbert Farrow his life, in October 1902. His mother Marie, of Ducklands, Hitchin, was washing clothes in the kitchen one Wednesday afternoon while Herbert, aged only 14 months, played around her.

Marie, whose husband Alfred was horse keeper for Mr Nicholls, carried some boiling water from the copper to a bath sitting on the floor. "I went to put some coal on the fire and when I turned round he was on his back in the bath," a weeping Marie told the inquest.

"There was only about two quarts of water in the bath. I got his clothes off and wrapped him up." But it was too late, the screaming baby was so badly scalded he died of shock.

## The frantic girl screamed as she burst into flames

It was a careless moment that destroyed servant Sophie Lewin as well. Fifteen-year-old Sophie, who came from Henlow, was warming cleaning fluid with turpentine on the stove when it caught fire. She snatched the pan, spilling some of the liquid on her apron, which immediately ignited.

Sophie panicked, running round the kitchen and then into the garden, her clothes ablaze. A horrified Ralph Hill watched from the other side of a fence, which he had to smash to reach the screaming girl.

The rug he threw burst into flames, injuring his hands, and he had to use water to douse the fire. "It was seen at once it was a hopeless case," reported the Express in February 1905. Sophie died a few hours later.

The Bible Class Meeting held on Sunday afternoons at Hitchin's Town Hall was one of the most popular in the county, thanks to the vicar, Canon Jones. It attracted men of all denominations, enthused by the Canon's delivery, by his practical sympathy and his interest in their lives.

But on one Sunday in January, 1911, the fare on offer was unusually sensational when one of the long-standing members, Arthur Aylott, died in his seat just as the afternoon's activities started. Poor Mr Aylott was not in the best of health but he had just told Canon Jones he was feeling better.

There could be no question that he was mistaken though as his laboured breathing alarmed the men around him and those who possessed ambulance certificates rushed to his aid.

As Mr Aylott fell into unconsciousness, Mr Grellett was sent for and the sick man was carried into an anteroom. By the time the doctor arrived he was dead.

"Canon Jones, when it became known that death had entered the classes in such a swift manner, impressively offered a prayer and the whole of the men stood and sang the hymn *Days and moments quickly flying blend the living with the dead*," reported the Express.

The police ambulance arrived to take poor Mr Aylott's body to his home in Lancaster Road.

Mr Aylott, who was 60 and a tailor, had undergone several operations for cancer but that afternoon "he had appeared particularly cheerful and gave reassuring news of his health."

Poor William Hare was too muddled and sick to get a doctor after he was hit on the head by a cow he was trying to feed. He staggered out of the cowhouse where he worked at Temple Farm, Preston, and stumbled home. He was seen on his way, swaying as if he were drunk, his face smeared with blood that trickled down his neck.

Because it was only two days after Christmas, in 1910, his wife and son were away. Mr Hare, who was 62, lay down in bed to wait for them.

His son Arthur came home first, followed by his wife Emma, who bathed his head and then decided a doctor was needed. It did no good. Mr Hare grew weaker as the days passed and died on January 15, 1911, of a brain haemorrhage.

Working on a farm was obviously hazardous. Another inquest heard that shepherd Jesse Stapleton of High Heath Farm had been crushed against a wall by a bull four weeks before his death in October, 1912.

The jury had to sit on bales of straw in a barn and then interview Jessie's elderly wife Lydia at her fireside. She told them 65-year-old Jesse had not been well since the accident with the bull, when he was helping to ring it.

But he was not one to complain and continued to leave for work at 5.15am every day. On the morning of his death he had fed the sheep and was going back to the farm when he felt ill and lay down in a field. He died there, on his back, of heart failure.

There was nothing odd about the death of George Dering of Lockleys in Welwyn, in February 1911. It was the reputation he left behind him that caused comment, with national newspapers taking up the tale of the eccentric recluse who left a tremendous fortune in cash and properties.

Although a widower, he lived a bachelor life and had not seen his daughter for several years. There were five carriages in his stables, including two early Victorian travelling coaches, one in bright yellow with leather upholstery, gold braid and brocade.

They were covered in dust, which was hardly surprising as they had not been used for 50 years, when the last horse left the stables. There had, oddly, been a coachman for a further four decades but he was long gone now.

For the last 10 years Mr Dering's household had consisted of his butler and his butler's wife. Presumably under instructions, they had let the building go, with pictures stacked three or four deep, their faces turned against the wall.

Large rooms were filled with marble statues, mostly from the 1862 Great Exhibition in Paris – one had cost £2,000 – and there were Dresden vases and enamel clocks everywhere.

But a creeper grew across the front door and over the coat of arms, where just a trace of gold and blue paint could be seen. The coach house, surmounted by a big clock tower, was covered in thick ivy from the face of the clock to the ground. The hedges in the park were uncut, the trees uncared for and the terraces unmown. It was a scene of desolation.

It had not always been so. Once Mr Dering had been hospitable and entertained at Lockleys. Blondin, the famous tightrope walker, had been a friend and taught him his art. Mr Dering had walked across the water in front of Lockleys on a rope, watched by the villagers and tenants. He had even wheeled a venturesome guest over in a barrow. As a hobby he had studied electricity.

*An idyllic rural scene at Weston in about 1900*

"Latterly however he grew to dislike any connection with the outside world," wrote the Express. "He would not have sheep and cattle in the park for fear he might hear the bleating and lowing of animals. Finally he diverted the main road, which ran near the house, and built a new one, making a gully 30-feet deep and 300 yards long through the hill, so the road was effectively hidden from the house." His privacy cost him £20,000.

On his death another mystery emerged as it became clear that Mr Dering, who had once lived in Brighton and married there, used a different name in Sussex. His son-in-law thought his double life was simple eccentricity.

His tenants were scathing about the notoriety conferred on Mr Dering by some of the national papers. He was just eccentric and retiring, they said, with a positive dislike of change.

Although he dealt with them in an arbitrary way, he was rarely deaf to a genuine appeal for help and usually responded liberally. They looked on him with respect – after all, he could trace his linage directly back to a Saxon thane and had an unfailing, old world courtesy.

Schoolboy Clarence Hills came to a sticky end while running errands for pocket money at a slaughter house in Bedford in 1913. He got a little too involved in what was, after all, only a part-time job, and begged one of the men to let him despatch a bullock with a humane killer.

The man said no but Clarence went on and on until he lost patience and gave in, handing Clarence the gadget set ready to fire. Clarence took aim, pulled the bolt, and fell down dead.

For some reason never satisfactorily explained, the cartridge went into the boy's head instead of the bullock's. The inquest verdict was misadventure.

Another death proved to be illusory. When John Hills was admitted to Hitchin workhouse in January 1904 he said he came from Norton, but had left the village 15 years earlier and been "knocking around" ever since.

A sister was traced to Baldock but when told that her brother was back, she almost fainted. "He was killed on the railway 15 years ago!" she cried. She rushed over to the workhouse and recognised him at once, partly because of a distinctive scar on his nose.

The man buried as John Hills 15 years earlier had been killed in a train accident, leaving his body badly mutilated.

As the general description fitted John, it was an area where he walked and he was missing, his relatives assumed it must be him.

Poor Rachel Holloway died in Royston workhouse early in 1901. The 43-year-old burned to death after her dress caught fire and she ran screaming into the yard. The coroner was told:

*"At the time of the accident there were two other inmates in the room but they were classed as imbeciles and no information could be obtained from them."*

The grisly end of Emily Dimmock occupied a good many column inches in the Express in September, 1907. Her body was found in her Camden Town flat by her 'husband' Bertram Shaw after he came back from work in the dining car of the Leeds train. Her throat had been slashed with such force that her head was almost severed from her body.

The particular interest for Express readers lay in the fact that Emily was a Hitchin girl, who had gone to St Mary's School until she was 13, and still had a brother in the town, at Blackhorse Lane. Her father William ran a candy stall in the market.

Emily, it transpired, had gone into service in London and not behaved as well as she might. Bertram, who freely admitted he was her lover, told police that when they met:

*"She had confessed she had not been living a virtuous life but she willingly agreed to live under his protection."*

As evidence emerged it became clear Emily had not mended her ways. She may have greeted Bertram with warmth and affection when he came home from work, but as soon as he went on overnight journeys, she was entertaining new men friends.

She was a frequent visitor at a nearby pub and had been there the night she died, escorted by a man with a beard.

The scene that greeted Mr Shaw when he came home was a terrible one. The parlour was in confusion and the bedroom locked. Forcing the door open Mr Shaw found Emily in a huddled heap on the bed, her naked body covered in blood-stained sheets.

The killer had wiped his hands on her clothes and then washed them in a basin of water, leaving red smears wherever he went.

At first it appeared that Emily had put up a fierce struggle, since furniture was overturned and ornaments smashed. But the landlady had heard nothing and the doctor later said she had been attacked, with tremendous force, in her sleep. The murderer had ransacked the drawers and taken Emily's few scraps of jewellery.

He left behind him a gruesome clue – his fingerprints in blood, which were photographed by eager police, just embarking on the challenging science of forensics.

Poor Emily, whose age was variously given as 22, 23 and 24, was buried at St Pancras Cemetery by the Economic Funeral Company. A large crowd gathered to watch the macabre ceremony.

Their appetite was further titillated when police summoned a clairvoyant to help them with the case, taking the man to Emily's room. He sat on the bed and immediately fell into a heavy trance. "He then proceeded to give a startlingly vivid display of the actual commission of the crime, pictured in detail the appearance of a certain man and said: 'The man you want is on his way to Melbourne'," reported the Express.

Emily's sister added fuel to the wild atmosphere surrounding her sister's death. Mrs Rose Martindale, of Langley Street, Luton, said she had been visited by the spirit form of Emily the very night she died. Emily appeared at her bedside along with the figure of the murderer, Jumbo (a gentleman friend of Emily's called Mr Large). Jumbo, thought Mrs Martindale, had caught a train and then escaped by boat. She also revealed that Emily had been knocked down by a horse on Hitchin Hill when she was 11 and it had affected her mind.

However both the clairvoyant and Mrs Martindale were left looking rather silly when a Robert Wood of Grays Inn Road, London, was charged with the murder.

"He passed with jaunty steps into the dock, smiling at his acquaintances in court," reported the Express.

His jaunty steps proved justified and he was acquitted in December, after he was defended by the famous Marshall Hall. "It would seem that the hope of discovering the perpetrator has disappeared," wrote the Express. "Even that is better than that an innocent man should suffer."

Only good was said of Ed Woods after his death. The 52-year-old signalman for the Great Northern Railway died very suddenly while at work near Peterborough in January 1908. As he felt himself sliding into unconsciousness, Mr Woods set all signals on danger to prevent any accidents.

His body was found after a train was held up for an unreasonable length of time for no reason. "Thanks to the heroic conduct of a signalman ...a terrible disaster was averted," recorded the Express.

*Perks and Llewellyn grew lavender around Hitchin, distilled the flowers and manufactured products. This picture was taken behind their High Street premises in about 1912.*

# Favourite Express-ions – 1904

*The new Hitchin fire station in Paynes Park, built in honour of Edward VII's coronation, in 1904*

✴ The Express decided it would be a good idea to give some advice to readers. Gems included: "All flesh may be grass but the lawnmower will never supplant the carving knife," "Men may be bribed but you can't induce women to take hush money," and "A big head doesn't always prevent a man from coming out at the little end of the morn."

✴ Perhaps Herts County Council should have taken some advice before they issued a driving licence to Samuel Sharpe. There wasn't any problem with his character – he was a fine upstanding chap. He was healthy too, but he did have one draw-back as far as driving was concerned – he was blind.

✴ Fine old buildings were at risk from the modern commercial spirit, raged Express columnist Spectator. He condemned "vulgarisation or vanishment of ancient landmarks" such as Bedford Priory, the subject of recent "wanton destruction." Public bodies, with no reverence for the past, should not be allowed to commit such outrages, he said.

✴ Standards were low in an unnamed Mid Beds village in 1855, when women were said to be thoroughly immoral and most had illegitimate children. Four out of five were opium eaters and all were in a fearful state of ignorance and vice – so recalled the Express, looking back over almost half a century.

✴ The solution for many poor families was to emigrate, usually to Canada. A correspondent from Quebec condemned the standard of some of his new countrymen, in a letter to the Express. "I have seen some very poor specimens, who don't like work and want to go back to mother. There are lots of this class come out here. The Greenhorn, if willing, always gets a good show. The class of man wanted is those that have grit, especially in lumber camp."

✷ Paying unmarried men less than colleagues with responsibilities was a common practice, even in professions such as teaching. But Express columnist Spectator thought it "Neither just nor expedient" adding "If we want to have work well and cheerfully done we should pay the fair market price for it."

✷ A mother and father pleaded guilty in court to keeping their son away from school. They told magistrates they could not afford breakfast for the lad so they: "Kept him at home so that if he was hungry he would at least be warm." The same problem was highlighted a few weeks later when an editorial in the Express criticised compulsory education for poor children, who had to walk a long way in all weathers and sit in wet boots and stockings: "With a mere snack of food at dinner time. They need hot soup and somewhere to dry their clothes," declared the compassionate writer.

✷ A Stevenage householder got a shock when she found a sheep in the back room of her cottage one afternoon late in January. The flustered sheep, which had escaped from a field, upset the table and a lamp fell on the hearth rug, setting it alight. Fortunately the situation was sorted out "with no danger."

✷ A moral dilemma confronted Hitchin guardians when they debated whether to give out relief to the mother of two illegitimate children. Mr Cook, the master, advised them not to – out relief should only be available in cases of good character and it was important to keep up that standard, he said. The guardians were more compassionate and made a small payment.

✷ Buffalo Bill's Wild West show attracted 24,000 visitors to Butts Close in Hitchin on June 23. Colonel William Cody brought with him a cosmopolitan army of 700 men, women and children who camped out preparing their acts. Buffalo Bill was the star of his own show, holding the crowds spellbound as he rode his horse while firing his Winchester so accurately that he hit balls thrown up into the air.

One of the main acts was a cowboy named Carter, who had adapted to modern technology and rode a bike through the air, leaping for distances of up to 56 feet.

There were also performances from Russian Cossacks, Bedouin Arabs, the Imperial Japanese troupe and Mexican Vaqueros and Ruraries.

A few months' later, when John Sanger's circus came to town, Hitchin footballer Bertie Leggatt won a cup in a goal-kicking contest between men and an elephant.

*The junction of Bridge Street and Queen Street, pictured sometime after 1930*

✭ Poor John Walker appealed to the Hitchin Board of Guardians to take him into the workhouse, even though his wife had a regular income. "I cannot get any of it; she sticks to it and drinks it," he told them. They were not to be swayed – she was obliged to support him, they declared .

✭ A bull being driven from Hitchin to Baldock careered out of control, lurched towards the Rose and Crown and then rushed into a draper's shop. "Here it was quite at home," reported the Express. Fears that it might depart through the plate glass window proved unfounded and it was finally induced to leave quietly through the door.

✭ Primrose McConnell gave advice on turnip singling in May and weeks later a cowslip was found on Norton Common with 188 florets.

✭ A Stevenage tradesman became anxious after two ladies' bicycles let out on hire were not returned. Only a small deposit had been secured. "A postcard has been received from the hirers but some circumstances about the case have led the police to make enquiries and it is said that these are not altogether satisfactory," reported the Express in August.

✭ A 12-year-old boy who went missing from his home in Kentish Town turned up the next day in Paynes Park, Hitchin. At first Percy Ellis told police he had been kidnapped by gipsies but later he confessed the truth – he had run away to go blackberry picking, thinking he could live on that 'luscious fruit.' Apparently he had been reading too many stories of the penny dreadful type.

*Mr W O Times*

✭ Hitchin's new debating society discussed council housing. President Mr W O Times suggested: "It might be asked it it were fair that the sober thrifty working man should have to pay increased rates in order to provide houses for the thriftless and the drunken."

*Farmers look at the animals at Jackson's Yard, Paynes Park, Hitchin, in or soon after 1903*

# The thirty-year vigil in one room

The train was crowded with people going home for the festive holiday. Tomorrow would be Christmas Eve, 1876, and everyone was warm with good humour, gazing at the first threads of snow.

Martha Burbridge and her husband, on their way to Nottingham, were settled in the middle carriages of the train. Darkness was beginning to fall as they passed through Hitchin and on towards Arlesey Sidings station.

"That's where the Three Counties Lunatic Asylum is," said someone in the carriage. He went on in a loud whisper to his companion: "It serves Hertfordshire, Bedfordshire and Huntingdon – that's why it got its name."

Everyone looked out of the windows as if expecting strange and manacled figures to appear.

The train ran on at 60 miles an hour. Driver Thomas Pepper, recipient of 44 premiums for good conduct, was well known to be a steady, careful, sober man. He had worked for Great Northern Railways for 25 years, many of them as a driver.

That very afternoon he had spoken to Mr Cockshott, superintendent of the line, at King's Cross, and nodded sagely over the need for caution in such wintry weather.

"My confidence in the man was unbounded," Mr Cockshott was to say later.

At Hatfield the signalman sent word down the line that the express had passed. Cadwell near Hitchin received the message and so did William Graves, manning the box at Arlesey Sidings. It would be 22 minutes before Pepper reached him.

Signalman Graves looked out at the 25 goods trucks waiting to cross the line into a siding, and he considered. There was time, he explained to the enquiry later – 17 minutes would have been too tight, but 22 was enough. He told the men waiting below to go ahead and set the signals at danger.

*The Arlesey train crash of 1876 as depicted in a drawing made at the time*

The men laboured over the trucks. One went across, two, three, on and on they rolled. Ten, 12, 19. Graves sat in his box, waiting for the all clear, to remove the danger signal in time for the express to thunder through. At 20 to 4 it was growing dark and beginning to snow.

The express was racing up to Cadwell, it was over and on.

Station Master Phillip Walter stood on the platform, watching the trucks as they were shunted across. He heard the cry as first one truck, then another, followed by a third, left the rails. The men cursed, they fumed. The line was blocked – but all was safe, all was nuisance but order, for the home and distant signals were both set at danger.

Porters ran to summon the platelayers, who scrambled onto the track and began furiously trying to right the heavy trucks – two full of sand and one of coprolites. Their breath hazed the bitter air as they strained to lift the weight, struggled, panted, sweated – and failed. Guard John Martin dropped below the trucks and under to try and uncouple them.

The roar came on a drift, it rolled along the line, growing as their disbelief grew into certainty. The express, the carriages full of passengers going home for Christmas, the train that was to stop at the distant danger signal, the driver with the reputation of a canny saint, the express that could not be there, roared into view.

Martin, the man beneath the trucks, scrambled out and ran. The platelayers, stunned with shock, dived for cover.

On the platform onlookers gasped, cried out, shrieked in terror. Nothing could be done. William Graves in his signalbox stood helpless by, the station master's wife flew out of her house, and down the line a porter ran with a red flag trailing in the wind like flaying blood.

On the express Driver Pepper saw the home danger signal and whistled, twice, sharply, for the brakes. Guard after guard gave evidence that they heard, they applied the brakes, they knew something terrible was wrong.

William Thacker was sorting parcels in his van. "I heard the driver whistle for the brakes," he said afterwards.

"I immediately applied my brake and had got it hard on. The train was travelling very rapidly at this time. I looked out and saw the home signal at danger. I was at my brake when the collision occurred and I held the wheel as the best means of saving myself from what I feared might follow immediately.

*"I was slightly hurt but not badly enough to prevent me attending to my duties."*

Driver Pepper was not so fortunate; neither was stoker George Smith and fireman Lovet. Smith was killed as he jumped from the train.

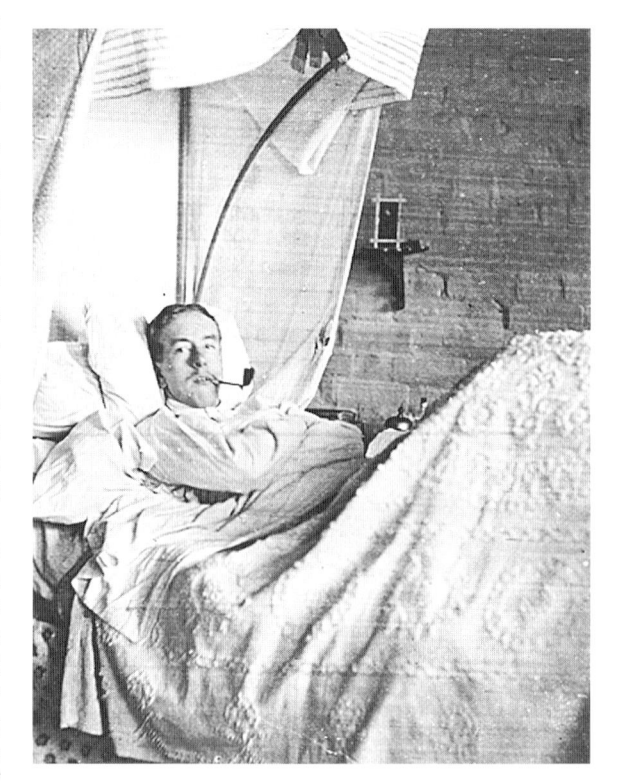

*Mr Welch, one of the survivors of the 1876 train crash, pictured recovering at Hitchin Infirmary. Other patients were taken to the Sun Hotel*

Witnesses saw Pepper hurl himself through the air, swathed in steam, to fall with a resounding, terrible crack onto his head, in the station master's garden, near where Mrs Walter stood.

Others watched fireman Lovet step from the footplate at the bottom of the engine as it passed the home signal, just before the signal box.

Porter George Bygrave said: "I ran at once to the fireman. He was insensible and nearly dead."

The driverless express, slowed by the brakes and with its steam shut off, hurtled into the trucks at about 30 mph. It jumped off the metal and ploughed several yards on, grating and grinding with a terrible sound.

There was silence, and silence, and a long, gasped quiet, until the first scream came. "For some time all was hushed and terror pervaded the mind of all present. Presently there arose from underneath the ruined carriages the cries of the wounded and imprisoned passengers," reported the Bedfordshire Times.

"The collision was of the most terrible character, totally destructive of those carriages which suffered."

One passenger, a police officer, scrambled out of the wreck and ran to the signal box, where he helped Graves stop all traffic, up line and down. Other passengers followed, turning in their hysterical confusion on Graves, as they tried to invade the signal box.

The station master telegraphed to Hitchin and Peterborough, relaying news of the disaster and pleading for medical help and more labourers. He sent messengers on horseback to Biggleswade and surrounding towns asking for every doctor in the area to come at once.

As the men rode into the darkness and snow, the platelayers scrambled back onto the tracks and began working furiously to release the trapped and injured passengers. "They worked with a will and before any surgeons had arrived several cases requiring their medical attention had been extricated from the ruins," reported the Beds Times.

"Mrs Walters threw open her small residence for the reception of as many as it would accommodate and the landlords of local inns and the villages vied with one another in ministering to the comfort of the sufferers."

Arlesey's vicar, the Rev F Ffolliatt Scott, arrived to do what he could, closely followed by doctors from Hitchin including Mr Grellet, Mr Foster and Mr Shillitoe, as well as three from Arlesey lunatic asylum and others from Biggleswade.

Simeon Woodhouse, the head guard, saw the platelayer with his useless red flag still in his hand and, knowing another train was due, sent him off to make sure it stopped.

He saw firemen Lovet lying by the side of the track and lifted him gently, resting his body against the signalbox. Thinking he was dead, Mr Woodhouse went on to the front of the train and began knocking on the doors of the vans, calling out.

The other fireman appeared, stunned and confused. Mr Woodhouse looked at him in surprise. "Why do you not come out?" he asked. "Pull yourself together."

Everywhere was chaos. It was 10pm before any trains were allowed through – leading to

> 'For sometime all was hushed and terror pervaded the minds of all present'

> 'The collision was of the most terrible character'

strong complaints from travellers who were not told of the disaster at King's Cross, but allowed to board trains and start abortive journeys. They spent hours outside Hitchin station.

One passenger, from Boston in Lincolnshire, protested about: "The reprehensible conduct of the GNR in sending passengers north when they knew they there was no chance of them getting to their destination for many hours, and increasing the agonising suspense of friends who expected them."

One three-hour journey north took more than 12, bringing another stinging rebuke about: "The usual selfish policy of railway companies in general.

*"The officials of the GNR not only kept silence as to the accident but booked passengers through King's Cross to the north as if nothing was the matter, knowing they would be detained for some hours."*

When news reached Biggleswade, crowds flocked to the town's station, many concerned and many more flushed with excitement.

Relatives and friends began to arrive as the hours went by: "Eagerly enquiring for every scrap of information, telegraphing to other stations for intelligence and anxiously waiting for many weary hours for news of absent ones," reported the Herts Express in 1876.

*"Nor was the suspense over until about two o'clock, and in some cases even later on Saturday morning, when the missing passengers arrived."*

Many were exhausted by the crash and chaos but: "Although tired, cold and hungry they happily arrived in safety."

Others were not so fortunate. Among the injured was Lady Ida Hope on her way to stay with Mr Aubrey and Lady Alexis-Coventry at Rutland. She suffered from two broken ribs and was very bruised and cut. Her maid was also "much hurt." Five people died in the crash and at least one soon afterwards.

They included Abigail Longstaffe, a 29-year-old parlour maid; Lucy Thompson from Grantham who was not identified until the next day; Maurice Michael, a German tailor; Thomas Pepper and stoker George Smith.

The inquest into their deaths was opened on Christmas Day at Lamb Inn in Arlesey; the five coffins were laid at the back, in a stable.

The accommodation was woefully inadequate and the hearing was short, with the coroner, Mr J Piper, declaring better premises must be found for the next session. Foreman of the jury was the vicar, the Rev F Ffolliatt Scott.

They met again during the second week of January, in the board schoolroom. Witness after witness came forward, to testify to the cold run through the darkening afternoon, the sequence of events, the routine journey that suddenly became a disaster.

The jury blamed Pepper and the the inefficient carrying out of the block signalling system, exonerating the station master and signalman Graves from any criticism.

*There was "a want of caution on the part of the deceased driver," they concluded.*

*He was going too fast for the conditions and could not have seen the distant signal was unexpectedly set on danger.*

The surgeons and doctors who had rushed to the scene were thanked and the inquest broke up, having set the official seal on yet one more grim railway disaster. Thousands attended the funeral of Thomas Pepper at Peterbough, following his coffin in a procession to the grave.

Among the passengers were Mr Burbridge and his wife, travelling home to Nottingham for the holiday. Mrs Burbridge was just 32 years old when she was dragged from the wreckage and laid on Arlesey station beside her husband.

A doctor, examining both, determined that Mr Burbridge had a badly broken and lacerated leg, but was basically sound. He sent him to the infirmary at the Three Counties Asylum, squeezing him into the packed space.

Mrs Burbridge, he quickly decided, was not likely to live. Her spine was damaged and her pelvis broken. She was taken to Lamb Inn.

As they were hauled away, on their separate routes to divergent treatments, they muttered their hasty goodbyes. They feared they would not see each other again.

Mr Burbridge had a serious leg break and the doctors decided to amputate. At first all seemed well but within days he died, a victim of tetanus. His body was taken home to Nottingham for burial and his death was briefly recorded in the Bedfordshire Times of January 27, 1877.

"Mr Burbridge, the gentleman who, with his wife, sustained fearful injuries in the GNR accident at Arlesey, lingered until Saturday last when death terminated his suffering. Mrs Burbridge is still in a precarious state. The husband and wife have been unable to see each other since they were suddenly separated by the terrible accident."

At Lamb Inn, Mrs Burbridge was not expected to live; five doctors examined her in turn and said she could not recover, but still she lingered on. Her relatives came to care for her but as the weeks became months they returned home.

She drifted on, defying all forecasts, until it became clear she would not die at all. After three years her relatives held a family conference and decided to move her back to Nottingham but, since she was so frail and always in such pain, they would make the journey in a series of stages. They planned the route meticulously and booked rooms and nurses along the way. The first stop would be in Hitchin at 40, Walsworth Road.

When they brought her to stay in the house, intending to move her quickly on, she was distraught with exhaustion and pain. So serious was her condition that her family, in another hastily convened conference, determined she could not be moved again.

They took out a long lease, hired a nurse, bought in furniture and settled her down in her new home.

It was a long, dreary, monotonous round of days merging into identical nights. At first the ladies of the town called, both curious and full of pity. Mrs Burbridge, shrinking from inquisitive eyes, would refuse to see them all.

But when visitors came asking for subscriptions for charities and good causes, she would make a donation. The Express reported:

*"Her plight, combined with her generous nature, won great sympathy. Flowers were often left at the door for the invalid lady who lived with just her sick nurse and a servant girl for company."*

Martha Burbridge died in September, 1909, aged 65, and a memorial service was held at St Saviour's Church. Her doctor told the Express she was patient and even cheerful in her affliction. At last, in death, she completed the journey she had begun on December 23, 1876, and her body was taken to Norwood for burial.

*Walsworth Road, Hitchin, in about 1890. As this picture was taken Mrs Burbridge lay in a room in one of the buildings, centre left near the curve in the road*

# How to be faux pas free at a coronation

Olive, the fashion conscious columnist of the Express, opens her wide and begloved arms to a long gone age.

The poor do not exist for her. There is no workhouse, no overcrowding, sewage does not fill her streams and noxious smells avoid her. This is the Edwardian dream personified.

Not that all went smoothly of course. In February 1900 she was very concerned about a society problem.

*"The prospects for the London season are not bright. The death of the Duke of Teck will probably cause the pre-Easter drawing rooms to be postponed until a later date than usual, thus shortening the season, and the number of distinguished families plunged into mourning will bring entertaining almost to a vanishing point."*

But she was up to date with latest scientific developments.

"It is confidently thought that Count Zeppelin's new airship which is shortly to be tried will really solve the problem of aerial flight.

"Flying machines are never likely to become anything but a costly hobby like ballooning, though the military authorities will no doubt make some use of them."

Such dull issues could not preoccupy her for long however. She was soon onto more serious matters, such as dress and etiquette.

*"One of the most difficult presents to choose is, undoubtedly, wedding presents. It's very difficult to hit upon something unique – something one can hope to venture will not be duplicated. A little time back a gift most in evidence was the tiny silver cruet, then came an epidemic of fans; now the prevailing idea seems to be to provide the happy pair with tables, fascinating little Louis XV specimens.*

*At a fashionable wedding I counted no less than 15 gifts of this description."*

A cheque would be much more satisfactory, thought Olive.

Clothes were her major preoccupation and she was soon advising women to dress "like our beloved Princess of Wales."

*"Her sleeves have always been of moderate dimensions, neither very voluminous nor very tight, her skirts the same; and no huge, extensively trimmed picture hat has ever been seen on her neatly arranged head."*

Olive was not alone in her obsession with fashion.

In January 1901 she wrote about the limits women might be driven to in their efforts to get a bargain during the sales. A blouse was ripped by two women as they fought over it in a West End store. She told shocked readers:

*"Both these women were well dressed and well spoken yet seemed in no way to realise the disgrace of their position."*

Olive decided to write on a new topic: physiognomy. "There is a general belief that small ears are a distinctive sign of aristocratic birth. Miss Ellis, who deals with this subject in her little volume on 'The Human Ear' says, for the comfort of those who have large ears, that this is a mistake and that, though they may be a disfigurement, big ears indicate neither plebeian origin nor lack of intelligence."

However, she went on, Miss Ellis did believe your talents could be assessed by looking at your ears.

Olive thought the days of coffee drinking were over. "It's so much easier and indeed cheaper to put out tea or cocoa on the breakfast table and make people give up coffee altogether," she wrote. Coffee was not made properly anyway, she added, advising:

*"It is important that the hot milk or cream should be put into the cup before pouring in the coffee."*

She was not much in favour of tea though, stating in February 1904 that:

*"Excessive tea drinking has been condemned as second only to alcoholism in the harmful effects it has upon those who indulge in it."*

A Royal Commission believed it was one of the causes of national physical deterioration and responsible for many cases of total loss of memory.

Olive also reported criticism of working class mothers who gave a bread-and-butter tea to their families. "It was almost universally resorted to because people would not take the trouble to cook," said Dr Hutchinson at a recent lecture.

Olive's fellow columnist Spectator was concerned about another beverage altogether – beer. He visited a pure beer event in Bedford in February 1901 and wrote:

*"He would have been a bold man who would have stood up in the meeting to confess a liking for foreign wines."*

He went on: "A man who drinks the wine of France and Spain instead of the honest beer brewed from homegrown malt and hops can hardly hope to escape the charge of lack of patriotism. It is as plain as a pikestaff that if we drink his wine we help to raise a foreigner from the state of abasement in which he naturally lives and to put him on a level with our more favoured selves."

Meanwhile Olive was finding life quiet – her only excitement was over the latest skirts.

*"They will fit perfectly over the hips with a flat box pleat at the back, springing out towards the knees from wide full folds, which fall about the feet."*

Being bored, she went on to talk about stationery. "As a rule the many attempts to improve upon the old fashioned style of mourning envelope have not been a success. They have usually resulted in some device equally hideous.

*"This can scarcely be said of a novelty which has been produced to meet a large demand for mourning stationery in consequence of the death of the Queen.*

"This consists of a small black bordered square in the corner where the stamp is placed so that it appears with a mourning band round it."

Queen Victoria died in 1901 after more than 60 years on the throne, but Olive had other thoughts to occupy her.

"It is no longer deemed correct to have a quantity of huge cushions in a drawing or reception room. In the boudoir, morning or bedroom they are permissible but as one does not lie back or lounge when receiving visitors, a small cushion is all that is considered necessary on sofas or chairs in drawing rooms.

*"The newest are in rich brocade and very delicate shades, trimmed with lace. Frills have long ceased to find favour with up-to-date folk."*

In her search for the perfect way of life, Olive was unceasing. She advised in 1901: "The most effective colour for a dinner table is pale yellow."

She then slipped into a rare DIY mood and continued: "Take a length of eura silk of this particular shade and puff it lightly and gracefully down the centre of the table, allowing half as much again as the actual space to be covered. Upon this place silver bonbon dishes and candlesticks, the latter filled with real silk shades. Trails of smilax or asparagus fern should edge the puffed silk centre, and the menu cards should be tied with narrow yellow ribbon."

Nothing however could rival clothes in her pantheon of interests. At the end of March 1901 she was warning: "Those of us who have not yet decided upon late spring or early summer clothes would do well to set about this task at once. In a very little time the rush will commence and modistes will then no longer be able to afford one that care and attention needed to make a display.

*"Black glacé silk promises to be extensively used for evening cloaks, little short coats, boleros, blouses, collars, reveres and cuffs."*

The coming look, she was confident, would be soft, cloudy and billowy to a degree "which means bad times ahead for the impecunious." Travelling gloves should be in antelope.

Anyone who had gone for the soft billowy look too early would have felt rather silly – it was a cold spring and Olive soon found herself advising readers to retain their warm winter undergarments for some weeks more – at least until the end of May.

The smartest of smart wear was suddenly a black tea gown, only recently deemed an impossibility from an artistic point of view. Short skirts were the vogue in Paris a year later, where they were worn by "the very smartest women for morning and even park toilettes."

Olive was not so keen on another fashion, for white gloves. It was only acceptable for the rich, who could care for them properly and who had small well shaped hands.

## Make sure to tie your menu cards with narrow yellow ribbon

"It is deemed vulgar to squeeze one hands into gloves that are too small," she warned, before issuing detailed instructions on mending them (where holes are concerned they should never be drawn together) and taking them off (to remove ones gloves by pulling at the finger tips spells ruination.)

Perhaps all these problems explain why there was a sudden fad for lace mittens instead. But trimming heirloom lace with jewels quickly lost favour – it ruined the lace and looked cheap and nasty.

The Panama hat was on its way out too among the wealthy – although pretty and becoming it was too "beloved of the masses much to please exclusive dressers." What was even worse, the upstarts trimmed their cheap copies with ribbons, flowers and lace.

They were unlikely to copy another hot fashion – wearing ostrich feathers up to 27 inches long. But the 'masses' were keen on open necked blouses which might, some feared, lead to pneumonia. "Others regard it with favour as likely to strengthen the throat and the chest," reported the impartial Olive.

She was totally against another occasional practice – for women to sit astride a horse while hunting. "It is anything but a graceful spectacle and those people who think the custom will become a fashion are quite mistaken," she wrote firmly in 1904.

She had no time for the argument that it was safer.

"What little truth there may be in this idea is not worth considering and it is far outweighed by the question of appearance," she added, with her never failing sense of priorities and form.

## The smart set wore ostrich feathers up to 27 inches long

It better befitted a women, she went on, to buy some short lengths of old brocade, silk or velvet in delicate shades and set about making a little theatre coat – much more in favour now than the old theatre blouse.

*The marriage of Mr Whaley and Miss Foster of Hitchin, pictured in 1909*

It wasn't only women who had to be rendered ridiculous – so did animals. The cold spring had given way to a stifling summer and owners were inflicting sun bonnets on both horses and fashionable dogs. Olive did not approve.

"Those who have much to do with horses are almost unanimous in their opinion that sun bonnets cause a great deal more discomfort than they prevent," she wrote.

*"It is the same with dogs, only in their case a sense of the ridiculous is combined with sentimental kindness, for nothing looks more funny than a fashionable woman with her toy pet in a sun hat."*

Fashionable women could do real harm sometimes and even frivolous Olive saw this. She condemned the practice of going "slumming" – visiting the poor in their slum homes. She had two reasons.

"The idea of making an exhibition of people's poverty is repulsive," she stated firmly. Also it encourages the professional poor, she warned. "Their homes present a ghastly picture of penury and want but the situation in many instances has been specially created with a view to the charitable donations of ladies who may visit."

It was not in her nature to be serious for long. Soon she was warning about passing on the name of a dressmaker or, even worse, a favourite holiday resort.

*"The ill cut sleeve or a badly hung skirt can breed the most bitter resentment. There have been cases, and many of them, in which firm friends have been driven into an enmity which has defied the softening influence of time."*

Travelling was another of life's hazards. Olive observed in August 1902 that American women "doing Europe" were now taking a valet with them instead of a lady's maid – the men were able to cope with tricky situations better.

Some of these tricky situations were of their own doing, as she acknowledged herself in September. "Women have to take the ordinary risks of life but how frequently we are reminded that our style of dress is designed to court dangers. It's especially liable to catch fire and cause others accidents such as falls and to generally place us at disadvantages.

"A lighted match thrown down by a careless smoker has frequently set a woman's dress on fire." As if that wasn't worrying enough – and the same issue of the Express reported the death of a Welsh girl whose clothes had ignited – even preparing food was full of hazards.

"Housewives should be careful of using cheap enamelled utensils for cooking, as soft and inferior enamels are liable to give off such deadly poisons as arsenic, lead and antimony." Home-made jam could make you violently ill, she warned.

So could scarves, apparently. Instead, Olive was pleased to report, the fashion was: "Not to muffle our necks this autumn. The big round fur boas, which were answerable for many a sore and weak throat, have disappeared."

She was full of envy for the American way of shopping, and critical of the English practice of only going in a store if you wanted to buy something.

"The shop walker at once requests to know the department one requires and he would probably begin to think of the police if told that one simply wanted to look about.

"One must say that one is requiring something, when one is forthwith conducted to a high chair and the sales person who serves these particular goods."

But everything was arranged more happily in America. "In some of the big establishments in New York there is not only a nursery with toys and nursemaids to look after the children, but also a band, a reading room and other attractions. One may spend an agreeable morning in getting some trifling amount of shopping."

Nothing, no diversion, no calamity, no political situation, war or strife, could keep Olive for long from the subject closest to her heart – clothes.

In February 1903 she told readers: "Many fashionable women are wearing with the tea gown an old lace lappet in the hair, secured by several antique pins and so arranged as to fall forward over the softly waving tresses."

This, she added, was particularly suitable for restaurant and theatre wear. There was good news for homely women too.

*"The flannel blouse, at one time a hopelessly dowdy garment, and impossible save for morning wear, is now donned by smart women in the afternoon, with dressy skirts that match and tone exactly."*

But the outlook was bad for the more mobile. "When motor cars were sanctioned by law, most of us had visions of being able to keep our own vehicle for almost nothing. There would be no horse to keep, no coachman or stable expenses, but simply a shed where the car could be kept for which nothing more than a barrel of oil or other motor fluid would be required.

*"Such dreams however have not have been realised and not only is the initial cost of a motor car almost prohibitive to people of moderate means, but the yearly expenses are seldom found to be less than that of keeping a horse and carriage.*

"Some margin should be allowed for accidents and possibly for fines for reckless driving."

Women drivers, she added, were rare but: "If women drivers become general there will, perhaps, be more difficulties than ever deciding the vexed question of speed when this is challenged by the police."

Olive however, was more concerned about the right clothes to wear while driving than any issue of safety. "For those women who 'mote' regularly nothing is more useful and comfortable than a three-quarter length coat of pony skin.

"A toque to match is the most desirable form of headgear and will be for several weeks to come. A veil of net lined with chiffon is, apparently, preferred before all others by those women to be seen tearing about in their fiery chariots and deservedly so, for it is very becoming and it protects the face well."

Olive was soon back on a favourite subject – stationery. She told readers early in 1903: "Fashionable writing paper is either soft grey or blue, the stamping being carried out in white. Quite small sheets and envelopes are not correct."

She finished: "It is curious how few people there are who possess letter scales. The absence can cause much anxiety and bother."

So could the lack of the right clothes. Olive advised women on February 28, 1903:

*"Coloured evening blouses that have not seen their last days must be finished out at home.*
*You cannot do better than run up a black lace coffee coat to wear over them."*

Brides were getting very adventurous and Olive was almost shocked. "There have been some startling departures in bridal toilettes lately. One very up-to-date bride appeared at the altar in a yellow and white gown, a hat trimmed with yellow roses and a bouquet composed of yellow blooms."

Another bold lady was married in her travelling dress with a large black picture hat and touches of black about her gown.

Servants were a constant source of vexation to the society lady. An item in the Express in 1900 recounted an unusual solution to the problem, under the headline "John Chinaman as a domestic."

"The simplest solution for the great servant question would, says Madame, undoubtedly be the introduction of the heathen Chinee – that is, if he could stand the climate and the British housewife could put up with him.

*"The Heathen Chinee is the most excellent servant but he has undoubted drawbacks. In the first place, although he will clean the house as it has never been cleaned before, he does not think it necessary to extend the same operation to himself.*

"Then, though he is a capital cook and, if he is carefully kept from any of his native delicacies, will turn out most appetising European dishes, it does not do to look into the kitchen while he is at work or to inquire for an exact inventory of all that he has used.

Of course his wages would be higher in England than in warmer climates but at first they would certainly be very low, for John can live and save on a most exiguous amount, but on the other side is a natural gift for petty larceny, forgery and other peccadilloes which may at any time break out and cause trouble.

"Moreover, though he requires no board or bedroom, many housewives might object to his introduction into the house of his favourite articles of diet, and still more to his simple way of putting down his mat anywhere – in the pantry or on the landing or, on warm nights, on beds – and just going to sleep on it without further ado."

Olive had plenty of advice on how to decorate your home. In November 1904 she warmly recommended apartments of pink and cream. Dark blue or a rich brown were also acceptable.

*"Terracotta is fatal to the generality of complexions and toilettes, so is rose colour, while green is terribly trying to those women inclined to sallowness."*

A new feature, Women's Realm, replaced the advice of Olive in the pages of the Express, in 1904. But writer Lorna was no more consistent or serious than her predecessor.

In an early column she commented on the Citizens' National League campaign to win more people the vote. Married women paid more income tax than men or single women, an injustice which disturbed her little as she immediately passed on to a more pressing subject – fashion.

*"There is a perfect rage for carved ivory this season. The latest vanity is umbrella and sunshade holders of ivory, beautifully carved, and these quite threaten to take the place of the beautiful jewelled parasol handles used by so many society women last year."*

She ends her column with a piece of pertinent advice. Hinting at Blue Peter TV programmes to come far in the future, she shows her lady readers how to make a hat pin case out of a tube of cardboard.

As the summer approached Lorna gave details of the perfect bathing costume, to be made of red bunting or serge with short puffed sleeves, a knee-length skirt and an edged collar.

*"The costume should be completed with black stockings and scarlet bathing shoes tied on with laces to match."*

In 1907 Lorna was telling her eager readers: "A high evening blouse is very useful when a low necked frock is not strictly necessary."

She advised taking jewels abroad in a small chamois bag, worn round the neck.

"It will hold many precious stones," she wrote, reassuringly.

Lorna's column was interspersed with one by Sylvia, who gave advice on dressmaking at home.

Readers could send away for patterns, such as the one in early 1905 for a boy's coat with a huge collar and a hat like Admiral Nelson.

The practical Sylvia advised that the "very sensible little wrap for a small boy which is both simple and becoming could, if wished, be used for a maiden of the same age, four or five." Soon afterwards Lorna made one of her rare social comments, on vegetarianism, which:

*"Once a peculiarity of a small section of the middle classes, has recently made many converts in aristocratic circles. It promises to become as fashionable as bridge."*

It was obviously a quiet time for Lorna, who went on: "While waiting for the new fashions for the coming season to make their definite appearance, it's advisable to overhaul one's lingerie and see that everything in that department of the wardrobe is in good order, so that later on one's time is free to devote to other garments."

Exciting fashion news came through a few weeks later and Lorna was able to get back to the serious business of what to wear.

She featured a simple afternoon gown that could be made in chiffon velours, crepe-de-chine or voile. Not simple at all, it had a yoke closely pleated between two rows of silk trimming, with the upper yoke composed of thick Irish crochet.

There were also details of a walking costume, including a bolero coat, edged with tiny knife-pleated ruched silk exactly toning with the cloth, and full sleeves with long cuffs bordered with pleated ruchings.

Men appeared to have little comment to make on female clothing, with one exception – the hat when worn in a theatre.

It caused complaints from people using Hitchin's new town hall and was a recurring theme during the Edwardian years – and apparently for many years past.

In February 1905, Lorna reported that a Parisian editor had launched a competition to design a becoming and unobstructive theatre hat – in 1786!

The Paris prefect of police had ordered his constables to eject any lady whose hat incommoded the playgoers.

*The real world, as in Thorpe's Yard, Hitchin, did not touch Olive, Sylvia and Lorna*

Sixty-four years later the issue was still causing immense problems, but the wily Mayor of Lyon had found a solution.

In 1850 he authorised: "All ladies over 30 years of age to retain their hats in the house and secured a bare-headed audience."

Frank Curzon, who worked at London's Prince of Wales Theatre, was not so clever a politician but had a practical turn of mind.

He wrote to the Express in 1910 on the matinee hat question. Suggestions that boxes be provided at public places and ladies forced to remove their hats were unrealistic, he said.

The boxes would need to be two-feet square to hold the fashionable creations, which cost from 10 to 20 guineas, and theatres would not have room.

No doubt men were glad to be free of such a tedious array of clothing. But Lorna reported in 1905 that, despite these restrictions, women were more wide awake than men in the morning.

"He is never so cheerful, so alert, so swift in his toilet as a woman can be – when she pleases – and he never seems so well and amiably, or at least patiently, prepared to begin the trivial round, the common task. That is why women have succeeded so well in those fields of labour which they have invaded and why the "boy" would never be a satisfactory substitute for the female domestic."

*Women were rather different in Letchworth. This picture is of the Spirella Folk Dancers, dated May 1911*

# Favourite Express-ions – 1905

★ The Rev W Norton preached in Hitchin and Stevenage on the subject of an English revival, to combat drunkenness, profanity and gambling. "As English people we are too icily regular and faultily faultless, too undemonstrative," he declared. A greater spirit of feeling and emotion would be a good thing for the nation, he believed.

★ Nearly 400 guests flocked to Kings Walden Bury for the coming-of-age party of Jack Harrison in January. Jack was heir to the popular JP, master of foxhounds and "generous and unbegrudging benefactor of the poor," T Fenwick Harrison.

"The scene was a very animated and brilliant one, the dresses being greatly admired," reported the Express. "Dancing was kept up from 9pm to 3am."

A 120-feet long temporary room was created, with the walls draped in green and white and 36 lights burning from three chandeliers. Floral baskets and ferns were suspended from the ceiling "while the ends of the room were tastefully hidden in a profusion of floral loveliness."

The tenants were invited to a separate dinner and servants' ball, with the 200 guests receiving Jack with long and prolonged cheers. The modest young man said if they saw any merit in him it must be on account of the reflected glory from his father.

★ As cars became increasingly common on the roads, so did accidents. In April two children were knocked over and killed in Welwyn and another injured. A letter to the Express stated: "Will the sad fatality be a lesson to the owners of these infernal machines commonly called motor cars, in the reckless manner in which they rush through our villages and on the main roads?"

The jury presiding at the inquest recommended a new 10mph speed limit.

The driver of the car, Mr George Pauling, "did all he could at the time and has promised to pay all expenses," reported the Express, adding that there was applause in court when this was announced.

Speeding cars were also causing concern in Stevenage, where a dog was run over in London Road.

*A stone gatherer, pictured at work*

"Complaints are very rife on the rate motors travel through and it is thought a byelaw regulating the speed through the town might be sensible," reported the Express. "The motor traffic is very considerable and increasing."

The aristocratic Lord Queensbury detested cars so much he wanted all civilians to be armed with revolvers, so they could shoot drivers who were endangering the lives of the public.

"Judging by the pace some cars have rushed through Stevenage, a bullet fired from an ordinary revolver would scarcely catch them up," commented an advert in the Express acidly.

Bikes could be dangerous as well. Poor Mr W O Times, clerk to Hitchin Urban District Council and in charge of almost every town organisation, fell off his bike in Cemetery Road and was found lying unconscious and bleeding in the road. He stayed overnight at a nearby house and was carried home to Bedford Road the next morning where he set about recovering "with absolute rest."

During a lecture at Hitchin Town Hall on radium, the audience handed round spinthariscopes of radium bromide, the tiny lethal shards darting with light.

The fire brigade were furious when they had to watch two cottages burn down on Hitchin Hill while their hoses spouted only a pathetic trickle of water "totally inadequate for the purpose."

The water engineer had refused to increase the pressure because a young messenger was sent to him and not a fireman.

"He could not take notice of a boy," he declared, coming in for some heated criticism. The Express even featured a cartoon headed Flames and Formality, a lesson in etiquette from H-----N firemen.

Public sympathy was not evident for the brigade in August – indeed firemen were jeered when they arrived at a flourishing blaze in Nightingale Road, Hitchin, after a delay of nearly half an hour.

Three thousand people gathered to watch the conflagration, some travelling from nearby villages, and the flames lit up the sky for miles around. Small print could easily be read by the light in neighbouring streets, declared the Express.

When the firemen finally arrived there were ironical cheers and hoots. The embarrassed men explained they were delayed getting horses from the Sun Inn, and needed them stabled nearer the new fire station in Paynes Park.

The British Society for the Propagation of the Gospel Among Jews met in Hitchin in February. The congregation heard that 500 Christian pulpits were occupied by converted Jews.

"May the ever hospitable gates of Great Britain never be shut against the persecuted Jew," declared the Rev Paul Dressler.

"Dr Barnardo is an outstanding example of the great work that can be done by a converted Jew. His work saves England many thousands of pounds annually by gathering up waifs and transforming them into good citizens of the dominions."

Poor Pc Unwin came a cropper in June when Hitchin officers decided to practice ju-jitsu for self defence, at the town hall. He broke his leg and had to be admitted to hospital. The other officers benefitted from the lessons however, when two drunkards caused an affray in the town. Pc Burrows was able to tackle one of the violent men and successfully ju-jitsued him.

The pathetic story of the poor rector of Clothall, Rev George Meyler Squibb, upset many Express readers in March. The 78-year-old rector, who was in failing health, became so worried about not doing his duties properly that he shot himself.

He had fainted in church six weeks earlier and was, said servant Matilda Jaggers: "Very anxious about his church duties." He confided to a friend that he was breaking up and would never be of any use again.

Numerous telephone posts were put up in the neighbourhood of Nightingale Road, Hitchin, prompting the Express to comment: "The town will soon resemble an American city in this respect."

At the end of April, Miss May Lucas, one of Hitchin's most eligible girls, married Arthur Wood in a "pretty ceremony." 1,500 spectators turned up to watch despite a cold and keen wind as May, in white satin trimmed with Bedfordshire lace and chiffon, was attended by four maids and a train bearer.

★ Mark All strolled into town in May, visiting Hitchin as part of his 10-year, 60,000-mile walk, which had already covered much of the Continent. Mr All, who was described as a tall spare man of 77, wanted to demonstrate to employers that a man is not old at 45 and can still work long after that. The high point of his walk, which had already taken seven years, was when the King gave him £2 at Newmarket.

★ An exhibition of cheap model cottages in Letchworth drew some snide comments. The Daily Sketch wrote:

*"First you must build the cottages, then you must teach the yokel to use them properly. Hodge likes to live in the kitchen and he keeps his sitting room for Christmas Day and burial or wedding festivities."*

One of the architects at the cottage exhibition was Miss Elspeth McClelland, whose sex caused a sensation in the profession.

She designed a £150 old English cottage with dark timbers and a picturesque verandah. On the principle that women spent most of their time in the scullery, she had made it as pretty and cheerful as possible with two windows.

Maybe Hodge would have thought the cottage a bit fancy and been happy to let a landlord keep six pigs, 40 fowl and a heap of manure in his Hitchin pub yard, but council officer Mr Blood wasn't. He ordered an agriculturally minded landlord, who did just that, to get rid of the nuisance.

Shortly afterwards another publican asked Hitchin council for permission to keep a horse in his yard.

When Dr Day, the medical officer of health, discovered that the horse and its manure would have to be taken through the living room, and the yard measured only 10 yards by three, he soon persuaded councillors to refuse the request.

★ The London Weekly published an article on Stevenage, commenting that it was gay for its size, with a fair number of dances in the season.

"Stevenage is remarkable for its broad high road and its open bowling green, surrounded by quaint old fashioned houses. It is a favourite summer resort for city gentlemen who are unable to get right away from town but like to stay with their families in the country."

*Bancroft pictured when Hitchin was still a rural town*

✴ The weather was so hot during the summer that two people died from the heat. Sales of ice cream soared, causing problems for Mr Blood, Hitchin's inspector of nuisances.

He found one vendor in Queen Street selling from dirty premises, with little or no furniture, wafer biscuits kept in the living room and an open bowl of cream cooling on the table while a young Italian woman swept the dusty floor.

When Mr Blood got her to understand that she must cover the cream bucket, she put a dirty towel across the top. To complete the hygiene nightmare there was a pony crammed into the small outhouse and the drains were blocked. The contrite owners promised to clean up.

✴ The famous vegetarian writer George Bernard Shaw, who lived at Ayot St Lawrence, wrote to the Express in July to complain about women who used birds as ornamentation in hats.

At a Covent Garden performance of Mozart: "This lady, who had very black hair, had stuck over her right eye the pitiable corpse of a large white bird, which looked exactly as if someone had killed it by stamping on its breast and then nailed it to the lady's temple. I am not I hope a morbidly squeamish person but the spectacle sickened me.

"I presume that if I had presented myself at the doors with a dead snake round my neck, a collection of black beetles pinned on my shirtfront and a grouse in my hair, I should have been refused admission. Why then is this woman allowed to commit such a public outrage?"

✴ An article in *The Schoolmaster* publication condemned a campaign in Hitchin. Posters in the town told children aged 11 to 13 they could be exempt from school all summer if they were needed to work on a farm.

The Schoolmaster commented: "Evidently there is in the rural district of Hitchin a dearth of juvenile farm labourers just now and the above advertisement is intended to quicken the supply.

"We earnestly hope that it will completely fail in its object as it deserves to do." Unemployed people should be used for the work, it added.

Curiosity did the daughter of a Stevenage tradesman no good at all in August.

"While sitting with relatives she meddled with a chaff cutter while nobody was near and got her arm so severely injured that she had to be taken to hospital," reported the Express.

✴ The vexed question of the Baldock man who had married his aunt caused a dilemma at St Albans quarter sessions in August. James Brown, known as a disorderly person and a vagabond, had been sent to prison for three months' hard labour for deserting his wife and two children. Now 'the incorrigible rogue' was back in court on the same charge but had come up with a novel defence.

His wife was, he said, the widow of his uncle, and such a union was illegal. If he was not married he could not have deserted his bride. The court were reluctantly forced to acquit him.

✴ Electricity mains were being laid along Walsworth Road in Hitchin and a farmer was offering a £10 prize for a digging competition, to promote interest in this branch of agriculture. Contestants had to turn over 40 poles of ground, although whether they belonged to the same farmer was not made clear.

✴ Otter houndsmen from Essex came into Hertfordshire for a three-day spree at the end of August, killing twice. There was a good field including several ladies who stuck to the hounds all day.

For two hours they chased one otter bitch until she became exhausted, whereupon the brave Mr Rose jumped into the river and threw her onto the bank, to be quickly dispatched by the hounds.

Mr Rose professed himself well pleased with Hertfordshire and the Express returned the compliment, stating that the hunt had provided much pleasure for local sportsman. All were resolved to return and repeat the pleasurable experience.

✴ An enterprising salesman took the opportunity to display a new invention to housewives visiting Hitchin market in September. Many were taken with the Canadian washing machine, which would revolutionise the erstwhile laborious task of washing linen.

Now they had only to depress a lever to activate two sets of rubbing boards which would squeeze soap and water through the clothes and turn them "exactly in the manner of hard work but quicker and better." One lady from Bancroft tried the machine, and was apparently very taken with it. Sales were reported to be heavy.

# The convict's fortune and his heir

A transvestite mother, a murderer on his way to the scaffold, two kings and a massive fortune in gold – that was the intriguing tale published in The Express of March 9, 1901.

The story, which encompassed three continents, started many years' earlier in 1819 when 35-year-old William Farrar was caught poaching. The motive, explained the Express, was poverty – his wife and child were going hungry when plenty of food could be had for the taking in the woods near their Millbrook home.

Three gamekeepers caught Farrar on the Duke of Bedford's land. Farrar, who was armed with a gun, did not intend to go quietly.

There was a furious struggle, the gun went off, and one keeper was mortally wounded.

Farrar stood trial for murder, was convicted and sentenced to be hanged in the very woods where the offence had been committed.

The day was set for January 29, 1820, a gibbet was erected and the Sheriff stood waiting for Farrar to be led from his cell at Bedford Prison.

It was not to be. A messenger arrived from London urgently requesting an audience with the Sheriff. His news was grim – George III lay dying.

Indeed, so imminent was the death that the messenger believed another rider would follow in hours. The sheriff must be ready to proclaim the ascent of the new king, George IV.

The execution was postponed. Farrar did not walk out of his cell to the gibbet but sat and waited until the sheriff was ready.

The messenger had not been mistaken; a second horseman followed hot on the heels of the first and the Sheriff was thrust into a flurry of official business.

When he was at last free later in the day: "He took it into his loyal head that it would be an insult to the dead king to send the soul of a common poacher to the bar of God on the same day that the Almighty would have the honour of receiving the soul of George William Frederick, King of England and Defender of the Faith."

The execution was postponed again and rescheduled for the next day. The Sheriff rose ready and eager to take Farrar to the gibbet – but his efficient city recorder had bad news for him. If he hanged Farrar now, he was told, he was liable to indictment for murder himself – the execution had to be on January 29, as named in the official documents, or it was not legal.

The Sheriff was in a terrible position, paralysed with embarrassment. What was he to do with his prisoner, a convicted murderer? How could the situation be resolved?

He turned to the new king for help and George IV, no doubt ecstatic that his long regency was over, displayed regal magnanimity.

He reprieved Farrar, ruling that instead he would be transported to Australia for life. Farrar was hustled away from his home, never to return or see his wife and child again.

He prospered in Australia, although the years of hard labour took their toll. At 55 he looked 70 and was alone; he had never heard from his wife and believed she had married again, being legally deemed a widow.

Of his son, also called William, he knew nothing. But in other ways he flourished, receiving a ticket of leave after 25 years, allowing him to earn his own living.

He was a free man again, with just one proviso – he could not return to England. Farrar, lonely and bereft of his family, put all his energy into his work. By the time he died in 1855, aged 70, he had acquired a piece of land worth £5,000.

In the event of his death, the land would pass to his male heirs. William, now a middle-aged man, stood to inherit a great fortune – but was ignorant of his good luck. If the estate remained unclaimed it would eventually pass to various charities.

Enquiries were made, advertisements inserted in newspapers, but to no avail. The years passed and still William did not contact the Australian solicitors. The charities became fractious and importunate.

Then something happened to make the search for William more vital and urgent than ever – gold was found on Farrar's land in substantial quantities.

The £5,000 inheritance increased rapidly in value – to almost £1million by the end of the century.

If William could be found, he would be one of the richest men in the world. Time was running out for the Farrars, a solution would have to be found.

Just as the gold seemed within the charities' grasp, the tale took another dramatic twist – William's son Robert came to Melbourne.

Robert had documents to prove his story, he knew things only a family member could know and he swore he was the grandson of Farrar and defied the world to prove the contrary. His claim looked indisputable.

He had come to Melbourne from the east coast of America, with papers proving that his father William had emigrated to the USA and worked in the mills of Connecticut and Rhode Island.

Strong as his claim was, it had to be investigated. Austin Brain, an Australian lawyer, made the long voyage round half the world to see if anyone in Bedfordshire could remember the Farrars and throw any light on Robert's tale.

He discovered a clue in the archives of the most aristocratic family in the county. At Woburn Abbey itself he found references to the Farrars. It seemed Farrar's wife – legally his widow – had taken another husband and started a new family. Farrar's son William had grown up, married and had several children, but every one had been a girl.

William was long dead and, according to everything Mr Brain could discover, there had been no male heir to inherit the vast estate.

There was no reference to an emigration to America and no grandson called Robert – or anything else.

The English trail was cold and the hunt now switched to America, where George McClean was appointed to investigate Robert's claim.

## The discovery he made was nothing short of sensational

It rested partly on the evidence of a family from Hitchin, who had come to work in Boston several years earlier.

They knew the Farrars of Bedford-shire well, had attended the son William's funeral, and were somewhat surprised to learn that the dead William appeared to be resurrected and living nearby with a son unknown to them, called Robert.

They lost no time in calling and immediately realised the truth. They recognised 'William' all right – it was his sister Sarah, born to Farrar's pregnant wife after he was transported.

Farrar had lived 35 years in Australia and never known he had a daughter.

Sarah had married, borne one son, Robert, and been deserted by her errant husband. Presumably learning of her father's inheritance and the punitive terms of his will, she devised her plan to dupe the lawyers.

She dressed herself as a man, called herself William, took Robert to America and shared a home with him as father and son. She built up a firm background as William, ready for Robert to lay his claim when the time came.

The visit from her Hitchin friends must have been a cruel blow; at one stroke all her meticulous plans were at risk. Despite her talent for deception, Sarah could offer no reason to explain her disguise.

Instead she appealed to her friends not to disclose her true identity and they, moved by her entreaties, kept the knowledge to themselves. Only in death did the truth come out, when the undertaker discovered the deception and duly reported that 'William' was not a man.

This surprising news created some interest but was discreetly smoothed over. The truth was only officially confirmed when 'William' Farrar's body was exhumed and the skeleton in the casket was declared to be that of a female.

Poor Robert. As the Express stated, he was certainly the grandson of Farrar the convict. But he was not the male heir of the male heir and neither he nor William's daughters were entitled to a single penny of the £1million fortune.

It was a different story for Mr McClean, whose sleuthing skills had unveiled the deception. He was paid a fee of 200,000 dollars, making him very wealthy indeed.

## Dirt and grime behind the gipsy myth

A party of "so-called Macedonian gipsies" was escorted through the area in June, 1905. The travellers, with two vans but no horses, had come from Stopsley at the expense of the ratepayers and were passed from the care of the Beds police into the hands of their Hertfordshire colleagues.

The party reached Offley, where the gipsies camped by the side of the road for the night while the police procured horses to take them on to Hitchin.

The group lived in one van which was "very old and excessively dirty," said the Express. One had no windows and the other, seemingly better equipped, had no glass.

Inside was a stove, a few cooking utensils and a medley of old rags, which apparently served as bedding. There were two families, with nine children between them, all very dirty and without boots, stockings and warm clothing. Despite this they looked, said the Express reporter, strong and healthy.

The families were actually German and had sailed from Hamburg to Grimsby seven months earlier. One father told the reporter: "I haf no horses, I haf no money," but "judging from his calm demeanour, these facts worried him not at all."

The police took the vans with their borrowed horses to the Highlander in Tilehouse Street, where a crowd gathered while the women took the opportunity to beg before they went on to Biggleswade. There Mr Ernest Huckle spoke to them in their own language "and found the women to be more intelligent than the men. Both the women and men smoked, as did a little boy about three years of age."

The next morning the family were moved on yet again, to Gamlingay.

Their standards of hygiene would not have struck many of Hitchin's townsfolk as especially poor. In the same issue of the Express the town surveyor Mr Blood reported a nuisance he had successfully dealt with.

It consisted of a pub yard with six pigs, 40 fowl and a heap of manure kept in dangerous proximity to nearby cottages.

Sometimes the poor had a chance to escape to a better life, however briefly. A letter in the Express in 1905 appealed for funds for seaside camps, which took in London working boys of good character and small earnings.

The lads, aged 14 to 17, stayed for one or two weeks discovering the delights of country walks or playing one of the games "which are dear to the heart of an English lad."

Almost 25,000 boys had been helped under this scheme since 1889 and "they are shown how their enjoyment is enhanced by the possession of a clean and healthy mind and of a clear conscience."

**The boy of three was smoking**

# An adventure with Dr Livingstone

In his youth the Rev Lowell J Procter had been an adventurer. By 1900 he was established as the rector of Radwell village, but he was a man who had known Livingstone – and not known him in the calm of England but in the drama, heat and adventure of Africa itself.

In January 1900 he shared his reminiscences with readers of the Express. His tale sat strangely among the minutiae of local government, entertainments and debate.

The Rev Procter joined the Universities' Mission to Central Africa shortly after Dr Livingstone discovered the lakes of Nyassa and Shirwah in 1859, a time when, in his words: "The whole of the surrounding countryside was a very hot bed of the slave trade.

"Caravan routes passed to the north and the south of the lakes, to and fro between the far interior and the settlements of the Portuguese, hidden tentacles from the sea appearing inwards in vigorous conjunction with the Arabs."

In May, 1861, the Rev Procter travelled with Livingstone up the Zambesi on the steamer, Pioneer. There they split up, Livingstone leaving to explore the Nyassa country and the Rev Procter taking a different direction under the leadership of Bishop Mackenzie. The two parties arranged to rendezvous by January 1862.

The Mackenzie party boasted one freed slave known as Charlie and six bearers to carry baggage, including calico and beads for exchange on the journey and to offer as presents for chiefs.

Charlie was not the best of guides. In quite a short time the party found themselves lost and wandering into an unknown native camp.

Things went wrong from the very start. As they approached the village they noticed that the small huts outside the perimeter were securely fastened. An elderly man set off a warning howl.

"The path leading into the place was peculiar, to say the least of it," wrote Rev Procter. "Running through almost impenetrable thicket, at intervals of 20 yards or so, were found narrow gateways, or rather barriers." Only one person could pass through at a time and poles could be used to block the way at several points.

The village appeared prosperous, with several large and well appointed huts. But it was not welcoming. A huge fellow appeared menacingly and motioned the travellers towards: "A hut of such size as almost to deserve the name of a house – evidently that of a chief – where he blandly invited us to sit down on mats under the verandah while he went to call the owner."

> The country was a very hotbed of the slave trade

Meanwhile Charlie had wandered off and started chatting to some of the villagers. He came back in a panic with a sinister tale. The villagers were "rank slave traders" and gangs of slavers passed through regularly, explaining the fastened huts and the fortified pathway into the village.

"This disgusted us," declared the rector and the party got together and prepared to leave. But they found that easier to plan than to achieve.

Natives barred their way: "Shouting at us not over civilly that the chief would be angry if we did not come back. This, after consulting together, we thought it better to do, in order to avoid a breach of etiquette and probably of blood at the same time."

The men's meeting with Chief Manasomba did not reassure them. He was:

*"A sinister looking individual with a cunning leer in his eye and wearing a dirty, broad-brimmed Portuguese straw hat. He wondered why we went off in such a hurry and in the most gracious manner possible promised to do anything in the world for us."*

Bishop Mackenzie struggled to make the best of the situation, explaining the party were English travellers lost on their way to Tombondira's camp: "Giving him full particulars and adding pointedly that our journey was not to buy slaves. To this he made no remark."

Any hope of leaving quickly was dashed when the chief: "Said brusquely it was a long way and we must eat and sleep with him tonight." After their midday meal the party again tried to leave but no guide was to be had "for love or – calico."

"Evening was soon upon us, so that at last nothing was left us but to go in and reluctantly agree with the chief to stay there for the night. Certainly the prospect looked anything but comfortable.

"Our host's manner was not attractive. The people were inclined to be insolent, offering things for sale and demanding exorbitant amounts of cloth for them. We could not move a yard without being watched while, to make matters worse, the number of evil looking savages we had noticed in the place in the morning kept on increasing all the afternoon."

But for all this the Bishop's party were reasonably sanguine. They had met many Africans in varying situations and none had ever offered violence.

Indeed: "The natives hitherto had shown such invariable good feeling that, whatever suspicions we may have entertained regarding Manasomba's people and our barter goods, we could not believe that they would think of attacking us."

This innocent trust was soon dispelled. Once again it was Charlie who grasped the truth of the situation, informing them that: "To a certainty mischief was brewing, that the sight of our goods had excited Manasomba's people, but being afraid to attack and rob us in the day time they meant all the same to do it at night."

In the darkest hour before dawn the tribesmen would strike, setting the Bishop's hut ablaze and spearing the men to death as they fled the flames.

"We had been led into a tight corner and a desperately ugly one too," wrote the Rev Procter from the safety of his Radwell home. But no one panicked and they quickly decided their only choice was to leave straight away. Secretly they got their luggage together and, in the rays of the setting sun, prepared to flee into the darkness.

"I told Manasomba that we had made up our minds to go on, as time was precious, politely begging him to excuse us and, at the same time offering him a gorgeously coloured scarf out of our barter goods as a propitiatory parting gift, walked boldly out of the village," recalled Procter.

Alas, Manasomba was not to be diverted by frippery. With a howl of rage he set his men in pursuit. Still the steady Bishop and his party did not falter.

"Sharp was the word, but taking care to show no hurry or excitement," wrote the rector, as they walked quickly away with their guns cocked.

"The savages started on every side and the village seemed alive with them, uttering the most fearful cries and yells, mixed with sounds – how produced I have no idea but this much I only know, it has never been my lot to listen to anything more hideous and blood curdling.

"I shall never forget the scene. Infernal is the only name for it. A crowd of half-naked figures with wild, glaring eyes, rushing to and fro among the huts, taking long, straight-legged strides so as to give them the appearance of flying along rather than running."

As the natives rushed forward, the bearers fled. "We found ourselves alone with only our rifles and the clothes upon our backs. I was the last." Around them were 100 natives, shouting, running and fixing arrows to their bow strings. Still the party kept their nerve.

> 'I was soon quite out of it and was no more than a mere looker on'

"We walked along, our guns on our shoulders, without the least hurry or nervousness, only now and again, when one of the fellows came too close, stopping to fix him with our eye and quietly cover him with our rifles."

Looking back over the years the Rev Procter recalls exactly how he felt, trapped and hounded in the middle of a foreign land by strange men. "I had the oddest sensation," he wrote from the calm of Radwell Rectory.

"It was not funk. There seemed no occasion for that, for whilst in a fever of excitement that made me forget everything except that our escape depended upon ourselves, still it didn't appear as if there were anything to be afraid of because, whatever happened, I was quite soon out of it, and was no more than just a mere looker on. That is how I felt. I have often thought since that men going into action must feel something of the same kind."

For half a mile the intrepid party walked on but the rector was soon roused from his daze. A huge native grabbed him from behind and seized the rifle, still held in Procter's hands. "We didn't want to kill anyone if we could help it but I must confess I felt my patience fast becoming a negligible quality. A fierce struggle began," he wrote, almost 40 years later.

In the tumult and the noise no one realised Procter's dilemma, as he struggled to keep hold of his gun, until it went off, grazing the native's skin. The effect was electrical.

As the gun exploded the native threw up his hands: "Horror and consternation depicted on his face, and flew like the wind to his companions who were making their way back with equal precipitation."

There was one final drama as the party fled with dignity into the night. A last arrow, unleashed by the parting tribesmen, lodged in the stock of Procter's gun and stayed embedded there, held by evil spikes – "A grim souvenir of our escape from Rundu Manasomba's slave trading horde."

*Adventures were quiet affairs for this group in Ashwell during the last years of Victoria's reign*

# Favourite Express-ions – 1906

★ Hitchin was "a substantial little market town" and "one of the most pleasant, salubrious and accessible residential centres," according to an illustrated guide to some of London's choicest suburbs, published by the Great Northern Railway Company in May.

★ In July the Express published two photographs of a car which had hit a telegraph pole between Welwyn and Hatfield. "We learn by telegram from Dr Hull shortly before going to press that Mr Harmsworth is making satisfactory progress," reported the paper, referring to the injured driver and pleased to pass the latest information on to eager readers.

★ A Letchworth idealist revealed her plans for The Cloisters to the Express in August. Annie Jane Lawrence had designed an open air school, not for children but for teachers.

"The end is to get people to adopt the open air life," she said, adding she was anxious to reach the leisured classes who had little to do but eat and dress.

The building would include a wide roofed verandah, a semi-circular courtyard and a roof supported by green marble pillars.

"Hammocks would be available for those who desired them, although the weak-willed could sleep in a bed.

"As a protection against the wind, Venetian shutters have been provided and these can also be utilised as screens at night," added Miss Lawrence, enticingly.

The bath, in the true spirit of the venture, was in the open air and there were no carpets "to harbour dust." But there were under floor hot water pipes and open fires. The building was due to open during the following year.

★ A noisy vendor of fly papers was trapped in a garden for 10 minutes in Hitchin when five dogs surrounded him. They had taken exception to his cry of "Catch 'em alive o," and he had to beat a hasty retreat, leaving some of his merchandise behind.

★ Working and travelling on the railways was a risky occupation – 1,099 people had died in accidents in 1905 and 459 had been injured. It wasn't as bad as it seemed though, the Express stated. Only one passenger had died for every 34 million journeys, and just one was injured for every three million, leaving a lot of unfortunate workers to make up the numbers.

★ Poor Captain Digby heard tragic news while in Australia in August. His 25-year-old wife had died giving birth to a premature girl, who did not live either. The captain, from Pirton Hall, cabled the words: "Goodbye darling, I am heart broken – your husband" to be etched on a plate on the coffin.

★ The Express newspaper made news itself in September when there was a fire in its works in Exchange Yard, Hitchin. A piece of tissue paper caught in a gas jet and fell, ablaze, onto sheets of paper. "Almost instantly one end of the machine room was in flames," reported the Express.

The fire was helped along by cloths soaked in paraffin which flared up to the ceiling. But the brave workers fought back, throwing water on the blaze until the fire brigade arrived, while a chain was formed to keep them supplied with full buckets.

The firm acknowledged their indebtedness to Mr Lee, machine foreman, and his fellow workmen, who "stuck to their post without thought of personal safety."

★ A London clerk who appeared at Hitchin county court in September must have had a great fondness for butter and eggs – he owed £12 for dairy produce supplied to his household in Rabley Heath although his income was only £2.5s a week.

He had sold some furniture to try and pay his debt but raised very little cash. He was told to give the farmer a pound a month.

✶ The oddest story of the year was told in the pages of the Express in November. It concerned little Clarence Brown, aged nine, who lived in an awning outside his home in Co-operative Terrace, Arlesey. Clarence had a hip disease that left him crippled and had spent a long period in hospital. When he came home in January, 1906, he persuaded his parents to put his bed outside.

The Express reporter found him "a merry eyed, fair complexioned little boy," well wrapped up and only driven inside if it was foggy or rained very hard.

His friends came along to chat and he could watch them play, he explained. "At night I have curtains put up round the garden."

His mother seemed happy with the arrangement, saying he was the pet of the village and lots of people stopped to talk to him. "There's plenty to take his attention out here," she told the reporter.

*Bystanders in Hitchin Market Place in 1906 watch the electricity cables being laid*

# The schoolboy who killed his mother

Winifred Rodgers was reading in the breakfast room when she heard the shot. As she looked up in surprise, not yet alarmed, her brother Frank walked into the room. He was perfectly calm but held a revolver in his hand.

"I have shot her," he said, looking straight at Winifred. "It's for the best."

Georgina Rodgers lay in the hall, half crouching against the sofa. A trail of blood led back to an easy chair in the breakfast room, where Frank had found her. Mingled with the smell of blood and of gunpowder was the overwhelming stench of alcohol, sodden on her breath.

Winifred got up and tried to pass Frank, to tend to her mother, but he stopped her. Although he had been too ill to go school for 12 months past, he was stronger than her. "No," he said firmly, gripping her wrists. "No. Someone had better go for a doctor." They stood in the doorway, looking at each other, both knowing it was too late.

Mrs Thurley was behind the bar of the British Queen, opposite the Rodgers' home in Meldreth. She looked up as Frank came in at about 9pm, carrying his younger sister Queenie in his arms. She knew at once that something must be very wrong, but the lad was quite composed, looking older than his 15 years. "Would you mind taking Queenie for the night?" he asked with his unfailing courtesy. "There's been a little upset at home."

He paused and Mrs Thurley never took her eyes from his pale, composed face. "I have shot mother," he said.

"What?" she gasped, moving towards him. "I have shot mother," he repeated, adding quickly: "Don't worry, it will be all right. I shall go over to Melbourn tomorrow."

He turned away, leaving Mrs Thurley with Queenie. A little while later, the child settled upstairs, Mrs Thurley looked out of the window.

Below her she saw Frank standing in the road outside The Gables and she went straight out to him. "Can I do anything?" she asked gently.

He looked at her with relief.

"I wish you would go in Mrs Thurley," he said. "The servants are afraid."

Inside the house there was panic and despair. The doctor had arrived, finally fetched by Winifred and a servant. Afraid to cross the front hall, to pass the body with its rush of blood and gaping neck wounds, they had fled from the back. Everyone was milling around; it was impossible to do anything.

Mrs Thurley went back to the British Queen, followed by the still calm Frank.

"Can I see Queenie?" he asked as they entered the bar.

*The Gables still stands in Meldreth, an imposing house with a nameplate beside the gate*

Against all logic and all sense she agreed.

Together they mounted the stairs to the girl's bedroom where, taking her gently in his arms, he kissed her twice.

Downstairs Frank handed Mrs Thurley a cartridge, settled himself in one of the chairs and picked up a newspaper. He proceeded to read for the best part of an hour, until Sgt Salmon arrived from Melbourn to arrest him.

News spread fast, and the story of the 15-year-old schoolboy who had killed his mother filled the national papers in April 1904. The inquest verdict of wilful murder only increased the frenzy and titillation.

The inquest was heard at the British Queen. A reporter travelled from Hitchin to the Cambridgeshire village to report in person. "The pretty village of Meldreth, with its long straggling old world street a mile or more from end to end, dotted at irregular intervals mainly with thatched cottages, is not a fit setting for such an awful tragedy as occurred there on Tuesday evening," he wrote with fervour.

He painted in the background details – the four children ranging from 21-year-old William to little Queenie, the father who worked away from home as a solicitor and the mother, who was frequently, distressingly, drunk.

Her husband had sent her away for a cure, but to no avail. He had brought the family out to this idyllic, quiet village a year ago, in an effort to stop his wife getting hold of alcohol. The move was entirely futile and, in a further blow, his third child, Frank, had lost his health and his good humour, becoming anaemic, weak and morbid.

Far from being able to prepare to be a solicitor as planned, Frank had been too sickly to attend school for the past year.

The beauty of the Gables – a picturesque, old-fashioned house near the village green – was completely lost to the family. Instead they were plunged into misery and distress. Eighteen-year-old Winifred, facing the inquest jury with composure, explained:

*"For the last few years we have been
very unhappy because my mother
had given way to drink."*

She told them something else, muttered by Frank as their mother's body lay in the hall.

*The British Queen, pictured
in November 1998*

"Frank said Queenie could not be brought up to the life we have led the last few years," confided Winifred, who won the sympathy of everyone in the court.

"She gave evidence clearly and with complete self possession, although she showed some signs of emotion when speaking of her brother," reported the Herts Express.

A few days later, when she was again called on to testify at her brother's committal, the strain was clearly showing. Dressed in deep mourning and with an ashen face, her: "Large full eyes looked for the most part at her brother Frank sitting beside her but he did not raise his eyes to any one of the witnesses," reported the Express.

Frank had been kept at Cambridge Jail and fed on meals brought in from outside. To try to foil the large crowd of curious sightseers who had gathered outside the courtroom, he arrived at Melbourn early, in a brougham. Despite the drama of the proceedings and the enormous interest in him, he walked with a firm step, wearing a dark grey suit with brown boots and a black tie.

He was allowed to sit during the proceedings and looked very pale, although he was calm and collected. His sister was not so composed.

"Miss Rodgers toyed nervously with the iron bar before her as she gave her evidence clearly and without faltering and her affection for her brother was plainly seen," wrote the reporter for the Express, occupying one of the benches packed with journalists and artists.

Again Winifred talked about how miserable the family had been at The Gables: "Very very unhappy through mother taking drink. Frank had never complained about his mother but had said he was sorry and it had seemed to worry him a great deal."

Frank, she explained, was very fond of his mother – in fact he was so much her favourite that his nickname was Mother's Boy. At this point Winifred seemed to forget the gravity of the situation and where she was, giving a smile. It did not linger long.

For the past month Frank had been very quiet and frequently ill with bad headaches, she said. He had suffered from nose bleeds every morning and seemed very depressed and unstable when his mother drank.

Her evidence was reinforced by the family GP, Dr Octavius Ennion, who was called to the house after the shooting. He saw Frank in the kitchen and the lad said: "I have done it."

The doctor asked for the revolver and Frank took it out of his coat pocket and handed it over, asking: "Did my mother suffer any pain?"

As Dr Ennion gave his evidence Frank looked up and took a keen interest in what he was saying. But his attention waned as other witnesses spoke and he stared steadfastly at his feet. The only exception was during the testimony of Mrs Thurley, when she recounted Frank's farewell to Queenie. This he listened to intently.

Dr Ennion's statement caused a sensation. He knew the family well, having cared for them since their arrival in the village a year earlier. He was aware that the mother was 'frequently under the influence' and had been concerned about Frank's health.

> 'The family were very very unhappy through mother taking drink'

> Frank changed, lost all interest in life and gave up his studies

His growth was exceptionally marked, he had violent headaches and suffered from nose bleeds. The doctor went on to describe events after the shooting. Frank, he declared, had not seemed sorry for what he had done – he did not seem to realise the gravity of the situation at all. Far from making any attempt to escape, he had sat quietly at the British Queen reading the newspaper.

The next day, testified Dr Ennion, Frank had told him he had shot his mother because of an overwhelming impulse. At first he had resisted but it returned and voices told him distinctly to do it quickly.

He did not remember pointing or firing the pistol, only feeling giddy and hearing a muffled retort. Then he tumbled against the door.

That dreadful night was the culmination of three months' anxiety and stress.

He constantly thought his mother was behind him and when he looked over his shoulder, he would catch a glimpse of her. Then she always disappeared.

Frank, stated the doctor grimly, had a history of insanity and alcoholism in his family, on his mother's side.

The next witness was the oldest child, William, who had owned the fatal revolver. He recalled asking Frank soon after the shooting: "Do you really know what you have done?" only to be told in exasperation: "Oh, don't worry me!"

The brothers shared a bedroom and for the last few weeks Frank had been irritable and restless in his sleep. On several occasions he had got out of bed in the middle of the night and locked the door – but he could never recall what had happened later. He had changed, lost all interest in life, abandoned his studies in shorthand and even given up tending his beloved garden. Three weeks before the tragedy Mrs Rodgers had been exceptionally intoxicated. That night Frank had dreamt he stabbed her.

But when Mrs Rodgers, no longer aware of what she was doing, had almost fallen under a train at Royston Station, it was Frank who rescued her, risking his life in the process.

There was never any question of the outcome of the committal – Frank was remanded in custody for trial at the Assizes. He appeared there in June, charged with feloniously, wilfully and of malice aforethought killing his mother on April 12, 1904. He was described to the jury as a schoolboy.

Once again he entered the court with a firm step and pleaded not guilty, without faltering. Throughout the three-hour hearing he was alert and listened keenly to all the evidence.

The judge, Mr Justice Phillimore, said it was a very sad, very melancholy and very grave case. He repeated the word sad three times in as many lines, speaking to a packed court with a large crowd of disappointed spectators waiting outside. A number of women in the gallery took particular interest in Winifred, the chief witness against her brother.

For a third time she described that last evening, when her mother had missed the evening meal "because she was not mistress of herself."

Dr Ennion discussed the family's problems – how Frank, anaemic and greatly under the influence of his mother, had been under tremendous strain because of her behaviour. His nervous system was so upset: "That he had acted under an imperative idea and shot his mother, thinking at the time it was the right thing to to."

He advanced the theory that Frank's mental state was hereditary – his mother and her father had been of intemperate habits, an uncle and great uncle had been sent to lunatic asylums. Not only did Frank hear voices encouraging him to kill, he saw visions as well.

Other medical experts testified about Frank's mental health. They were unanimous – it was fragile. "He did not know right from wrong when he did it. His senses were dormant," said one. "He was in a morbid state of excitement and yielded to an impulse to commit the crime for which an immature judgement had for some time led him to believe there was moral justification," testified another.

Frank's Uncle James was more succinct – he said the lad had changed and his lively nature become morbid.

It took the jury just four minutes to reach their verdict – that Frank was guilty but insane. The schoolboy killer heard the words impassively and was quickly removed from the dock, to be detained at His Majesty's pleasure.

# Favourite Express-ions – 1907

✦ Lace making should be taught again in Bedfordshire schools, three county councillors recommended in April. They suggested Saturday afternoon classes were set up and girls be allowed to practise during a portion of their needlework hours at school.

✦ A "very serious event" took place in September, according to the vicar of Pirton. 'Parliament has passed a bill legalising marriage with a deceased wife's sister and thus lowered the standard of marriage which has been uniformly adopted by the Holy Catholic Church."

God forbids such a union because of the nearness of kin, declared the vicar, adding: "Such marriages have been considered to partake of the nature of incest."

✦ The icy weather in early February drew thousands of visitors to Biggleswade, where they skated on 20 acres of flooded meadowland. Cheap excursions were arranged by Great Northern Railway. Others made do with the ice that had formed at Walsworth near Hitchin but it was "limited and not of the best quality."

✦ The possibility of building a Channel Tunnel was discussed by Hitchin Debating Society, with Mr W F Langford concluding the revenue would never yield a profit for shareholders.

✦ An accommodation crisis was looming at Stevenage police station, where there were only two cells for prisoners and no toilet facilities, even for the officers.

✦ A terrified stag, chased by hounds, plunged into a garden at Kneesworth in March and through the small parlour window. It was badly cut and dashed about, frightening the wits out of two ladies sitting in the room at the time. Chairs, mirrors and pictures were all smashed and blood from the stag's wounds stained the carpet. Eventually the huntsmen, from Cambridge, managed to get hold of the animal and take it away – but not before the hounds had plundered the kitchen, eating food off the table and breaking the dishes.

*Hitchin railway station, pictured in about 1866*

✦ Shillington was all agog after the parish nurse was jilted at the altar in April. Poor Miss Periera was due to wed Thomas Stevens of Bournemouth in the village church in April. But on the very day of the ceremony, with the bride and two bridesmaids waiting, the bridegroom, speaking in a strange and incoherent manner, said he wanted the ceremony postponed.

The nurse ran to her house, locked herself in the attic and refused to answer the door. Eventually her worried friends broke a window and found her huddled in the corner of the attic "in a prostrate condition." The bridegroom fled back to Bournemouth and poor Nurse Periera was taken to a rest home.

✦ The death of 86-year-old Mrs Arthur Ellis achieved extensive press coverage in May – she was the nurse employed by actress Ellen Terry to care for her son Gordon Craig, who was born in Orchard Road, Stevenage.

Mrs Ellis, known as 'My dear Essie' by the great woman, was one of a farmer's 13 children and had seven of her own.

Always on the lookout for sales, the High Street shop Chambers advertised "splendid" photographs" of Ellen Terry, available for 2d each.

✦ Should Hitchin be covered by a 10mph speed limit for cars? That was the question discussed by urban district councillors in June. Mr Gainsford, vicar of St Saviour's and a member of the council, preferred not to impose a restriction but prosecute fast motorists for "driving to the common danger." After all, he said, 10mph could usually be too fast and sometimes two was quite enough.

Mr P A Sharman, secretary of the North Herts Automobile Club, was horrified at the very idea of legal limits. "It resolves itself into an absurdity," he wrote to the Express. "We could have all sorts of fancy limits all over the country." Indeed.

✦ That would not have suited cyclist 26-year-old G A Olley, who established a new record in June by riding 1,000 miles in four days nine hours three minutes. He started his marathon from the Cock Hotel in Hitchin on a Rudge Whitworth and toured East Anglia, braving gales in the Fens, flocks of sheep and a badly timed level crossing. He sustained himself on Welsh rarebit, poached eggs, stewed fruit, custard, tomatoes, egg, milk and hot tea, while being massaged with whisky. During his epic ride he snatched five minute cat naps by the road side, only going to bed twice for two hours. At the end of his ordeal he was judged "fit as a fiddle."

✦ Baldock was in a fever of excitement when the Prince of Wales and his equerry, driving from London to Newmarket, had to stop at the George and Dragon in Baldock while a burst tyre was mended. The chauffeur, with the assistance of the hotel's 'boots,' put in a new inner tube while the Prince waited in the car. News soon got around, a crowd gathered and, as the car finally pulled away, cheer after cheer was raised. The Prince stood up and raised his hat as he drove off.

✦ A slow-witted workman caused an explosion at George Spurr's drapery establishment in Hitchin Market Place (now the site of Churchgate and The Comet newspaper) after someone smelled gas in July. The man, searching for a leak on the top floor, lit a match. Two assistants were thrown across the room, a wall was demolished and another caught fire. Only the fact that firemen were already on hand saved a disaster but "as it is the damage is very heavy," reported the Express.

✦ A marked increase in cases of cancer was blamed on vaccinations by Beds county councillor Mr C Soundy, in August. His statement was greeted by cries of "hear, hear." Another man who was opposed to modern changes was Mr W Birch of Midland Cottages, Hitchin, who objected to having to pay more rent because his sanitation had been improved. It would be unfair, he wrote to the Express, to be penalised for "a mere fad." He had lived in the cottages for eight years and in that time only three adults had died (one in childbirth) and four children, including three of his own.

✦ The perils of intemperance were outlined at St Mary's Church in August, when Boys' School master Arthur Goodwin gave a talk. "Visitors are struck with the number of loungers about the Market Place and immediate neighbourhood who delight in getting intoxicated," he declared. "How is it that an apparently quiet country town like Hitchin has got into such a state? Obviously drastic measures would be necessary to effect reform."

# Dr Williams' pink pills save another life

Dr Williams' Pink Pills for Pale People could do anything. If only half their advertising were true, there would have been no need to set up the National Health Service.

They could cure anaemia, rickets, scrofula, decline, consumption, indigestion, palpitations, rheumatism, sciatica, St Vitus dance, paralysis, locomotive atazy, neuralgia and disturbances of the central nervous system – and all for less than three shillings a box.

Each week the Express newspaper would report the real-life story of someone saved by the pink pills.

Take William Bradley's eldest daughter, who had been a great sufferer with anaemia all her life, was inclined to be consumptive, could not eat and was sick if she took medicines.

The doctor said her case was so serious that nothing could do her any real good. Nevertheless, in the end Dr Williams' Pink Pills for Pale People not only cured her, they made her hale and hearty as well. Her mother declared:

*"It was wonderful to see what an improvement one box made."*

Her father took a more mercenary view – Dr Williams had saved him pounds in doctor's bills as well as saving his daughter's life after she had been despaired of.

Mr J Hoskins was quite a different kettle of fish. He was so grief stricken after his beloved mother died that he underwent a sort of paralysis "the effect of which was to deprive him of his memory."

The poor man, who was a school master, often found himself saying things which he knew to be wrong but he could not correct.

He could not concentrate, his mind wandered and the problem was not getting any better. But Dr Williams' Pink Pills for Pale People changed everything and his memory was completely restored.

It was important, stressed Dr Williams, not to be deceived into accepting substitutes.

Other patent medicines promised as much. A cup of Epp's Cocoa – grateful and comforting – was better than any apple a day. The delicately flavoured beverage might save many heavy doctors' bills.

If you were still unfortunate enough to succumb to an infection, Dr J Collis Browne's chloroydne might save you.

A great specific for cholera, it also helped epilepsy, spasms, colic, palpitations and hysteria.

Teenagers must have been especially keen to get their hands on Clarke's World Famous Blood Mixture because it promised:

*"A safe, permanent and warranted cure for pimples, scrofula, scurvy, bad legs, skin and blood diseases and sores of all kinds."*

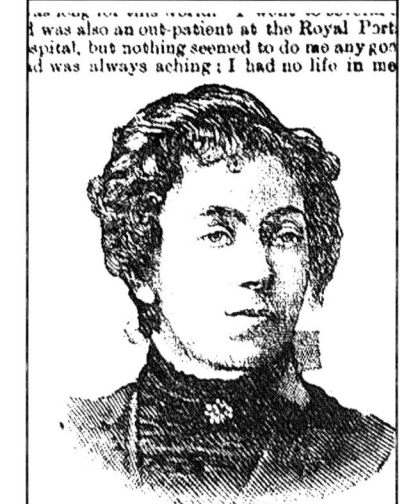

*Poor Mrs Hayles, only restored to good health thanks to Dr Williams' Pink Pills for Pale People*

*A notice to bakers – Mr J Barrett, yeast merchant of Baldock, had been appointed sole agent for the sale of genuine N G & SF yeast for Bedford and North Herts*

Zam-Buk was another indispensable addition to the medicine cabinet. It cured obstinate piles, eczema, sore hands and legs, wounds and burns. Nurse Greenwood declared she had used it daily for five years.

It worked wonders on a carpenter with a fearful gash across his thumb, cured burns and brought great relief to a housewife with piles. "I always carry Zam-Buk in my bag and never a day passes without the well known green box being brought into use," declared Nurse Greenwood.

Mrs Yeoman was actually dying when Zam-Buk was administered. Her family had been summoned to her bedside because of the state of her ulcerated leg, spreading poison throughout her system.

The problem resulted from a 40-year-old injury, when she had slashed her leg with a rip hook while harvesting. It never healed properly and she tried doctors, hospitals and remedies for years but nothing worked.

Finally the situation took a turn for the worse, Mrs Yeoman was confined to bed and her daughter was sent for by telegram.

She arrived clutching a box of Zam-Buk, pleading with her mother to try the magic potion. There was a sensation when it worked.

Not only did the swelling go down but the sore began to heal, clearing up for the first time in four decades. Mrs Yeoman was now 75 and flourishing "entirely free from pain."

Mothers were urged to check their children's tongues – if they were coated, or the youngster was sick or cross, they needed a laxative. California Syrup of Figs was the answer. "Keep it handy, mother," ordered the adverts.

Peps saved Sgt Major W Cole of Twickenham, who had joined the Army in 1854, aged only 15. Although young, he was tall and his commanding officers sent him to the Crimea, where he fought at Sebastopol and was injured by a shell. Along with other wounded and sick soldiers he was taken by boat to the Army hospital at Scutari, run by Florence Nightingale. The great woman herself cared for Cole.

"She was evidently astonished at my youthful appearance," he wrote in the Express in 1911.

*"She placed her hands on my shoulder
and with tears in her eyes said:
'My poor boy, you ought to be at home
with your mother, not here'."*

Miss Nightingale actually wrote to Mrs Cole, letting her know about his injuries.

By 1905 the rigours of fighting and warfare had caught up with the Sgt Major, who began to suffer seriously from congestion of the lungs, wheezing, choking, burning in the throat and bouts of bronchitis.

An early end seemed certain until a friend recommended Peps which: "Came to my rescue and brought me back to a comfortable state of health."

Bile Beans were the saving of one woman who allowed her embarrassing story to be told in the Herts Express in 1903.

It was headlined: "A young lady escapes from death. Constipation, if neglected, often leads to stoppage of the bowels." Her tale was indeed heart rending.

"I could not take nourishment and consequently grew too feeble to work," she wrote. "Having taken to my bed I grew weaker and weaker."

A risky operation was her only chance and she was admitted to hospital where, at the last moment, her parents stopped the proceedings and she was taken home.

"This was in consequence of what they had heard about the power of Bile Beans and I started on a course immediately," wrote the young lady. Fortunately the Bile Beans worked and she was saved.

*James Doan offered every reader of the Express a sample box of his backache kidney pills*

Doan's, which produced backache kidney pills, decided that using testimonials from people all over the country was a bit of a cheat, and ran its Hertfordshire Express advertisements with Hitchin residents.

In 1910 Mr E G Tuck of Highbury Road, who was "well known and respected," told the world about his long-term kidney problems and unnatural secretions while Mrs Gray of Kings Road explained: "My legs were as large as my body was formerly.

"It was impossible to put on my boots and I could not sit comfortably in an armchair." Mr J Day of Trevor Road had "found the pills to be a splendid remedy."

The case of Mrs E Manley of Hounslow was too good to omit from the Herts Express. The unfortunate woman had dropsy which became so bad she had to be tapped regularly for water – the first operation yielded nine gallons, with up to six at 30 more sessions. "In a short time I became an enormous size and I was so weak I could barely raise my hand to my head," she wrote. But there was no need to worry – Doans affected a complete cure almost over night.

Purchasers of Holdroyd's Gravel Pills could get their money back if they weren't thoroughly satisfied. The magic pills guaranteed a positive cure for gravel, lumbago, pain in the back, dropsy, wind, diseases of the kidneys, bladder and urinary organs, stones, gout, sciatica and rheumatism.

*If tablets and pills seemed a bit too much to stomach, sufferers could try Hunyadi Janos best natural aperient water.*

Not only did it cure constipation, it also took care of indigestion and many disorders of the liver, reduced weight in cases of obesity, gave relief to victims of gout and rheumatism and cured other diseases caused by the accumulation in the blood of irritating impurities.

One reason the testimonials for patent medicines flourished was that doctors charged for their services and money was in very short supply for most people, who were always grateful for the means to earn a little extra.

Adverts appeared regularly in the Hertfordshire Express offering to buy moleskins "for cash and in large or small quantities."

Brookers, the Hitchin ironmongers, sold traps, stating they would help you "Make money out of moles and rabbits."

Ferrets were another source of income. "Strong, sound, healthy ferrets wanted," declared a firm from Norfolk.

*If all else failed, you could always sell your teeth. "Old artificial teeth, any condition, 5d per pinned tooth on Vulcanite, 1/6d on silver, 2/- on gold, 4/- on platinum plates," was the offer from C H Merchant of Bradford.*

Bedwell Farm, Stevenage, pinned its advertising on the desire to bring up healthy offspring. In 1905 it advised mothers to give delicate children "pure rich milk from Jersey cows, absolutely free from dust, grit and other impurities, delivered daily (in sealed bottles if necessary)."

Getting the right job or hiring the right help were major problems. In a typical week in 1913 the Express carried advertisements for "two apprentices to dress make, thorough training under fully qualified costumier," and a draper wanted a smart gentlemanly lad.

"Learn the drapery trade, liberal pocket money given," was promised.

It was hard to get a good servant. "A comfortable situation is offered to a respectable young women to assist in the house and help with children. A willing and obedient girl will be generously treated and not made a drudge," enticed one potential mistress. Another was more businesslike.

## Sell moleskins, ferrets and false teeth to boost your income

## The magic pills would cure gravel, lumbago, wind, stones and gout

*An advertisement for Alfred Cutlack, a tailor in Sun Street, Hitchin*

*G C Flanders, motor, cycle and athletic outfitter of Tilehouse Street, Hitchin, advertising one of his exciting items for sale*

*"Required house parlour maid, three in family, cook and housemaid kept. Must be experienced, good wages given to capable servant, not over 27."*

Miss Rowley of Barnet wanted a "cook general, good wages, three in family, housemaid kept. Also man for boots and coals." Mrs Birrell's household of three boasted three maids and a man who did boots and knives, but she needed a parlour maid.

Another family of three also needed a housemaid, but they wanted someone experienced who was a good needlewoman. They had three maids and promised: "No downstairs work."

Employers had very clear ideas about their ideal employee. J Wright of Graveley was hoping to find:

*"A young married man to look after three horses, used to ploughs and binders."*

George Spurr, who ran a large store in Market Place, Hitchin, needed "an active obliging lad, who can mould, to assist in bakehouse, also with horses in yard. Breakfast, dinner and tea given."

A married man (with sons preferred) was wanted to work as a groom and make himself generally useful, while an advertisement for a between girl required a clean worker.

An elderly lady and gentleman were looking for a churchgoing domesticated companion to help their servant and a man looking for a job as a groom gardener boasted that he was an abstainer.

Others preferred to use their accomplishments to try and earn money.

Miss Emily Bunyard took classes at the Sun Hotel in Hitchin in all the society dances including the Boston, double, triple, French and Continental. She would also teach children over 10 and coach ladies in morris and country dancing.

Goods for sale were another important source of advertisement revenue for the newspaper.

In 1907, when cars were still a rarity, the Express was selling a "roomy light running four-wheeled dogcart with cushions and removal seats for luggage."

Readers could also buy a single brougham in good condition, phaetons and dogs carts.

An Edison concert phonograph was for sale and "a nice little turnout, light wood governess cart, harness, white pony."

Advertisements covered every field of life, down to the most trivial. Any woman worried by the condition of her soiled straw hat could make it as good as new if she just bought Paris non-gloss hat dyes, made in the latest shades and applied with a brush, available from Brookers of Hitchin.

In March 1909 Budd and Co of Market Place, Hitchin, advertised a small heeled boot-shoe with ribbon lace by Lotus, featuring:

*"A straight glace kid toe cap that always looks well and is always in good taste. It can be relied on to give unstinted satisfaction."*

An aspiring businessman could get a fruiterer's and greengrocery business for £100, with a horse and van included, in 1907. A few years later a small temperance hotel was on the market due to illness in Park Street, Hitchin.

If all else failed the brave could always set sail to Canada with an assisted passage, available for farm labourers and domestic servants:

*"Work guaranteed. Only reliable persons of good character need apply."*

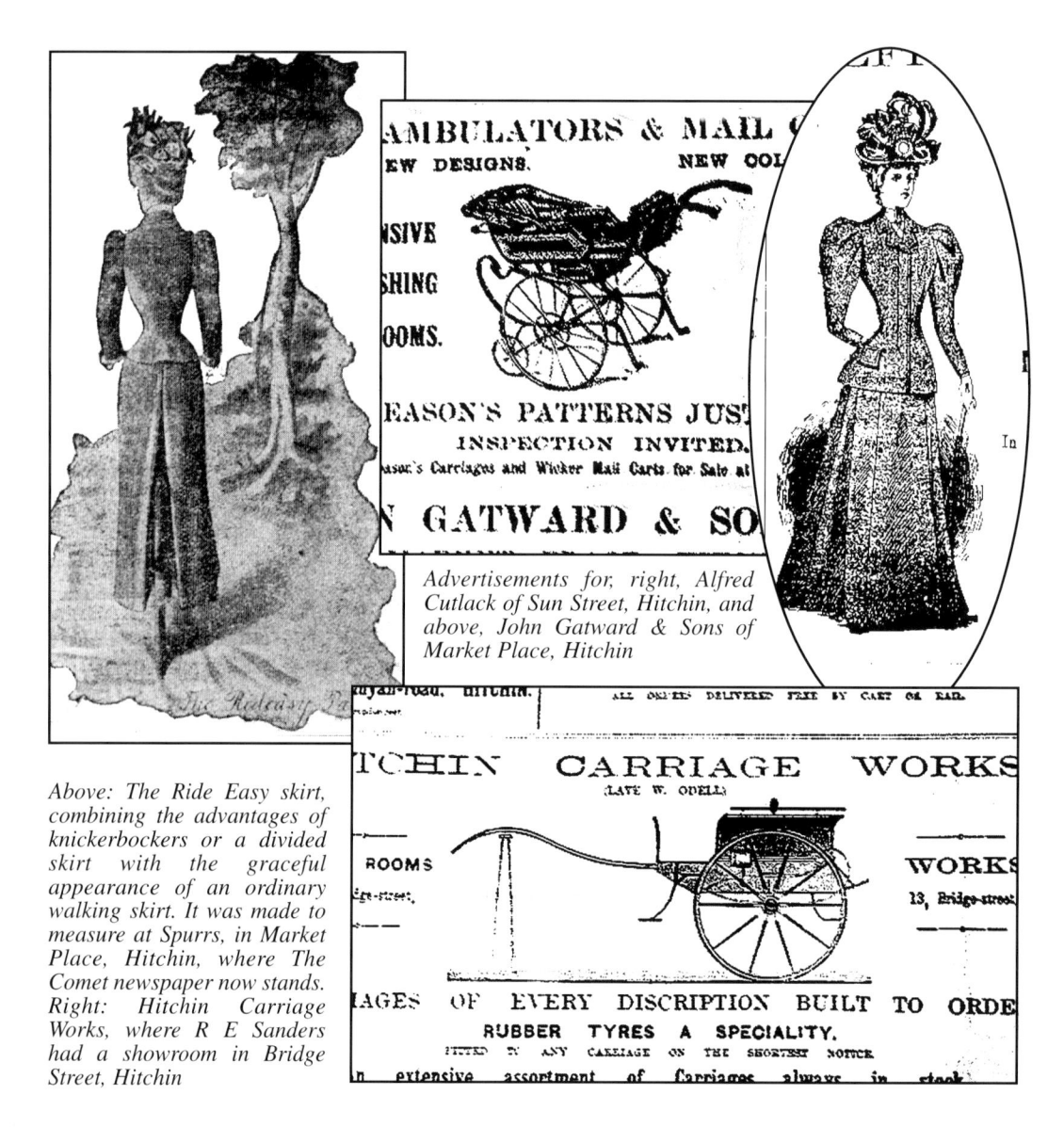

*Advertisements for, right, Alfred Cutlack of Sun Street, Hitchin, and above, John Gatward & Sons of Market Place, Hitchin*

*Above: The Ride Easy skirt, combining the advantages of knickerbockers or a divided skirt with the graceful appearance of an ordinary walking skirt. It was made to measure at Spurrs, in Market Place, Hitchin, where The Comet newspaper now stands. Right: Hitchin Carriage Works, where R E Sanders had a showroom in Bridge Street, Hitchin*

# The cabbage patch baby

Rose Young was, for the Edwardian age, a lady of extremely easy virtue. She was also an appalling mother. By the time she met Frederick George Beeton she was 35 years old and had two illegitimate children. Her exasperated sister had issued an ultimatum – she would not help Rose "if she got into trouble again."

Beeton was a different matter altogether. He was a good looking man of 27 who could almost have been mistaken for a youth, with his clear cut intelligent features and slight build. He was in steady work, as a railway goods clerk, and something of a snappy dresser – a reporter was to carefully describe his dark grey suit and mauve tie when he stood trial for murder.

That was far in the future when Beeton came looking for lodgings in Letchworth in September 1907, leaving his wife and three children living elsewhere. He rented rooms in Pix Road, settled himself down and let his roving young eyes wander freely. Before long they settled on one of the neighbours – the lush and loose-living Rose Young.

Beeton found life dull. He had a vivid imagination and preferred its dramatic conceits to reality. When he introduced himself to Rose, he prudently pretended to be single. But that was simply common sense for a young man with his eye on an extra-marital liaison, even with the likes of Rose. It was panache and a streak of pure drama that made him introduce himself as C Charlesworth.

It was not his only alias. First he substituted Charles for George as his middle name and then he began to invent other identities. "It was for a fancy," he was to say at his trial. He had done it for "two or three years."

Another fancy made him tell Rose he worked for W H Smith's when in reality he was employed by the Great Northern Railway. He was to be caught out in lie after lie but for Rose they mattered little – she was charmed and rapidly conquered.

Their affair ran on apace, he moved in as one of her lodgers, and then the inevitable happened – Rose became pregnant. In the summer of 1909, she gave birth to a baby girl, to be called Margaret Ruby Young.

Rose was not a woman to be overconcerned at losing her reputation – that had been decisively lost several years before. But she had to live and "a child might interfere with her business," as the court was told later.

For Beeton the situation was quite dire. He was desperate to keep his family from hearing about Rose and the baby. Rose was forever nagging him for money, writing importunate letters, threatening him with exposure. He could not stretch his meagre wages any further.

He tried to lull her with flowers and chocolates, but they would not serve. She knew now how grossly she had been deceived and that he had a wife living and other children, to whom he sent the bulk of his salary each week.

Beeton wrote to her, asking her to keep their affair secret from his wife.

"How I managed to keep it to myself I don't know," declared Rose at Beeton's trial, very pale and dressed in a striped pink print dress.

*"From what I could see
she was getting very suspicious."*

Whichever way Beeton turned he could not make his money stretch far enough. His pay of 28 shillings a week was almost completely committed, with 18 shillings going to his family and eight spent on lodgings.

Rose was demanding five and he had promised a florin but seldom paid her the two shillings. He wrote to her once:

*"I am extremely sorry, I was never
worse off myself than now,"*

He became increasingly impatient, accusing her of being overreaching in her demands. "Have not I always helped you in the past?" he wrote on another occasion and then again:

*"Will you not save my wife and children
from the disgrace of my folly?"*

He was a frantic and a harried man.

Margaret was still only a few weeks old when Beeton came round to see Rose, on the night of September 10, 1909.

He had good news. His brother was prepared to adopt Margaret – the problem was solved.

In fact, it was solved immediately – his sister-in-law Susan was waiting at Hitchin station to take the baby now.

Rose lacked a strong maternal instinct. Without hesitation she quickly prepared Margaret for a final goodbye, giving her the breast, wrapping her in a shawl and tying on her bonnet.

Beeton lifted the baby from her arms, loosened his overcoat and placed Margaret inside, warm against his chest. With a brief farewell he left Rose, walking rapidly away, the child invisible and hidden inside the thick coat. She would never be seen again.

Human life had less value in 1909 than it does now. The life of a child was worth very little at all.

There were no social services to check up on Margaret, no adoption agencies to approve Beeton's brother and his wife, no concerned neighbours to raise the alarm.

But there was one arm of officialdom that reached exceeding far and with great accuracy – the vaccination officer.

Every baby had to be vaccinated against various diseases or be granted an exemption certificate. Parents were regularly hauled before the courts for transgressing the rules. Rose knew this but gave it no thought. Beeton knew it too but it went right out of his mind.

It did not however go out of the mind of Mr Prater, the vaccination officer, who wrote to Miss Young in October 1909, informing her he would be calling shortly to treat her new baby. And call he did, catching Rose at home but failing to see her child. Rose made an excuse and, panicking, wrote to Beeton asking what she should do.

Beeton must have been a man of considerable charm, verging perhaps on charisma. How else can one explain what happened next? Or did Rose, never accused of any crime, know much more than she appeared to? Either way it is not surprising that she became the object of intense dislike and that a crowd of women and girls gathered outside the Pixmore Institute during Margaret's inquest, hooting and hissing at her.

First Beeton persuaded Rose to travel to Whitechapel workhouse with him to try and get hold of a baby girl there, pretending it was a missing child of theirs.

On December 3 they made the journey to London but, for once, Beeton's silver tongue failed him. Despite his best entreaties the staff at Whitechapel workhouse would not hand over the child to him, declaring there was not sufficient evidence she was his.

Beeton seems at times to have lost all touch with reality. He wrote to Rose after they got back to Letchworth: "I am now convinced since my return the baby is my little one."

The evidence for what happened next was much the same at both inquest and trial. Rose explained how Beeton, accompanied by his wife, had come to her house with a baby girl in his arms.

"She knew it was not her child but they asked her to look after it and get it vaccinated," reported the Hertfordshire Express at the inquest, in March 1910. This the obliging,

> "She knew it was not her child but they asked her to look after it"

> 'The man, the pram and the baby were nowhere to be seen'

gullible Rose did, never seeming to question why Margaret could not be returned or the adoption revealed. What fanciful tale Beeton had told his wife one can scarcely imagine.

One of the incredulous jurors asked Rose: "When they brought a strange child in did you ask where the other one was?"

"No," she replied.

"On the following Sunday Beeton came and said the child was the wrong one and I should have to go with him to London and take it back," Rose told the inquest jury. True to past form, Rose went.

Taking the child had proved quite easy. Returning her was another matter entirely and Beeton's undoing. Phoebe Locke was the youngest member of a family who lived in Canning Town. On the day of her strange adventure she was being pushed in her perambulator by her sister Dorothy.

They were suddenly accosted by a very personable man, smart, slightly built and with clear-cut intelligent features. He gave Dorothy a doll and then asked her if she would like to have some apples and nuts – could she just pop in the shop and buy them for him? Certainly Dorothy could. When she came out, smiling and eager with her arms full of treats, the young man, the perambulator and, most worryingly of all, the baby, were nowhere to be seen.

Phoebe spent several days with Rose Young in Pix Road, Letchworth, making the acquaintance of the vaccination officer. Then, just when she was getting settled, Beeton arrived to take her home again.

But when he tracked down Dorothy Locke and gave Phoebe back to her, the ungrateful girl raised such a ballyhoo that he was forced to make a dash for it, a crowd in pursuit.

He was caught at Aldgate Street Railway Station and arrested. Frederick Beeton, a respectable railway clerk, with doting parents in Peterborough and three legitimate youngsters of his own, found himself standing trial for child stealing. The evidence was overwhelming, his excuses patently false and, on December 27, 1909, he was sentenced to three months' imprisonment.

Beeton, with no chance of remission, served his sentence at Wormwood Scrubs. At first he was a model prisoner, quiet and well behaved. But as the weeks went by he became more restless and, finally, quite frantic. "On March 5 so desperate was his state of mind that he escaped from prison and ran a little along the road in his prison clothes before he was recaptured and brought back into custody," reported the Express newspaper at his trial, in June 1910.

Edward Lord, an assistant warder, gave evidence of the abortive escape. Mr Lord was a fit man and not only caught up with Beeton but passed him, swung round and grabbed him from the front. As he took the prisoner back to jail, Beeton said: "What a fool I am, this will drive me mad."

But he said nothing else, keeping the reason for his bizarre flight a secret. It remained a mystery until a fellow prisoner asked for an interview with a warder and, looking very anxious and concerned, said Beeton was not just a child kidnapper but, much worse, a child murderer as well.

Thomas Stockall was allowed out of Wormwood Scrubs to give evidence at both the inquest and the trial.

He caused a sensation when he first appeared at the Pixmore Institute, accompanied by two warders, to tell the coroner that he had become friendly with Beeton while they were in Wormwood Scrubs together.

They were in adjoining cells and got into the habit of talking, to pass the time. As the weeks went by Stockall realised that Beeton was becoming more and more nervous and anxious.

He knew Beeton was in prison for child stealing but one night, in a faltering voice, Beeton told him why he had kidnapped Phoebe Locke. "He said he had stolen the child because he had lost one of his own, an illegitimate child," Stockall recalled.

> 'About this affair of mine. I did away with it and buried it'

> *"I said that it was a funny thing to do –
> to steal a child to replace one of your own.
> You could not get over fond of it."*

The revelations were not over. Three days later Beeton confided once more in his new friend, saying. "About this affair of mine. I did away with it and buried it" – it being poor Margaret.

The coroner and the jury were enthralled as Stockall went on. Beeton, he told them, had confessed to drowning the baby. He had burned her cape and bonnet and "wished he had done the same with the child.

"He said it would mean a rope round his neck if he was found out. He said he was afraid someone would find the body. He said he had buried it in his allotment with cabbages planted over it."

Beeton had rented the allotment until March 25, 1910. His tenancy agreement expired just two days before his release and "as a consequence someone else might be digging up the plot," the prosecution counsel explained at the trial. Beeton had confided in Stockall in "an agony of apprehension."

"He seemed very anxious to get out of prison before his tenancy expired," Stockall told the inquest. "He said he could do away with the body and get another child. I said it would make things worse."

Beeton's revelations had not been welcomed by Stockall – indeed they disturbed him so thoroughly he could not sleep.

"The worry of what Beeton had said sent me to the infirmary and brought these grey hairs," he told the trial jury, pointing to his almost bald head. He was so ill he stayed in the infirmary for 13 weeks.

Long before the end of his stay he had come to a decision – he could not be party to a murder. He told the authorities exactly what Beeton had said.

Within hours policemen had arrived at the allotments in Norton Way, Letchworth, and, finding out which was Beeton's, were digging it over thoroughly. They discovered what they were looking for – the body of a small baby, just a few weeks old, buried without a cape or bonnet. It caused a sensation.

*Hitchin railway station, probably pictured shortly before the First World War*

The Hertfordshire Express reported: "Numbers attracted by morbid curiosity thronged to the spot and the discovery was the chief topic of the hour."

The trial of Frederick George Beeton, charged with feloniously, wilfully and of malice aforethought killing and murdering Margaret Ruby Young on September 10, 1909, took place at Hertford Assizes the following June.

Lord Chief Justice Alverstone, who had decided to set aside a whole day for the trial and if necessary run into the next, heard Beeton plead not guilty. Outside a large crowd gathered, most waiting until the verdict was announced.

Mr R Muir presented the prosecution case and, on his behalf, Beeton employed the celebrated Ernest Wild, who had spoken for the defendants in the Peasenhall and Yarmouth Beach murder trials.

Mr Muir outlined the case and called several witnesses, including Rose Young. Then he introduced Thomas Stockall, the Wormwood Scrubs convict who had betrayed Beeton and was the most crucial prosecution witness. No sooner had Mr Muir finished questioning him than Mr Wild was on his feet.

Beeton's confession had worried him, had it not, he asked Stockall, who immediately agreed it had.

*Wild fixed him firmly with his clever eyes. "I put it to you, you were in a very worried frame of mind when you went into prison," he asked quietly.* Stockall shook his head.

*"I felt 50 years younger," he declared.*

Wild decided to enlighten the jury about Stockall's record. Had he not staged a 'robbery' in his office, going to the lengths of tying himself up and staying a 'prisoner' for five hours until he was found and freed?

Stockall admitted he had.

Did he not keep the 'stolen' goods in secret and pocket the insurance money to the value of £3,000? Yes, Stockall mumbled, he did.

Was he only caught when, three years having passed by and considering himself safe, he started to pawn the 'stolen' goods. Stockall nodded – he was.

Wild turned to face the jury as he delivered his coup de grace. This was a man who had gambled at Monte Carlo – he loaded those words with the heavy opprobrium of decadence and disgust – and had lied from beginning to end during the investigation of his 'robbery.' Was he not lying now?

"No," replied Stockall firmly. "I had my oath on this."

Wild called his first, most important, witness, bringing him to the stand in the afternoon.

Frederick Beeton walked from the dock in the full knowledge that his life depended on what he said in the next few minutes. His quick wits, his ready tongue, his charm verging on charisma – all were necessary now. He looked across the courtroom at his young wife and his parents, their eyes fixed on his face, and he told the story of Margaret's last hours.

Mr Wild took him quickly to the night she died, on September 10, 1909, when she was just two months old but already unwanted and a burden to all.

Beeton explained that he left work at 8.30 in the evening and went straight to see Rose Young, arriving at about 9pm. He told her his sister-in-law was waiting at Hitchin Station to take Margaret home with her. Was that true, asked Mr Wild? "No," replied Beeton, lowering his eyes. "It was not true."

Rose picked up the child, gave her the breast, wrapped her in a shawl and put a bonnet on her. "I took off my overcoat and placed the child in it. It could not be seen," said Beeton.

"What was your intention in taking away the child?" asked Wild. Beeton replied simply: "To get it out of Letchworth."

He elaborated. He thought he would walk to Hitchin Station and abandon her there, on a train, and when she was found the workhouse would have to take care of her.

*"Did you go the quickest route?" asked Mr Wild. "No," Beeton said.*

"I took the farthest route to avoid publicity. I carried the child as far as the golf links, about two miles.

"I ran down the hill on the Baldock Road. Having reached the golf links I looked at my watch and, finding it had turned 9.30, I knew it would be impossible to catch the train.

"I came back intending to take the child to Miss Young and tell her the truth."

The court was completely silent now, everyone gazing fixedly at Beeton as he went on with his story.

*"Having reached Norton Way, halfway back, I rested on a seat and while resting I looked at the child and thought it did not appear to be alive. I removed its shawl and bonnet to give it fresh air but to no purpose."*

Wild interjected: "Was it dead?"

Beeton: "It was dead."

He thought the baby had suffocated. "The child, when I looked at it, had moved a long way down the coat," he explained.

He paused a moment before going on. "Finding myself with a dead child I was in an awful straight.

*"Whether to take it to the doctor or Miss Young I didn't know. I determined to put it in the goods office at Letchworth sidings. There I placed the child amongst old invoices and letters in what was termed the book room."*

There was a sharp intake of breath throughout the court and Beeton lowered his eyes.

The body stayed hidden for three days. Meanwhile Beeton visited his allotment very early one morning, digging a small hole in one corner.

Using his key, he returned secretly to the goods office and removed Margaret's body from its hiding place. Carefully, when he was sure he would not be seen, he carried the tiny corpse to the allotment, buried it without tenderness or regret, and planted cabbages over the unmarked spot.

In the hush that followed Wild asked: "Why did you bury the child?" Beeton answered without hesitation:

*"I had no idea what to do with it. For fear I might be charged."*

Rose Young seldom asked about her child. When she did Beeton replied that "it" was going on all right.

Next Wild turned to the question of Stockall's evidence, which must be discredited if Beeton were to be acquitted. Beeton denied most of the convict's story, declaring what he really told him was: "I have not murdered it. It is in my garden at Letchworth and I am in a terrible way because it is sure to be found and they will accuse me of murdering a child."

Wild stood quietly for a moment, looking at the defendant. Solemnly he asked: "Did you kill the child?" With perfect composure Beeton looked back at Wild.

"No, sir, I didn't," he said.

It was Mr Muir's turn to cross examine Beeton. He asked the question in everybody's mind. "Why, if you had accidentally smothered the child, not come forward and rely upon your character?"

"Because," replied Beeton, "I was afraid I should be charged with the murder of the child."

"Why should you be afraid?" queried Mr Muir.

Beeton told him: "Being found with an illegitimate child."

"Which," thundered Mr Muir, "You had got with Rose Young with a false story."

"Yes, sir," agreed the contrite Beeton.

Mr Muir pressed on. "How many false stories have you told about this child up until today?" Beeton mumbled: "About three."

Why had he not given evidence at the inquest, asked Mr Muir?

"Because I was ashamed of myself," replied Beeton.

This was too much for Beeton's wife, who collapsed and had to be helped from the court.

One character witness came forward to speak for Beeton. Arthur Johnson, who had worked with him for about seven years, declared "he was known as a very abstemious man."

It was time to sum up. Mr Muir began, talking to the jury about the "wonderful stories" invented by Beeton. Could the jury believe a story suddenly told in the witness box that had never been told in public before?

> **'I was afraid I should be charged with the murder of the child'**

Mr Wild followed, making what the Express described as "a powerful speech" for the defence. He addressed the jury for over an hour, saying there was a great gulf of difference between getting the child out of publicity and out of the world.

It would be suicidal and wicked to rely on Stockall's evidence: "a creature such as that."

"However many Beeton's faults, and they were many – however many, his lies – and they were not a few – the explanation he had given was perfectly feasible and one which they could reasonably accept as the truth."

Lord Alverstone summed up, telling the jury that they were not in attendance at a court of morals.

"However profligate a life the prisoner had lived, however grossly he had lied, only if the jury was convinced beyond all doubt that the prisoner had actually murdered the baby" could they convict.

*"We are not casuists or philosophers or theologians, but men of the world. It is a sordid and terrible story, with lie upon lie running through it, and it is up to you to unravel it."*

It did not seem a task that worried the jury a great deal. They took just 18 minutes to find Frederick Beeton not guilty.

But he did not walk free from the courtroom. His own testimony convicted him of a lesser crime and he was jailed for nine months without hard labour, for unlawfully and contemptuously burying the body of poor Margaret Ruby Young and obstructing the course of justice.

He left Hertford Assizes to begin yet another jail term.

*Pix Road, Letchworth, where both Rose Young and Frederick Beeton lived*

# Favourite Express-ions – 1908

✴ The "awfully sudden death" of 52-year-old William Jones of Codicote in January resulted in the inquest verdict "that the deceased died by the visitation of God, from natural causes."

✴ The parents of a sick 14-month-old girl in Essex, who belonged to the Peculiar People, were tried for her manslaughter after relying on the prayers of the church elders to save her. After telling the court they did not believe in the intervention of doctors, they were acquitted but severely censured.

✴ Dr Day, the medical officer of health, urged councils to lay tar over the dusty roads, or at least to water them more often on dry days. They were a hazard to health, he said, adding: "Dust contains numerous noxious matters."

He was also unhappy about the number of slaughter houses in the district – 13 – and wanted to replace them with one public abattoir. He said:

*"The indifference which English people display in the matter of the quality and condition of their food is extraordinary, as is also their ignorance of the dangers of unsound meat."*

Dr Day faced an uphill battle to persuade people that they would be healthier if they changed their habits. In October he was haranguing Baldock fairground workers for letting 150 hens loose on the streets.

✴ Arthur Arnold, of Old Park Road, Hitchin, was so desperate to feed his family that he stole watercress from the beds at Ickleford on Good Friday. He told the court he was out of work and his wife and children were starving. The cold-hearted magistrates fined him, with seven days' imprisonment in default.

*The German Hospital in Benslow Lane, Hitchin, opened in 1908, and now Pinehill Hospital*

★ The Hitchin branch of the International Anti-Cigarette League had almost doubled its membership during its first year, to 104. The Rev H E Jones of St Mary's Church declared that cigarettes: "As well as strong drink, has a very injurious effect upon both body and brain."

★ Mrs Mary Willoughby Osborne was convicted in St Albans of beating a 13-year-old Nigerian girl. No reason was given but she had been overheard to say: "I will flog them every minute, every hour and every day if they do not obey me." The magistrate, despite the lack of any evidence from the Nigerian girl, said that in view of the provocation offered he would merely ask for costs.

★ The first old age pensions had been agreed in the 1908 budget. By September, 70 year olds were being told whether they would get the pension to make up their income to 13 shillings a week. "Pensions are not for everybody, not even if the qualifying age of 70 is reached, but only for those who attain to certain standards of thrift and other conditions," explained an article in the Express. Many felt it would encourage people to be profligate. But at least one elderly couple in Baldock were happy – they were overheard announcing they could now afford to marry.

★ Socialism was a new force in the land. In May the Independent Labour Party set up a branch in Hitchin, holding regular public meetings in the Market Place on Sunday nights. The first one in June was disrupted by Conservatives singing under a Union Jack while 50 policemen stood by to stop trouble breaking out.

There was a lot of confusion as to what the new party stood for – the Express reporter said many of the 1,000-strong crowd seemed "to be in doubt as to whether Socialism meant sharing out or was something nice to eat."

They got another chance to see Socialism in action in October when 150 men passed through Hitchin on their way back from lobbying their MP in London.

They carried a blood red banner proclaiming: "Nottingham unemployed. We demand the right to work." Most were foot sore, many were hardly in shoes and the majority were emaciated and pale. They were treated to a good tea of fish and chips as they arrived in the town thanks to the generosity of Canon Jones of St Mary's Church. They were also given tobacco.

The three leaders were Socialists: "But they kept their views strictly in the background, concentrating themselves on the right to work principle," commented the Express reporter, with approval. They had been treated better in Hitchin than anywhere else, said the men.

*The first nurses employed at the new German Hospital, ready for work*

✷ The famous writer G K Chesterton almost missed a public engagement at Stevenage Town Hall in November. When he finally arrived he regaled the audience with the humorous story of all his delays and problems. "I was determined to get here even if I had to hire an airship, for I think it a caddish thing to leave people in the lurch," he told them.

✷ Life was much quieter in Arlesey but the girls attending the Country and Colonial Training School for Ladies were preparing to swap the calm of Bedfordshire for a tougher regime. They were being coached as brides for the 40,000 bachelors in Canada, where they would arrive in due course with the skills they needed for their new life, including 'carpentering' with various woods, tree lopping and lighting bush fires.

✷ Christmas was coming and food and drink were the main subjects on people's minds. About 25,000 had visited a currant and banana exhibition in Holborn, no doubt looking for ideas for tasty suppers.

Meanwhile some Letchworth residents were accused of getting round the lack of licensed premises in the garden city by bringing vast quantities of alcohol into their homes. A few had even been known to sell a glass of beer, according to shocked whispers. But the Total Abstinence Society were very keen to stop inmates at Hitchin Workhouse having a drink of beer with their Christmas dinner.

A letter was sent to remind the guardians that most people were there owing to their consumption of intoxicating drink. One of the guardians objected violently, saying that was just not true, and his view prevailed by a narrow majority.

✷ An unusual touch of excitement came to Express readers in December, when an account of Dr Richard Shillitoe's exploits reached the paper. A former Hitchin resident, the doctor was practising in Canton in China when one night his bachelor establishment was attacked by pirates.

"But for his personal intrepidity we might have had to record mournful instead of cheering news," reported the Express. Chinese pirates, they added helpfully, often cut people's throats.

This 30-strong gang lived in a bamboo town and had crept up to Dr Shillitoe's home, tying up his servants and threatening to kill them. Brandishing flaming torches they pushed open the door of his room. Undaunted the doctor seized his revolver and, shouting at the top of his voice, boldly charged into the midst of them, firing as he went. Thoroughly alarmed, the pirates fled and he was saved.

✷ Christmas was unseasonably warm, forcing butchers to delay slaughter until the last minute. "Millions of animals enjoyed two days more of existence," reported the Express at the end of the year.

*Hitchin swimming pool in Queen Street, pictured in 1908*

# The new-born baby dying in the garden

Of all the scandals to blight the life of a young Edwardian girl, pregnancy was the worst. In their desperation, panic and ignorance, many kept their condition secret. When they gave birth, some killed the child.

One such was Kate Kiddle, whose nightmare plight enthralled readers of the Express newspaper in the autumn of 1909, who heard of "a sad occurrence at Biggleswade, where a servant girl gave birth to a female child under distressing circumstances and, according to the evidence to hand, threw the infant out of the window, causing her death."

Kate's story was first revealed at an inquest, held at the Royal Oak in Biggleswade. Nineteen-year-old Kate lived with several other servants at Fairfield House, where she slept in a room near the cook, Jane Simpson.

One Saturday in September, Jane heard a noise at about 11.45pm, as if someone was ill, so she lit a candle and went to investigate.

As she moved into the corridor outside her bedroom she heard the lavatory window opening and Kate Kiddle called out: "I have been sick but I am better now." Kate unlocked the lavatory door, came out and the women returned to bed.

But all was not well. Jane could not get back to sleep; she heard water running and the cry of a child. Eventually she got up again, woke the parlour maid, Nellie Lane, and the pair of them went back to the lavatory. They found blood on the floor.

The cries of a child continued as the women tackled Kate, who could only mutter distractedly: "Oh, don't say anything. Leave me alone."

All the house was awake by now and Nellie and the housemaid went into the garden, searching for the child they could hear crying in such distress.

They found her, lying naked under the lavatory window, almost frozen to death. Tenderly they took her inside, where Jane wrapped her in an old woollen vest, put her in a basket by the kitchen fire and sent for a doctor.

She tried bathing the baby to warm her but it was to no avail. The child died at 8.15am on Sunday morning.

By midday the police were at the house. Sergeant Vincent gave evidence that Kate, the daughter of a chauffeur, had been at Fairfield House since April and had arrived with an excellent character from her former employer.

The baby had died, said a doctor, of exposure, congestion of the lungs and a fractured jaw.

## The weak and cold baby lay outside

It all seemed, as the coroner said, extremely simple and very grave. It was perfectly plain that the unfortunate girl was confined with this child in the lavatory and in a frenzy threw the baby out of the window.

He could only direct the jury to find a verdict of wilful murder against the mother – there was no other course open to them.

The question of whether the mother was responsible for her actions at the time was not for them to consider, it would be left to another court.

He added that it was the most extraordinary thing that there were no less than seven servants in the house, one actually directly working with Kate Kiddle, yet no one had noticed her condition.

The jury obliged the coroner and returned the only verdict open to them, that of wilful murder committed by Kate Kiddle.

But they were not happy and added that they sympathised with the girl and felt she had not meant to commit murder and hoped she would be strongly recommended to mercy.

They went further and the foreman, Mr W B Aubrey, expressed their sympathy to the owners of Fairfield, Mr and Mrs Sartoris, who had only come to the area recently.

He added the regrets of all the residents of Biggleswade and said he hoped this unfortunate affair would in no way interfere with their previous hopes of a long residence in Biggleswade.

This incensed one reader who wrote to the Express the following week, saying the sympathy should really go to Kate's parents and to the girl herself.

"I pray that her life may be given to her," she added, going on: "I would ask people not to send their young maids to carry breakfast up into their young sons' bedrooms, for it is there often a girl finds her first tempter.

"This is not what I have heard but life as I have found it, I can stand by what I say, and my master was one of the most learned of men and as good as he was clever, holding high office in the church while his wife was a lady in every sense of the word.

> *"This is 30 years ago and judging from the daily papers the conduct of the upper classes do not improve."*

The letter was signed "Sympathiser."

Kate appeared in court late in October, to plead not guilty to a charge of feloniously, wilfully and of malice aforethought killing and murdering her newly born female child at Biggleswade on September 11, 1909.

The prisoner was pale, but calm and collected in her demeanour, reported the Express. She was attended by a nurse.

As the trial started the judge ordered all women and children to leave the court – he did not want them to hear the case. It was indeed heart rending.

Much of the evidence from the inquest was repeated. then Kate took the stand. She told the jury that she had become acquainted with a footman while working at Lord Henry Grosvenor's house in London, and intercourse took place between them.

She left London in March, taking up a position in Biggleswade, chiefly to get out of this man's way.

It was not until some time later that she realised she was going to have a child.

Next she talked about the terrible night her baby died. She told the jury she could remember very little about what had happened but that she had an idea she put the baby on the window sill when she heard someone coming.

Ryland Atkins was prosecuting and he put in a plea for a manslaughter charge, arguing that Kate had behaved in a perfectly rational way after the baby had been born.

"He contended that the frenzy brought about by the pain and childbirth passed off the moment the child was born," reported the Express.

Defending, Charles Stimson was having none of that. He made an eloquent appeal on behalf of the prisoner, who was now crying.

"Everything was weighed against her as if she was a mature matron," he declared, turning to the spellbound jury. "It was absolutely absurd to tell anything the girl might have said in her frenzy against her."

He had no right to appeal for the sympathy of the jury but they all did feel deeply for the girl, he went on.

> *"Foolish and sinful as she had been, she had been terribly recompensed and she intended no harm to the little life that had come so unwelcomely into the world."*

Mr Stimson's oratory was to good effect. The jury found Kate not guilty and, to a burst of applause that was instantly suppressed, she was discharged.

# 'I pray that her life may be given to her'

# 'Everything was weighed against her as if she was a mature matron'

# The long arm of the law

It was a typical day at the petty sessions court in Hitchin in 1902. The chairman of the magistrates was the town's premier citizen, Francis Delmé-Radcliffe of the Priory.

The first case the bench heard concerned children. Eliza Pestell, of Adam and Eve Alley, Hitchin, was charged with neglecting Daisy Stratton and William Pestell, in a manner to cause unnecessary suffering and injury to health. The prosecution was brought by the-then SPCC, the Society for the Prevention of Cruelty to Children.

The youngsters, aged 10 and six, were Eliza's grandchildren. Daisy, who was the older and illegitimate, was found wandering near the gasworks on a bitterly cold night in November, with very few clothes on.

She was obviously ill and could hardly speak as a result of a severe throat infection. When David Sterry, the SPCC's inspector, took her home he tried to remonstrate with Eliza but, before he had got three words out, her son Arthur set a lurcher on him.

Mr Sterry was not to be deterred and, accompanied by Police Sgt Freeman, he went back. Arthur was as threatening as ever but Mr Sterry was determined to look at little William, who was obviously filthy. He managed to get hold of both the children and carried them triumphantly off to the workhouse where Mr Grellett declared they were grossly neglected.

Daisy was a familiar sight around Hitchin, following the abusive Arthur through the streets as he lit lamps. She was often out at 11pm before going back to her grandmother, who was a rag and bone gatherer.

Eliza was indignant at the charges brought against her. Daisy she declared, had suffered from birth with an "affection" of the throat and her mother, who was blind, had never given her a penny towards her keep. William's father was working in Edgeware as a hawker and was no more generous than Daisy's parents.

As the magistrates tried to get the facts clear they were interrupted on several occasions by a furious Eliza, declaring her innocence and citing examples of her care for the children. Contradicting herself, she stated that she had been ill recently and could not manage to look after them.

The magistrates fined her £1 or 14 days' imprisonment in default of payment. William was handed over to his father and poor Daisy taken back to the workhouse for a week. 'The court missionary was interesting himself in her welfare," reported the Express.

The next case involved speeding, with a motorist summoned for travelling above the 12mph limit. Supt Reynolds gave evidence that he had seen Tom Underwood drive through Baldock at eight minutes past 10am and telegraphed to Royston, asking for him to be observed there. Pc Knight testified he arrived at 10.30, covering a distance of nine miles in 22 minutes. Mr Underwood was fined £3.

*Superintendent Reynolds*

On another typical day Walter Beard, a 14-year-old boy, appeared in court at Bedford in 1904 for cruelly ill treating a horse. He was charged along with his employer, Samuel Maynard, a dealer. Beard had been seen driving a sick horse, harnessed to a manure cart. The case against him was dismissed, but Maynard was fined.

Soon afterwards William Turner, a labourer from Walkern, was summoned before Stevenage Magistrates for a breach of public health.

Mr Turner was living with five other adults and four children in a tiny two-bedroom cottage. Two daughters had now left but the magistrates were not impressed – only two adults and four children could stay in the cottage, they said. They gave him four weeks to sort out the problem.

Charles Sisserman was the next defendant that day but he sent his wife to explain why they consistently kept their daughter off school – she was needed to help at home because of sickness. Mrs Sisserman got a ticking off and was told to mend her ways.

Unemployed labourers Frederick and Alfred Parker were charged with trespass at Graveley on December 21, 1903, under the game laws. Shepherd George Walker testified that he found them rabbiting on land near the Great North Road. One of the defendants said they just wanted a rabbit for Christmas dinner, as he had a wife and four children to feed, but his pathetic story did not move the magistrates and the Parkers were fined.

So was Walter Miles, a Walkern drayman, who admitted driving an unlit vehicle on the highway at night time. He apologised, saying he had run out of oil.

The penultimate case concerned George Carpenter of Stevenage, who was summoned under the Wild Birds Protection Act for using nets to take a wild bird and unlawfully keeping a goldfinch he had caught. He denied the charge, claiming the 10 birds found in his barn were not goldfinches at all, but he was found guilty.

Walter Knott fared no better. The Stevenage labourer was charged with stealing a dead duck from outside a butcher's in Stevenage. He was caught when the owner chased after him, not leaving him much room for denial.

The resourceful Mr Knott blamed his action on a funny head and begged for mercy as he had never done such a thing before. When the magistrates heard it was his 25th offence, they sent him to prison for six weeks.

In June, 1904, Elizabeth Barker, the wife of the keeper of the Star and Garter pub at Silsoe, was charged with attempting to commit suicide. The poor woman had cut her throat with a razor one May afternoon while in bed. She told the magistrates that she had hoped to bleed to death before she was found, adding that she dreaded the night. She was bailed to appear at Bedford Assizes.

Frederick Gatward, a 57-year-old horsekeeper from Therfield, appeared in court on a charge of attempting to commit suicide, in January, 1907.

It was a sad but simple case, declared the prosecution. Mr Gatward, who had married a women 19 years his junior, had seven children to support on a very small income.

He had been ill for six weeks and the police court missionary, appointed to look at the case, told magistrates: "I really believe that the man was starving for want of food."

Mr Gatward had run down his garden path and jumped into a pond before being rescued by his wife. He told Pc Hart: "I am sorry I did it. My head was so bad." Hearing that his employer of 26 years was prepared to take him back, the magistrates bound him over.

> "I really believe that the man was starving for want of food"

Herbert May, of no fixed abode, was charged with destroying his own clothing while an inmate at Hitchin Union workhouse on October 28, 1907, and pleaded guilty. Described as a refractory tramp, May had torn up his trousers during the night. He told the court he was ashamed to walk about in them.

He took issue with the official description of him, stating he was a sawyer by trade who had been invalided out of the Navy and was making his way north to go back to sea. He was imprisoned until the rising of the court.

In October 1904 engine driver George Catchpole of Ickleford was fined on a long charge, that: "Whilst driving a light locomotive on the highway at Biggleswade he did unlawfully neglect to stop and remain stationary when requested to do so by a person having charge of a restive horse." Mr Catchpole's impatience led to the horse bolting.

Brothers Wilfred and Harold Tomlin were in trouble at Hitchin court the same week for wilfully damaging oak trees – they had thrown stones and sticks into the branches to dislodge acorns. The lads were fined two shilling and sixpence – exactly half the amount that Mr Catchpole had to pay.

Other youngsters "thirsty for conquerors" (as they were called) were also fined for damaging chestnut trees.

In August 1904 Florence Crawley of Sandy was summoned for failing to notify the right official that her 15-year-old daughter Violet was suffering from scarlet fever. The Medical Officer of Health, Dr John Prior, said he visited the family as a consequence of information received and asked if Violet had scarlet fever. Her mother "denied it in the most positive manner." She refused to let Dr Prior see the girl, saying she was out. The chairman of the magistrates, Mr C Payne, told Mrs Crawley that it was a very serious charge with a heavy penalty, but there was not sufficient evidence that she was guilty.

Mrs Spicer walked for seven miles from Bendish to Hitchin to get to court in February 1905, carrying an infant in her arms. She was charged with not sending her daughter to school and explained that she needed her to look after the baby while she tended her husband, who had been hurt in an accident. She was fined.

Frederica Walker was a regular at Hitchin Court, always on the same charge – being drunk. In November 1904 she appeared yet again. She denied that she had been drinking and using abusive language, blaming her condition on being annoyed and excited after a number of boys attacked her. The magistrates, quite unconvinced, sent her to a home for inebriates for nine months.

At the end of August 1904 William Gray, a painter from St Andrew's Street, Hitchin, appeared in court charged with being a wandering lunatic at Hitchin on August 21.

The surgeon William Grellett testified that Mr Gray had apparently been insane on the Saturday evening, but he was kept under observation and recovered.

Supt Reynolds told the court that Gray had turned up at the police station at about 11pm that night, declaring he had murdered his mother. He was very violent, a state of mind the superintendent blamed on intoxicating drink.

Mr W Tindall Lucas, chairman of the magistrates, warned Gray to abstain in future and discharged him.

Alice Page, of Peahen Yard, St Andrews Street, Hitchin, appeared in court in July 1909 summoned for malicious damage to growing wheat in Willian Lane. Alice was seen with two other women one morning picking poppies by Mr Delmé Radcliffe's gamekeeper Henry Simmonds, but only Alice was honest, or foolish, enough to give her real name – it cost her dearly in a heavy fine. Chairman of the magistrates, Mr Salusbury-Hughes, told her she must not think she could go trampling other people's corn down and the magistrates were determined to put a stop to it.

Another curious cash crop could be collected from farmland. George King was sent to the Assizes in early 1903 accused of injuring horses as he cut off their manes and tails in an Elstow field.

*Seasonal agricultural work was one legitimate way the poor could boost their wages. These labourers are harvesting lavender for Perks and Llewellyn in about 1900*

Stealing 6d worth of walnuts was the charge against labourer Henry Field of Baldock in October 1905, after he picked them up from under a tree. He was fined two shillings and sixpence or seven days in prison.

In May, 1909 four men were cautioned for playing football on the highway at Bedford Road, Hitchin. They had been spotted by the vigilant Pc English and one had a previous conviction for the same offence.

There wasn't much you could do on the highway – gaming was an offence and 15 young men in Pirton were fined for playing cards by the side of the road in January 1903.

You couldn't even rest on it – in April 1903 Alfred Pryor of Welwyn was sent to prison for two weeks for sleeping out one night. He had some money but "instead of getting himself a bed he spent it on drink," the magistrates were told.

Women and children may not have enjoyed the same rights as they do now but you couldn't assault them with impunity, even in domestic situations. In May, 1903 Walter Salt, a tailor, of Wratten Road, Hitchin, appeared in court charged with unlawfully wounding his wife Emily.

The magistrates were told that Walter came home drunk and Emily, furious with him, grabbed a hammer. Walter seized it from her and hit her over the head.

When Inspector Spriggs saw her she was covered in blood, but protesting that it was all her fault, Walter was in a good mood when he came in but she was cross and pushed him away.

"If he went to prison she did not know what she would do with the children," reported the Express. The family was seven months behind with the rent.

The Salts' daughter gave her version of events. "Mother had said she would hit father with the hammer if he knocked her about much more," she testified, adding that Salt had pushed her over.

The magistrates sent him to assizes for trial where Mrs Salt appeared in such an upset state that she had to be given a seat and a glass of water. After her husband was persuaded to plead guilty he was bound over and allowed to leave.

Drink was at the root of the terrible tragedy which engulfed Alice Pallett, who let her five-week-old baby Frederick starve to death while she took to the gin bottle.

The judge, moved by her youth and inexperience, showed her mercy and sent her to a home for inebriates for three years.

In February 1905 schoolmaster Ernest Startup of Shillington was charged with unlawfully beating Annie Simkins, aged nine, after complaining about the girl's handwriting.

"He gave her two blows on the side of her head with the back of his hand," reported the Express. Annie's face was bruised, she had headaches and was in a dull and dazed condition, with symptoms like meningitis.

Mr Startup, who had been at the school for 20 years, said Annie was slow and covered her work in mistakes.

The magistrates were not happy, commenting that there appeared to have been a good deal of punishment going on at the school.

In the end they gave Mr Startup the benefit of the doubt but warned him to change his ways. He didn't really get a chance, because he was dismissed from his post shortly afterwards.

*Biggin Lane, Hitchin, pictured in about 1930*

# Leisure and pleasure

*Sanders Garage in Walsworth Road, pictured in about 1912*

Gay Paree, just a train ride away for modern Brits, seemed almost as close in the heady days of 1906, when a weekend excursion was introduced from Hitchin Railway Station.

The bold adventurers dismissed the 500 miles as nothing and were quite undaunted by having to work on Saturday before they could set off. They set off on the 7.12pm train, confident they would be back early on Monday morning.

For 14 glorious heady hours they would walk the boulevards and watch the Seine ripple by. One passenger recorded the trip in detail for Express readers too timid or too tired to make the journey for themselves.

They caught a special boat train from Victoria at 9.10pm, reached Newhaven at 10.30 and were sailing within the hour. But a big disappointment awaited them when they finally arrived, tired and very hungry.

"Breakfast, as we understand it, is unknown in Paris (especially at 7.30am) and we had some difficulty in persuading the dapper little proprietor of a café restaurant that we were hungry and coffee and rolls were of no use to a hungry Englishman. We spoke to the garcon in school-acquired French and it was distinctly humiliating to have him hint in good English that, if we would only speak in that language, he would be happy to oblige!"

Finally fortified the party went to the Arc de Triomphe, drove down the Bois, took a boat on the river past the Eiffel Tower and Notre Dame and went to the morgue to see the bodies – one corpse they recognised as a man they had just seen fished out of the water.

Not surprisingly the travellers were hungry again, so they devoured a good and cheap dejeurner before going to the Rue de Rivoli, visiting the Louvre, Napoleon's tomb and Les Invalides, followed by dinner on the street of the Grand Boulevards.

Their adventures were still not over, as they now enjoyed some free time – or "go as you please" as they styled it, before meeting at St Lazare Station at 9pm.

"We were not very tired," declared the intrepid traveller on returning home just over 12 hours later.

The Hitchin Blue Cross Temperance Brigade Cycling Club went on a weekend trip to Clacton, in August, 1902, leaving at 6.30am. From the first all did not go well.

They had two punctures before Buntingford, took a wrong turn at Puckeridge and then A W Hunt took a bad spill. "Luckily those behind him managed to steer clear of his machine," one of the cyclists told the Express.

"We bandaged up his knee and hands, which were cut rather badly, and he continued his journey." But their adventures were not over – a few miles further on one of the men rode into the handrail of a bridge "which soon brought him to a standstill."

They arrived at Clacton just before 3pm and immediately wired their captain in Hitchin before finding lodgings. Although a heavy storm brought the evening to an abrupt end the intrepid band were on the beach by 6.30am next morning, ready for a dip in the briny. There a last adventure befell them.

"After bathing for some time an amusing incident occurred. One of our number, mistaking his machine, found himself in the presence of four Clacton belles! Imagine his position – of course he had no idea mixed bathing was allowed," reported one of the cyclists with glee.

Poor Hunt was too injured to cycle back and caught the train. But no one was put off repeating the adventure and other outings were planned.

Even a solemn occasion could provide an excuse for a jaunt. CGM from Potton took the opportunity to watch Queen Victoria's funeral procession in February, 1901, and then shared the experience with Express readers.

Anxious to get a good position, CGM arrived at Kings Cross Station at 9pm the night before and travelled at once to Victoria "looking at the splendid decorations of purple and white en route."

When he tried to book a room at the Buckingham Palace Hotel he found he was not alone – they had received 3,000 more requests for accommodation than they could cope with. CGM was not deterred. "I had come to London determined to see this great pageant, the like of which would probably never be seen again, and so I made up my mind to brave the cold and wearisome hours to walk around London at night.

"Shall I ever forget the succeeding 10 hours' tramp in the practically deserted streets?"

For a rest he took a ride in a hansom cab but "the hours dragged wearily on" as he became exhausted and cold. It was not until about 8.30am that the longed-for spectacle began to materialise, with soldiers arriving for duty.

At Piccadilly the crush became fearful and the crowd was pushed roughly back by Hussars.

"The perspiration on the faces of the men and the pale tear-stained faces of the women told of the crush they had been subjected to," wrote CGM.

He was pinioned against a lamppost, struggling to breathe, "so determined was the onslaught." Mounted police moved ruthlessly to keep the crowd back, riding at them again and again, and dozens were carried off fainting.

For all the chaos and discomfort, everyone kept their good temper and were rewarded with an amazing and impressive spectacle.

As the Queen's coffin went by: "Every head was bared and everyone's breath seemed to be held. It was gone all too soon.

"With eyes rivetted on the silken pall, I scarcely had time to notice the gorgeous trappings and the cream colour of the ponies...I saw the King! Yes he looked every inch a King!" Despite his grief "his bearing was very dignified."

When the procession was finally over, CGM realised just how hungry he was – he had last eaten at midnight. He joined a long queue outside an eaterie in Piccadilly, finally sitting down at 2pm. "But I felt I had been repaid a thousand fold for the fatigue experienced," he finished triumphantly.

Social life in Hitchin was given a huge boost in March 1901 when the new town hall opened in Brand Street. A special key of silver ornamented with turquoise, blue enamel and mother of pearl

*Excursions could be made in this wonderful cycle, sold by G C Flanders of Tilehouse Street, Hitchin*

*Cyclists pose by their machines in Brand Street, Hitchin, around 1880.*

was used for the ceremony. The first production, by Hitchin Musical Society, was a selection from the Messiah and Hiawatha's Wedding Feast.

The town hall became the main venue for a large variety of events, proving so popular that in August a commercial traveller contrasted the town's Wednesday afternoon quiet, oppressive, deadly stillness with the evening's uproar at the town hall. He waited amongst a swaying crowd of hundreds, all eager to enter the portals of a "somewhat ugly building."

Sometimes the crowd was not so well behaved. One playgoer wrote an angry letter to the Express after going to see the Silver King in September, 1907.

He complained that he was "subjected to a prolonged struggle," to get in, "the people crashed up the steps from every direction with no idea of order and the policemen on duty were powerless to check them. Indeed one had his helmet knocked off, while the other was lifted off his feet in attempting to rescue it." There would be a serious accident unless procedures were altered, he went on. "There was a disgraceful scramble to get in, men and women struggling together in an unseemly manner." The play was disturbed by latecomers pushing to seats at the back.

Circuses and shows came to town on occasion, always attracting huge crowds. In February 1901 it was the turn of the Mammoth Menagerie Combinations, who showed a lovely Yankee milk white horse, a hairless or india-rubber mare from the Transvaal and a bell-ringing monkey from Mafeking.

Zarniella, a tramp contortionist, and Lady Lulu, the equilibrist and juggler, came down with other London variety artists to entertain a 1,500-strong crowd at Hitchin Football Club fete on Bank Holiday Monday. A fun match was staged between 'tramps' and 'ladies.'

A different style of football match was held in November when the John Sanger Circus visited town – this time the main attraction was a game between the elephants and T W Barnes of Hitchin FC. Red Chinese boxers were also high on the bill.

Purwell fete included a washing and a hat trimming competition in 1901, 'which was productive of some wondrous and fearsome creations.' The proceeds went to the St Saviour's Working Men's Club.

In July 1909 the Hitchin Blue Cross Temperance Brigade held a picnic at Lilley Hoo. Their half-day holiday was blessed with beautiful weather and almost 50 people left the town early in the afternoon, some by brake (an open four-wheel horse-drawn carriage) and others riding bikes.

When they arrived they took part in several games including cricket, bicycle tent pegging, basket ball and tug of war. Tea and supper were provided before they left at 9pm. They finished the day by processing through Hitchin with Japanese lanterns hanging from their bikes "making a very pretty spectacle."

Practising temperance could be a time-consuming and highly social activity 100 years ago. A variety of organisations existed to fight the scourge of drink, such as the Hitchin Total Abstinence Society.

Not many people managed to travel abroad but sometimes the exotic was brought to them. In January 1905 the SPG "strikingly illustrated" its missionary work in India with a series of tableaux vivants or "living pictures including household scenes, life in a zenana, the work of the lady doctor and the mission school."

It might sound glamorous but it was not, declared the Express reporter. "The life of a lady missionary was one of constant self denial." Being a teacher was no picnic either. "A great deal of tact had to be exercised so as not to do away with the customs of the children too suddenly." Widows were looked on as a curse and often banished.

In contrast the ladies of Hitchin enjoyed a tea and bought examples of fancy needlework to boost missionary funds.

Another missionary exhibition was held in March 1909, including lecturettes, receptions, costume lectures and stalls.

Afterwards it was heralded as the event of the year with "hearts touched and thrilled by the earnest appeals of some of the missionaries in their final addresses from the platform."

But the most successful of the Edwardian exhibitions was the Japanese bazaar of February 1905, presented by the Queen Street Congregational Church at Hitchin Town Hall.

The entrance was converted into an archway flanked by soldiers and geisha girls while the hall had become a Japanese village celebrating a feast of lanterns.

Bamboo houses, a Buddhist temple and a volcano were just some of the attractions.

A series of living pictures were performed, rather deviating from the subject – they included Daddy's Ship in Sight, Cinderella, Sally in our Alley and Good King Wenceslaus.

Vistors learned about China, Japan, Zanzibar, Madagascar and India, saw a model of a Japanese god, studied medical missions and toured a

*The immensely successful Japanese bazaar of 1905, held at Hitchin Town Hall*

zenana – rooms reserved for women – "erected in a very life-like manner."

All this delight, opened by the Bishop of Barking, took place in Hitchin Town Hall.

Afterwards it was heralded as the event of the year with "hearts touched and thrilled by the earnest appeals of some of the missionaries in their final addresses from the platform."

A Wedgwood-style picture in sugar of the First Christmas won Bridge Street baker Leonard Garratt a gold medal at the Bakers and Confection-ers Exhibition in London in 1903. Six years later, at a dinner of the Herts Philatelic Society, a model in sugar of the dread-nought battleship was exhibited on waves of margarine.

Clubs and societies abounded. The members of the Union Jack Working Boys' Club gave an exhibition of repoussé work in 1903, showing off flower holders and fancy articles in copper.

Eight years later the Letchworth Men's Meeting held a strawberry social with entertainment including duets by the Misses Johnson and Waddams. Evening promenade concerts were held at the Sun, where a lawn tennis club met.

Hitchin ran a lively Friends' Adult School, which had 129 male students in 1901 who met on Sunday afternoons. At the AGM, members heard that four pupils had died in 1900 – two of old age and two killed in accidents on the railway.

A year later the Hitchin Society of Arts and Letters was founded, to embrace ancient and modern art and literature, with especial emphasis on local antiquities.

Speakers held frequent lectures. In early 1901 Percival Gaskell spoke at the Workmen's Hall, Hitchin, giving a series of talks on the Early Flemish and German Painters.

The same venue was used by the The Church of England Temperance Benefit Society, which held a smoking concert there six years later.

Letchworth, established as a town with an unusual spirit, entertained a different kind of speaker. Miss Martha Craig lectured on the People of Venus at the Howard Hall in 1907, going on to thrill visitors with a talk on Generation, Re-generation and De-generation and Success and How to Obtain it. "Miss Craig has an almost hypnotic power of compelling belief in her ideas," reported the Express.

But the supply could not always satisfy demand. Letchworth residents were apparently distraught at the end of a series of lectures on Dante by William Loftus Hare in 1906. The ensuing void "emphasised the woeful lack of any attempt to minister to the pleasure and entertainment of the ordinary man in the street," reported the Express.

> 'Miss Craig has an almost hypnotic power of compelling belief in her ideas'

Sometimes organisers provided what was good for people rather than what they wanted.

One Express correspondent wrote in October 1907: "It is not creditable to Hitchin that whereas only a moderate audience attended Professor Flinders Petrie's lecture on prehistoric Egypt on Monday and a very small one the lecture on the decimal system on Wednesday, the town hall was crowded in the cheaper parts on Tuesday when a silly sensational play with the idiotic title of "The Worst Woman in London" was the attraction.

*"It is evident that the public taste is of the poorest and the public idea of the relative value of things sadly distorted."*

Devotees of the terpsichorean art (dancing) who had little opportunity to show off their nimble footwork were thrilled when plans were made for an annual hospital ball to be held in Hitchin, in 1909.

Fundraising was as popular then as it is now with a wide range of events held to woo residents. In April, 1901, the fourth annual tea and entertainment in aid of the widows' and orphans' fund of the Amalgamated Society of Railway Servants was held at Hitchin Town Hall, followed within days by a conversazione at the Boys' Grammar School, run by Hitchin Musical Society.

But by the time of the First World War the major new entertainment was the cinema. In February, 1911, the first permanent picturedome opened in Hitchin, in Ickleford Road, following the popularity of the occasional cinematograph shows.

There were two performances a day, with a Saturday matinee, and the programme changed twice a week. Films were short and the first programme consisted of:

☆ An 'educative and amusing' look at how a cricket bat is made.

☆ The winning Miss Langdon.

☆ Fox hunting from leaving the kennel to the kill and returning home.

☆ Tweedledum and Frothy want to marry.

☆ His Mother's Thanksgiving, the story of an ambitious son who thought his aged mother too lowly for him but was turned back to the right course by his fiancée who, although a woman of fashion, also possesses a heart.

☆ Bobby the Bootblack – Bobby (a cinema regular) sees an advertisement for a negro page boy and turns himself into "a man of colour" by means of boot polish. He gets the position but he so wins his mistress's heart that she kisses and hugs him, the result being disastrous.

☆ Jean goes foraging – an intelligent dog who can find anything his master and mistress want.

This extensive programme, which lasted less than two hours, was accompanied by music.

The management aimed, declared the Express, to provide an entertainment free from any objectionable feature but at the same time foremost in instruction, interest and amusement.

## Town's first cinema aimed to provide a programme of instruction, interest and amusement

*The Playhouse, pictured in Hitchin Market Place, opened on Saturday, October 4, 1913 and was demolished to make way for Burtons in about 1938*

# Favourite Express-ions – 1909

✷ Employees at William Carling, the publishers of the Hertfordshire Express in Exchange Yard, Hitchin, complained about the noise from ragged urchins, employed to clear up the nearby market. The boys, aged from six to 12, were shouting and quarrelling to such an extent that work was apparently impossible.

✷ Poor Mr Bradley, in charge of Walsworth Road Post Office, lost £65 in a burglary just before Christmas 1908. In the new year he heard that unless he made good the deficiency at the earliest possible moment, he would be the subject of civil proceedings by the Postmaster General. "This seems very hard on him," commented the Express. The Rev George Gainsford of Woodside was practical in his sympathy and set up a collection to help Mr Bradley.

✷ In February Arthur Latchmore, one of the founders of the Hitchin Blue Cross Temperance League, died. "He upheld the standards of temperance and purity and all the manly virtues and duties of citizenship," declared the Express. Above all he set the example of a blameless life, keeping cheerful despite years as a invalid.

✷ Soon after Mr Latchmore died the town went into mourning for Mrs Gainsford, the wife of the vicar of St Saviour's, who was seized by a fit of apoplexy one evening after returning to her home at Woodside from a shopping trip in town.

She had married 55 years earlier, when aged 20, and had five daughters and two sons. "Her good works were unnumbered and unceasing," commented the Express in a heartfelt tribute.

"Her greatest happiness was in making others happy." She was: "A wonderful woman whose like here in the town of Hitchin none living can expect to look upon again."

*Annette Gainsford*

*Printers at the Carling works in Exchange Yard, Hitchin, where the Hertfordshire Express was produced. It later became the Gazette and merged into the modern-day Comet, just yards away, in 1998*

✴ Consumers were reeling after Lloyd George's budget raised the tax on spirits and cigarettes. Meanwhile girls were having to study an extended curriculum – the education code included not only cookery and midwifery but also sick nursing, the care and feeding of infants and elementary hygiene.

Hitchin's medical officer of health declared that the girls of today were the mothers of the next generation and, when properly trained in domestic economy and the care and feeding of infants, would rear up a healthier and physically stronger race.

✴ Letchworth residents were thinking on similar lines and a system of domestic economy was set up at one of the schools, aimed at girls who didn't want to go into teaching or the civil service.

They were taught separately for their last year, spending half the day on general studying (with specific reference to running their own homes) and using a workman's cottage for practical work the rest of the time. They learned cleaning, mending, sewing, cooking, gardening and the care of children.

There was some debate as to whether this experiment was a good idea, at Herts County Council. One councillor called it "risky and dangerous" while another commented approvingly: "It is to train them to be good servants."

Mr Stride said he was most gratified to learn that domestic economy was the modern name for washing and mending.

✴ Hitchin guardians discussed whether they should take two children into the workhouse, when they met in June 1909. Mr Baylis, the relieving officer, painted a very black picture of the father, saying he was dangerous. "He knew for a fact the man used to take his wooden leg off and beat his late wife with it," he told the guardians.

"Mr Jones (the vicar) once promised to buy the man a new wooden leg if he would take the pledge but he did not." In the face of such evidence the guardians reluctantly agreed to look after the children.

✴ The strange story of two bemused old ladies gripped the area in June. Elizabeth and Helen Stone, aged 60 and 61, began to behave in a very odd way after living together for many years in Codicote.

*The Hitchin Blue Cross Temperance Brigade pictured in 1908, a year before their tireless supporter Arthur Latchmore died.*

They became suspicious of the neighbours, feared a conspiracy against them and were possessed by religious mania. They believed God had commanded them to sacrifice a child for the sins of the people amongst whom they lived.

Eventually the spinsters were admitted to Hitchin workhouse, where they repeated the most extraordinary delusions – one claimed a neighbour had paralysed her arm by hanging out dirty washing. When they were undressed rolls of banknotes were found in their pockets, adding up to £287.

It seemed they had saved the money from an allowance of well under a pound a week. The women were sent to the Three Counties Asylum but their cottage was maintained and they were allowed to return later, when they had recovered their wits.

★ A flower exhibition in aid of Blind and Crippled Girls was held at Hitchin Town Hall in June, sending the Express reporter into raptures over the pretty sight. "To train afflicted girls to earn their own living is a great achievement but to train them also to make things of beauty that are almost joys for ever is something even greater," he declared.

The girls lived in homes with up to 500 others and their flowers were unusually faithful copies of nature, especially the chrysanthemums, which could easily be mistaken for the real thing.

★ Three lectures in farriery were delivered at the forge in Park Street, Hitchin in July, with a shoeing competition to be held later.

★ A shocking case of child neglect came up at court, with Eliza Brown of Norton Street, Baldock, charged with neglecting her children George, aged two, and one-year-old Joseph.

The woman, the court heard, had unfortunately given way to drinking habits. The NSPCC inspector Mr Bulton testified that the children and the house were in a verminous condition when he visited in November and he issued a stern warning to the woman about her duties and responsibilities.

There was a short improvement but by June 1909 the children were in a worse condition than ever.

Mr Brown, who had just returned from militia training, was trying to make the woman clean up the place but failing – the bed and clothing were just a mass of filth, Mr Bulton declared. Mr Brown described his house as a pig sty.

Police Sgt Gray told the court that he called round on June 13 and discovered the children alone, sitting in the garden. He asked a neighbour to look after the babies and found Mrs Brown weaving her way home from Weston fair with a man at almost 11pm.

Dr Robert Macpherson said the children were in a indescribably dirty condition, lying on black bedclothes and with sores caused by filth.

Mr Francis Delmé Radcliffe, chairman of the magistrates at Hitchin, was scandalised. It was one of the worst cases that had been before the bench, he said, and the defendant appeared to be utterly callous. She was sent to St Albans jail for a month.

★ Several valuable foxhounds belonging to Mr G Smith Bosanquet's kennels at Broxbournebury in Herts died after being fed poisoned meat in July.

★ A pony delivering milk to Hitchin Hospital in Bedford Road bolted and raced, complete with cart, along Brand Street, Bancroft, Ickleford Road, Bearton Road, round almost in a circle to Old Park Road and then into the town centre through Nuns Close and West Alley before it finally halted, with the shafts and part of the harness broken. Fortunately no one was hurt.

Only days later another pony caught one if its legs in a trap in Brand Street and galloped away on three legs, neighing wildly, before the driver managed it pull it up.

In September there was a dramatic rescue scene when a horse, standing outside a butcher's shop in Queen Street, bolted after the driver fell between the shafts.

The terrified horse careered madly through the town still trailing its cart, which contained three women and a child.

Bystander Charles Maylin, of St Andrew's Street, seeing the dangerous state of things, bravely tried to stop the horse, stumbling under the flaying hooves as he did so. The cart turned over, throwing the women and child to the ground but not seriously injuring them.

"The unfortunate man Maylin was picked up in a collapsed condition," reported the Express. One of the cart wheels had rolled over him, fracturing his ribs and injuring his lungs.

"With all haste he was conveyed on the police ambulance to the hospital. It appeared from the first that Maylin's case was hopeless." The poor man died soon afterwards.

Only days later there was a second fatal accident in the town when Andrew Watson of Walsworth was knocked down at the railway station while oiling the points. Sixty-year-old Mr Watson, who had worked half his life on the railway, died soon afterwards of terrible injuries.

There was a touch of excitement at a trades exhibition at Hitchin Town Hall in August when a strong smell of gas was noticed. "The escape became plainly apparent when a lady's dress caught on fire near Messrs Van Houten's stall," reported the Express. The lady, Miss Solomon of Chiltern Road, escaped uninjured after her quick thinking niece extinguished the flames – but the dress was ruined.

The poor wife of labourer Albert Franklin was badly injured when he attacked her with a pruning knife one evening in August at their home in Broom, Bedfordshire. The 32-year-old man, who had recently spent three months in the lunatic asylum, tried to cut her throat and, after she managed to escape, held the police at bay with a loaded gun from his upstairs bedroom.

They "showed tact and pluck and the bluff of Pc Gibson came off," reported the Express. He pretended there were more officers outside than the three actually present and that "a mythical being" was mounting the ladder to the window to shoot Franklin, who was finally persuaded to descend.

He looked terribly wild but they managed to search him, finding a razor and a considerable amount of money for an unemployed man. Franklin was sent back to the lunatic asylum and his wife was reported to be progressing very favourably.

The grim days of 1848 were recalled when a new water tower was opened at Windmill Hill in Hitchin in September. Black fever – a kind of typhoid – had raged through the town, said Theodore Ransom, chairman of Hitchin Urban District Council.

*The Sun Hotel in Hitchin once had gardens at the rear, where the car park now stands, in about 1870*

Out of the population of 6,000, 1,700 residents had become ill. A new pure water system had been introduced, with Hitchin only the second town in the country to carry out such improvements.

Everything had not gone smoothly and there had been major legal complications, leading to administrative chaos. But in 1909 everything was different and the townsfolk looked forward to an improved water supply.

Animal lovers were in mourning when "a very aristocratic figure in the canine world passed away" in the form of wire haired fox terrier Merrimac, who had a noble pedigree trailing back into the dim past.

Although he was described as probably the best terrier ever bred locally and was a show champion, he died when he was only 11 months old.

"He always bore himself grandly," reported the Express, adding that owner Mr M H R Grellet had refused several tempting offers for him. "Mr Grellet will have everyone's sympathy in his loss," stated the reporter, although whether this was for Merrimac or the several hundred pounds he had turned down was not clear.

Hitchin Debating Society grasped the thorny problem of divorce in November, when they discussed getting rid of some of the more glaring anomalies. These were weighted against women, who could not get a divorce simply on the grounds of their husband's misconduct, but had to prove cruelty as well. The husband automatically had custody of children.

Mr George Spurr said the subject was an unpleasant one but as an enlightened body they should not shrink from discussing it. He did not wish to advocate a general relaxation of the marriage vows, but some form of relief in cases of matrimonial turpitude was necessary.

Women who were granted a judicial separation could not get another husband, were probably apart from their children, and were prey to every temptation, often falling into misery and degradation. Divorce in such cases would be conducive to the general morality, he argued.

Mr W F Langford opposed, declaring family life was the most vital and important thing of all. If divorce was made easier we would have a very bad time indeed – people might get one after any quarrel, he said.

"Motherhood was a woman's greatest duty and if the women of this country would spend more time looking after the real object of their existence, instead of the silly agitation they made at present, it would be much better for all," he added, referring to the suffrage movement.

The society's next debate was over the standards of journalism – were they deteriorating? Mr Spurr argued that modern attitudes were deplorable and that papers were owned by too few people. The great powers in the land were the pulpit, the platform, the stage and the press, with the latter by far the greatest of all.

He also spoke disparagingly of the sensational and misleading headlines in some papers, criticised "light" reports on Parliamentary debates and slammed the habit of building some people up into heroes. He ended by asking if papers tending to uplift and advance the moral and intellectual condition of the people.

Mr W Holland did his best to answer this volley of abuse. Local journalism had considerably improved he said, then went on to weakly agree with much that Mr Spurr had said. The debate finished with a comment about the deplorable efforts of certain papers to create a scare that war might break out between England and Germany.

A plan was put forward to create a skating rink in a shed covering the whole of the garden of number 118 Nightingale Road, Hitchin. Seth Smith proposed cementing the floor, putting up a corrugated iron roof and making walls of old boarding across an area 40ft by 25ft.

The rink would be lit by paraffin lamps. Surveyor Mr A T Blood was not impressed, telling councillors: "In the event of this corridor roof catching fire, the means of egress would be very limited." There had been no plan to provide sanitary conveniences.

As Christmas approached Josiah Oldfield of Bromley wrote to the Express, begging readers not to eat a festive bird. "It is sadly out of harmony with the gentle founder of Christianity to celebrate his birthday by slaughtering millions of helpless creatures wantonly and needlessly," he protested. "The fruitarian diet is better, is more nutritious, promotes sounder health and long life and gives greater joy to those who adhere to this Arcadian feast." Mr Oldfield was a member of the Dumb Creatures Christmas League.

# The day Emily Pankhurst came to town

Through the town marched the suffragettes. The police stood on either side, half guarding, half derisive, ready to uphold the law if the large crowd got out of hand.

The women were undaunted, walking with pride and deliberation out of Hitchin's historic Market Place, past historic shops and along dusty streets towards the railway station. The noise was tremendous as they passed in a volley of hoots, the occasional stone blistering the air.

At their head were Miss Gawthorpe, Mrs Despard and Mrs Pethick-Lawrence, all leading campaigners in the movement, but all shocked by the virulent attack against them.

For 90 minutes they had fought to make themselves heard in the Corn Exchange, struggling against hecklers, ironical remarks and laughter from all quarters, while the police stood guard at the door and a large mob jostled outside.

The audience had been made to stand in a futile effort to reduce disruption and extra police were drafted into the town for the meeting. As the women emerged from the hall they were met with shouts and hoots. "The behaviour of many members of the crowd was most discreditable," reported the Express.

Miss Mary Gawthorpe wrote to the Express the following week, denying she wanted to be martyred and commenting on the hooliganism.

"So far Hitchin is the only place where such unreasoning and unfair hostility has been shown. In Letchworth, in Willian, in Baldock and in Stevenage, too, nothing but kindness and good feeling has been met with. Criticism, of course, there has been. We welcome that. Irrelevant horseplay is another matter."

*Hitchin Market Place in 1906, displaying a campaign poster for J J W Miller, who was standing as the Conservative candidate for Parliament – he was defeated*

The year was 1907 and the Hitchin area was a prime target for suffragette action, thanks to the outspoken views of its MP, Julius Bertram. But other townsfolk were to play fascinating roles in the long struggle for a female vote, reaching back to its earliest days.

Emily Davies, founder in 1868 of the first ladies' university college, off Benslow Lane, Hitchin, was a leading suffrage campaigner. She presented a 1,500-signature petition to philosopher, economist and MP John Stuart Mill, which he flourished in Parliament, urging votes for women.

It was all in vain, the 1867 Reform Act extended the franchise to more men, but there was never a moment when women were considered seriously as voters.

Bill followed bill in ensuing years and all were talked out, blocked or stalled, often by Gladstone. But with each disappointment and setback, the campaigners became a little more angry, a little less subdued, much more determined.

In a 1907 pamphlet published by the Garden City Press, Lucy C Dalley wrote:

*"Women have ground their teeth in silent, impotent anger for years when their claims have been flouted and their sex insulted in these farcical debates. The suffragettes have merely become articulate."*

Votes for women was no longer a side issue but one of central importance, splitting the nation. Support grew steadily but there were plenty of men, and quite a few women, to mock the very idea.

If women had the vote, they said, they would become corrupt and men would no longer treat them with chivalry. They might even abandon marriage and the population would die out. Anyway, everyone knew women were too emotional to make serious political decisions.

Twenty years later, in 1927, the Hertfordshire Express reported a funeral, paying tribute to suffrage campaigner Sarah Smithson. Time had transformed perspective; the former eccentric, once fit only for contempt and ridicule, was now a heroine.

Mrs Smithson was well-to-do, with a certain social cachet. She lived in one of the grandest houses in Tilehouse Street, was well connected both through birth and marriage, and could have led an idle life of gossip, fashion and charity.

But she chose quite another course, one that made her "a laughing stock to less acute thinkers and the butt of the vulgar sallies," reported the Express after her death.

She spurned soirées and balls to sit at a table addressing envelopes and organising meetings, working "steadily and persistently for the suffrage cause, ploughing a somewhat lonely furrow."

Her motivation was simple – a desire for justice, for right, for sense. She told a public meeting in Hitchin in April 1907 (billed as Mrs Edward Smithson):

*"So long as women are placed beside lunatics as the only case of people who are not allowed the vote, they will never occupy the position they ought in the eyes of men."*

At the very time she spoke one MP was proposing to introduce legislation to stop married women working.

Mrs Smithson was a seasoned campaigner, founding a women's suffrage society in York in the late 19th Century, and later becoming chairman of Hitchin, Stevenage and District Suffrage Society.

But she was not a supporter of Mrs Pankhurst's militant movement, which turned to violence when peaceful methods failed. "She was always a law abiding suffragist, believing that force was no remedy, even for a great injustice," commented the Express in its obituary on Mrs Smithson.

The loneliness and the vulgar sallies were long over by the time she died in 1927, a grand old lady of 83. Justice had almost been done, women of 30 had the vote and were about to win total equality with men. The Hertfordshire Express, the very newspaper which had on occasion mocked the suffrage movement, fawned at her funeral.

Hitchin's historian Reginald Hine gave an inspiring eulogy:

*"Her whole life was spent in search of things that are more excellent. At four score years she was still a seeker, still keeping abreast of the knowledge and the problems of the day.*

*The variety of that seeking was infinite."*

To every cause she espoused she brought "her sweet reasonableness and her exhaustless energy."

Exhaustless energy was vital to the suffragettes, whether reasonable or not. Edwardian women were second class citizens, earning less than half the average wage of a man, treated with a mixture of reverence and disparagement – and often just the latter.

This attitude showed in every field of life. A journalist writing in the Express in September 1902 commented on the increasing cruelty to children.

"It is merely the inevitable outcome of women labour in factories," he wrote.

"Instead of domestic service and a proper training in home duties, the young woman of today seeks employment at fixed hours in a factory and her evenings are spent in idling or unprofitable recreations.

"The result is ignorance of home management to a painful degree, an intolerable desire for idleness, a loathing of household duties and a keen enjoyment of gossip with the next-door neighbour. Children brought into the world have to care for themselves."

At the same time another column in the paper featured a dress pattern for an "essential" afternoon skirt that must be worn with a dainty blouse.

When Hitchin Debating Society was set up in January 1904, the first issue it discussed was whether to admit women (they decided yes.)

It was more than three years before they welcomed a female speaker and they made much of their gesture when Miss Gertrude Bacon, daughter of a famous aeronaut, lectured on Wind, Wave and Cloud.

Anyone who thought this a breakthrough for women's rights would have soon been disabused; chairman Mr W O Times went on to refer to a suffragettes' meeting in the town, planned for the very next day. He dismissed it casually, saying he:

*"Thought it more improving for the intelligence to deal with the laws of nature than condescend to think of the fleeting and fluctuating opinions of party political strife."*

Mr Times would have won approval from the town's Liberal MP, Julius Bertram, who successfully blocked Keir Hardie's suffrage bill in the last months of 1906. He earned the undying hatred of the suffragettes.

Christobel Pankhurst, daughter of leader Emily, declared: "Let any MP oppose our measure and he will live to regret it." Mr Bertram, far from being fazed or afraid, basked in the attention. It was reported that women imprisoned in Holloway had been heard to say: "Mr Bertram, MP for Hitchin, has become a marked man."

The Express was in raptures, calling him "our bravest MP" and asserting that he could claim to be the most courageous member in the House of Commons.

His argument was simple. "Taxation is not the whole basis of representation," he said. "The real basis is manhood – the ability to bear arms and defend the country if necessary from invasion." He tried a little flattery too.

"I think politics are best left to the more rough and disorderly members of the community," adding "Some day my arguments might be regarded as out-of-date but for the present I think those arguments would weigh with the majority of men and a huge majority of women."

It seemed he was right – Hitchin Debating Society members gave him victory by 28 votes to 14 when they discussed the issue in 1910.

It was their second look at the subject – in March 1907, members listened to Holloway veteran Irene Miller, who declared: "Women have done everything they could to show they do want the vote. For 40 years there have been petitions, processions and demonstrations."

*Julius Bertram, MP for the Hitchin area*

The audience listened quietly, especially when Mr G Crosoer intervened on the side of reason. "Whether women are the inferior sex or not is a difficult question," he announced. "But it is one that should be studied fairly. A very few women are, I should say, almost as good as I am myself."

Miss Miller lost her resolution "by a large majority."

North Herts continued to receive close attention from the Women's Social and Political Union. Early in January 1907, Minnie Baldock came with Flora Drummond to disrupt one of Mr Bertram's meetings, in Baldock. Both women were notorious after being imprisoned in Holloway.

At first they sat quietly in the hall but then, unable to contain herself any longer, Flora Drummond "burst forth like a tropical storm in all her fury," reported the Express. "With a frenzied bound, gesticulating wildly, her face a picture of uncontrollable passion, she reached a point near the platform and, with her back to the wall, poured forth a torrent of words in a manner which would not have disgraced – we were going to say a Kilkenny cat, but remembering she is a lady we will refrain."

All chivalry was forgotten as Mrs Drummond was hustled roughly into the street, followed by poor Minnie. Gales of laughter and cheers followed them. If they had been allowed to stay they would have heard Mr Bertram state he was sure women had no desire for the vote.

Many men could scarcely be rational when they discussed their wives, their mothers and their sisters. An Express columnist appropriately called Cactus told Express readers: "Woman is reverting to the primitive type.

"She is succumbing to the very same temptation as in the beginning. Why cannot she be content with the glories and undisputed kingdom assigned her by her maker? They should be content as ruler of the destinies of mankind in the nursery, home and schoolroom." His self interest soon showed as he went on:

*"It is a cruel and monstrous thing that men cannot be left in peaceful possession of their own rights and privileges. Are men to have no rights sacred to themselves? No sphere safe from feminine intrusion?"*

In contrast The Hon Mrs Ernest (Mary) Fordham of Odsey, stated her views clearly in 1909. "We women are members of a great family, daughters of God who has given us life that we may employ it for the benefit of humanity.

"We fight that women may be free, free as their fathers and husbands, to make their own lives, to live them as they please, to work at what they are most fitted for and for wages in proportion to their work, not in proportion to their sex, so much for men, so much less for women.

*"We ask, and it will be given to us, for the right and the protection of the vote, that has done so much for men, and which can't logically be withheld from women, who pay rates and taxes and who bear children and educate and fit them for citizenship."*

To many men the issue was little more than a joke. A handbill advertising a suffragette meeting in the Market Place caused Hitchin Urban District councillors great hilarity at a meeting in 1908.

The following November, when a meeting was held at Hitchin Town Hall, the speakers fought to be heard against a cacophony of irrelevant remarks, whistles and choruses of popular songs. The meeting ended with "a budding polyphonist" commencing a series of imitations of cats, ducks and other creatures, much to the amusement of his friends. The following week the Rev J Frome Wilkinson of Barley wrote to the Express to complain about the disorder, "A crime against public order and an outrage on English liberties." The suffrage issue was not a war against men, he declared, but a combined movement of men and women "into a Caanan of truer social order."

It wasn't only men who were opposed to extending the vote – many women were too and in 1907 they set up their own anti-suffrage society.

A year later MP's wife Mrs J A Pease accompanied Mr Bertram to a "distinguished political and social gathering" in London to protest against votes for women. "There is no demand for the great constitutional change on the part of the women of England," declared Mr Bertram.

*Two girls with bikes, dressed as suffragettes, pictured in a field at Pirton*

The depth of his thinking was revealed in another item in the Express, in 1908. Commenting on Lloyd George's groundbreaking social budget, Mr Bertram said: "The reduction on the duty on sugar is almost as great a thing as the establishment of old age pensions."

Lorna, who wrote a regular Women's Realm column in the Express, was incapable of any serious thought at all. She limited her comments to repeating Ella Hepworth's item in the Sketch: "Naive New York is seriously discussing whether a man should marry a woman with brains or not, for all the world as if Man, poor dear, had any choice is the matter."

But such attitudes were fading and the suffragette movement was indefatigable.

In June 1908 Robert Gernon of Letchworth declared in a letter to the Express: "The case for women's suffrage has been fought and won. There is no question about it at all, it is inevitable."

Mr Gernon's last words were certainly correct, but his timing was rather in error.

Emily Pankhurst herself came to Hitchin in March 1907, speaking of the low wages suffered by women. In answer to a heckler who called out: "You should have six months' hard labour," she replied:

> *"We would not mind imprisonment or even death so long as it is the means of doing something to help those who are too poor to help themselves."*

She was accompanied by Mrs Nellie Alma Martel, a seasoned speaker at the town hall and the catalyst for a raucous meeting in January. "Seldom in the history of the town has a political meeting caused so much excitement as one held under the auspices of the Hitchin Liberal Association," reported the Express.

"The news that the valiant members of the suffragette army were to attend drew crowds of people."

As Mr Bertram moved through his speech, Mrs Martel stood on her chair, followed by most of the audience who were cheering, hissing and groaning. "Amid a scene of boisterousness which has never been equalled in the town, she addressed the meeting," but no-one could hear her, and neither could they make out a word from Mr Bertram.

Six police officers threw Mrs Martel into the street, where she was greeted enthusiastically by a crowd of hundreds, who followed her to the Market Place where she held an alternative meeting. But peace did not descend on the town hall – as she left someone discharged acetylene gas and cayenne pepper bombs, choking half the audience. "For a long time after she had left the confusion continued unabated," commented the Express.

Mrs Pankhurst's favourite daughter Christobel chose to speak in Letchworth when she visited Mr Bertram's constituency, in July 1907. "Women are not free but edged in by all sorts of boundaries and laws made for them by men," she told an audience at the Howard Hall.

"They are regarded as something less than human and inferior to men."

Hinting at years of increasing civil strife, she ended: "We will make the men's lives a thorough nuisance until we get the vote."

One cause of nuisance was Mrs Elizabeth Impey of Whinbush Road, Hitchin, who went to Holloway for three weeks after a large suffragette raid on the House of Commons, in April 1907.

Charged with disorderly conduct, she was at first imprisoned in a filthy cell, given bread and cocoa, and searched in the middle of the night, before being allowed to sleep in cleaner quarters. She described her dull diet – milk for breakfast, dinner and tea, and one egg, two ounces of butter and bread to eat.

Her only utensil was a wooden spoon and her plate was a flat bit of tin. It was not the conditions that worried her though. "We had no work to do and the solitude was awful," she confided in the Express. "There was nowhere to rest."

But she was prepared to endure it all again. "I am simply working for the cause of women because I desire to help my sex," she said. Her answer to the old chestnut "many women don't want to vote," was equally simple.

> *"They do not have to use it. If in these enlightened days you are still content to be included in the same class as criminals and lunatics and denied the right of citizenship, we do not mind. But do not be offended when other women ask for something higher and nobler."*

Soon afterwards Mrs Impey was helping to run a literature stall at Hitchin on Market Day with Miss Gawthorpe, who was campaign organiser

> "We will make the men's lives a thorough nuisance until we get the vote."

for the constituency and described by a northern newspaper as "small, brisk and dainty." In July she travelled north to Jarrow, to campaign in a by-election.

On her return she told the Express she "had been struck by the large number of working men who have asked whether their wives would have votes in her scheme, and by their obvious relief when she replied in the negative."

A meeting at Letchworth reading room heard a speaker from the adult suffrage movement argue in favour of votes for more men as well as for women, increasing the number of voters from 7.5 million to 23.

"The anomalies of the present system are many and give too much weight to the propertied classes," he said. "A wave of unemployment extinguishes thousands of votes."

Male suffrage was certainly far from straightforward, with the vote limited to householders, some lodgers, property owners and graduates. Men had to apply for the vote and, where the case was in doubt, the Liberal and Tory party agents would argue for and against, depending on the political inclination of the man concerned. In September 1907 the Express reported a typical session of the annual revision of the Parliamentary, county and parochial election lists, held at the Sun Hotel before barrister Theobald Mathew.

It was decided Frederick Bysouth would lose his lodger's vote because he didn't have sole use of his bedroom but that Mr W B Watts, accused of sleeping in a bedroom with his father, could keep his because he only shared when there were visitors in the house. Poor William Knight was refused the occupation vote because he lived with his mother and she paid the rent and rates.

But it was the decision over Harry Blake's application that proved the most difficult. Harry lived with his wife and her father in a house in Radcliffe Road – the father had the vote so the barrister finally decided Harry couldn't.

No social security probe into shared housing was more intense and frequent anomalies affected even the rich and powerful.

In 1905 playwright George Bernard Shaw, of Ayot St Lawrence, lost his vote, as did the county's leading aristocrat, making national headlines in the process.

The Daily News commented: "Somehow or other it seemed quite natural for the present order of society to disenfranchise its most brilliant satirist. When again Mr Algernon Swinburne (the poet) was also placed among the voteless, while a known lunatic retained his suffrage, we could afford to smile and hold our peace.

*Stalls at Hitchin Market Place at the end of the 19th Century, facing towards Churchgate*

"But it is a very different matter when the Marquis of Salisbury, of Hatfield, Hertfordshire, finds himself statute debarred in respect to the Parliamentary franchise."

But for women this was an irrelevance – many were prepared to put up with the ludicrous system rather than be excluded completely.

They found an aristocratic champion in Lady Constance Lytton of the Knebworth House family, whose campaign won the support of her brother.

Like Mrs Impey, Lady Constance was prepared to go to jail for her beliefs and, in March, 1909, the Express reported the tumultuous welcome she received when she left Holloway with 25 other suffragettes.

A band greeted them, along with a large crowd of sympathisers, and they rapidly devoured a special breakfast. Lady Constance, who was met and embraced by her sister, Lady Betty Balfour, gave a speech she had written the night before. Denied the use of pen and paper, she wrote in her own blood on the back of an old letter.

She recalled the night of her arrest, when the behaviour of some of the crowd had made her desperately ashamed – she would never have believed that Englishmen would behave in such a way to women.

She had spent her sentence in either the prison hospital or a special cell, because she was deemed to have a weak heart.

She was sceptical about the reasons for her lenient treatment and frequently protested against the favours she was receiving "on account of her social position."

In spite of this she had been through a gruelling time.

One night Lady Constance was woken up by the terrible shrieks from a nearby cell, where a woman was rattling the gates and crying to be let out. She was under sentence of death for killing her child and her screams of despair went on for days. Ever compassionate, Lady Constance said:

*"I wish the Home Secretary who has defended the present system under which a formal sentence of death is passed in these cases could have been there to hear those cries."*

If the same Home Secretary thought Lady Constance would be daunted by Holloway he was sadly disappointed. She emerged from prison even more committed to the cause.

Two weeks later she was telling Express readers why she cared so much.

"The whole social surroundings of her life had been repellent to her, even the publicity of the ballroom having a sort of terror for her. She came of literary stock but had not made use of educational opportunities and never cared for books," the newspaper reported.

Her conversion came after meeting the leaders of the suffragette movement and she began attending meetings.

Her first impression was rather an odd one: "The word washing was always recurring. She heard the people crying out: 'Go home and tend to your washing'."

Several letters sent to her on her release from Holloway took issue with the authorities for letting her be imprisoned because she was from the nobility.

*"But Lady Constance said if there was anything in nobility, it must be nobility of action."*

She must have shocked many readers deeply when she declared her impatience with the idea of hereditary honour, stating: "These were things that could not be handed down by law and prestige."

Her brother the Earl of Lytton agreed to be the president of the year-old North Herts branch of the National Union of Women's Suffrage Societies in March, 1910.

*Lady Constance Lytton, wearing her WSPU medals*

The members' first job was to collect 737 petition signatures towards a quarter of a million collected nationwide.

Lord Lytton had already proved his commitment to his sister and the cause. He was the chief speaker at the third annual demonstration of the Men's League for Women's Suffrage, in early 1910.

The fact that his sister had suffered martyrdom (as one of the speakers termed her ordeal) attracted a large audience. The meeting ended on a high note as Lord Lytton moved the resolution:

*"The exclusion of women from the franchise is both unjust to women and detrimental to the best interests of the state."*

Only weeks later Lady Constance made her most courageous stand against the system she despised and became a martyr in truth. Wearing commonplace clothes, she was arrested once again as a suffragette demonstrator.

This time she kept her real name secret and instead told officials at Liverpool she was Jane Warton, an impoverished seamstress of no status or position.

Lady Constance had been diagnosed at Holloway as having a serious heart disease. Jane Warton apparently did not. Lady Constance was treated with politeness and respect whereas Jane was insulted by prison warders.

The aristocrat was not well enough to be force fed; the seamstress suffered this humiliation eight times.

At last Lady Constance had the evidence she needed to condemn the system and her brother called for an impartial inquiry.

He described the issue as "one of the chief political questions of the day" and told a meeting at Hitchin Town Hall in October 1910 that is was dangerous to deny women the vote any longer, their patience was exhausted. He declared: "The woman who had to obey the laws and pay the taxes should have a voice in choosing representatives."

But Lady Constance paid a high price for her moral victory. The doctors at Holloway had been right – her heart was weak and her health was irreparably damaged by her treatment at Walton jail. In 1912 she had a stroke from which she never properly recovered, dying in 1923 aged only 54.

Her brother, always a supporter of the cause, expressed his doubts about the methods being used in a moving speech he made to the House of Lords. Speaking of militant action he said:

"You see in it only the folly and the wickedness; but I also see in it the pity and the tragedy.

"I have seen the exhibition of human qualities which I consider to be as rare and as precious as anything which a nation can possess.

"I have seen these qualities given to a cause which is in itself as great and as noble a cause as you could well find, but given in such a way as to defeat the very objects that they sought to obtain....And that, to my mind, is tragedy."

*Lord Lytton*

The suffragette movement became more extreme and violent in its frustration. In March 1912 the Express reported that 200 women had broken windows in the West End and 20,000 had attended a rally.

Three months later Jane Short, a 31-year-old art student from Commerce Way, Letchworth, was charged with unlawfully, wilfully and maliciously damaging windows at Baldock Post Office.

She appeared at Hitchin Magistrates Court in a smart green costume, suggestive of the colours of the suffragette cause, and gave a lengthy and mostly inaudible statement.

She was caught walking away from the scene with stones in her bag and told police she had broken the glass, but she pleaded not guilty.

Her argument that "It was not a malicious act but a means to protest against the government in the matter of votes for women" cut no ice with the magistrates.

They sent her to prison for three months after she refused to be bound over.

It was not the end of Jane Short's protesting though. She reached national prominence the following year, after she was sent to prison for arson and went on hunger strike.

It was the period of the iniquitous Cat and Mouse Act, when prisoners who refused food (and often water) were released until they were stronger, then taken back to jail for the whole gruesome business to start again.

But Home Secretary Reginald McKenna decided Jane Short and fellow prisoner Mary Richardson would not be released under this scheme, but forcibly fed – a practice which had been abandoned because of its barbarity. The suffragettes were furious, blaming McKenna's action on his anger at the indomitable courage of the women. Miss Short and Miss Richardson, they pointed out, were not even convicted criminals, but still awaiting trial and presumed innocent.

Jane Short, also known as Rachael Peace, was duly sentenced to nine months' imprisonment – her third sentence – and the feeding continued.

Mrs Pethick-Lawrence, one of the movements' best known figures, spoke at Letchworth in December 1913. To cheers she declared:

*"This agitation is not a woman's movement; it is a movement for human liberty.*
*One hundred years ago four great classes were shut out from political liberty – the Jews, the Catholics, the working men and women. We have seen the barriers which shut out the first three swept away. We now wait to see the last great barrier of sex swept away."*

She spoke of the terrible tortures of forcible feeding, under which no woman's will has broken down. "As I stand here I think of one woman from this very town of Letchworth.

*"It is evident that she has been chosen in the hope that in her, woman's will may be broken down. It may be because she has not many friends, or because she is very weak in body."*

She finished her speech with the rousing words:
*"Nothing can destroy or sweep away this movement."*

Mrs Pethick-Lawrence urged residents to write to McKenna, asking him to receive a deputation from the garden city concerning the harsh treatment of Jane Short. Their letters were in vain: Mr McKenna replied that he could see no point in meeting them, adding that forcible feeding was only used in the case of three exceptionally dangerous prisoners, one of whom was now released.

Even Hitchin's then MP Robert Cecil, an ally of the suffrage movement, refused to sign a petition for Jane's release. He was not an admirer of the way in which the government dealt with the question, he said, but at the same time he thought criminals should be punished.

Twenty members of the WSPU created a scene in Westminster Abbey one Friday afternoon at the end of 1913, chanting for the release of Jane Short and Mary Richardson.

"Their enemies torture them for they know their cause is righteous," they sang, repeating the scene at St Paul's Cathedral the following Sunday. Mary Richardson became one of the most extreme figures in the movement when she slashed Velasquez's Rokeby Venus at the National Gallery in March 1914.

The situation was spiralling out of control and there seemed no solution. Only war was to restore civil peace to the nation.

Most supporters of votes for women abhorred violence, which they felt was putting the cause in

*Robert Cecil, MP for the Hitchin area*

jeopardy, but the public often judged them all the same. The women were also united in their growing frustration. There was a serious blow to the movement in February 1913, when yet another women's suffrage bill was shelved.

'An Englishman' wrote to the Express: "A woman to vote for those who have to make our laws? Having the power to do so, indirectly if not directly, they are made rulers of men.

*"I have looked into the inspired volume and I can find no warrant therein for women to have such a position. It is not necessary for women to have a vote of their own to remedy their grievances; as witness the white slaves bill."*

That must have reassured the female population enormously.

Even the WSPU held many peaceful activities. In July 1911 it swapped its violent and fierce campaigning stance for a very sedate event – a garden fete at Elm Tree House in Letchworth.

The stalls were tastefully arranged on the lawn, enticing buyers with handmade work, sweets, Russian goods and tempting articles of use or ornament. There were excellent refreshments, a palmist to look into the future, and hat trimming and sewing competitions.

Another fund-raising event, also in Letchworth, required every visitor to bring an item worth 3d to a bazaar, to pay 3d to get in and to buy something for 3d.

"There was much amusement in seeing what articles people put on their stalls and trade was brisk," reported the Express, adding:

*"It would be a libel to state that North Herts suffragettes are not domesticated."*

There were also entertainments including a political Punch and Judy, a comedietta and a concert. It was noticeable that a large number of men helped, added the Express.

But opposition continued unabated. In March 1912 a movement was set up in Bedfordshire to oppose women's suffrage. One of the founders was Samuel Whitbread of Ampthill, who signed the declaration:

"There must be many who are convinced, as we are convinced, that the extension of the franchise to women would be disastrous to the nation, disastrous to the Empire and, what is no less vitally important, disastrous to British womanhood."

Something must be done to resist the movement in favour of women's suffrage, they went on. An attitude of apathy was no longer possible.

"We appeal to those who still think that the duty of governing belongs to the sex which has the duty of protecting the home and defending the country.

*"We appeal to those who believe that women find an exalted sphere and duty in their state, a sphere which is not one whit less honourable, important and influential than that of men."*

Sir Robert Cecil, MP, did not agree and made his view clear in Parliament. He could not understand the view that giving the vote to a million women could seriously imperil the safety and prosperity of the Empire, and he said so.

Withholding the vote from women because a few went too far and broke windows was not a good reason, he added.

"The question had not been considered fairly by the House, but had been put off again and again with a variety of pretexts," he told Parliament.

Miss Wright of the WSPU, speaking in Letchworth's Howard Park, summoned up the anguish of women. "For gentlewomen, cultured and refined, to attend society functions and deliberately outrage the traditions of decorum requires undoubted pluck and determination," she said.

*"We have now arrived at a stage where nothing small is effective and we have to frighten people."*

In their effort to make their voice heard, women took to the streets. The North Herts branch of the National Union of Women's Suffrage Societies joined a march of up to 50,000 women in June 1911. They took pride in what they were doing and all carried distinctive banners.

The North Herts pennant of old gold coloured silk was woven at Letchworth with a device that declared: "Weaving fair and weaving free, England's web of destiny."

> ## 'Weaving fair and weaving free, England's web of destiny'

It was carried in turn by three men and Miss Wilkinson, secretary of the Letchworth division. Among the group from Letchworth, Hitchin, Stevenage, Knebworth and Welwyn, were Mrs Barry Parker, wife of the architect of Letchworth, and the Hon Mrs E O Fordham.

They were watched by numerous spectators but few supporters as they marched to bands playing tunes such as the Marseillaise and inspiring music composed by Dr Ethel Smythe.

One local marcher told the Express: "At Whitehall there was a curious experience of a depressed looking string of sandwich men bearing the legend 'Women don't want the vote.'

*"It was impossible not to feel some amused satisfaction at the contrast between our gay and cheerful thousands and those rather dilapidated deputies of the anti-suffrage party."*

The crowd were mostly quiet, she added, not shouting out the usual "Go home and mind the baby" or "Make dinner." "Nor were we asked if we did not want to marry," she added.

*"The last is usually voiced by an especially unattractive specimen of masculinity. Most of us returned to our homes with glad hearts at the great success of our endeavour to show the strength and intensity of our demand and with the conviction that the end of our long struggle cannot be far distant."*

It was yet another false dawn, one of the endless disappointments, prevarications and delays that pushed some women into violence. Many stayed resolutely law abiding however.

A peaceful march converged on Trafalgar Square from Edinburgh in November 1912, passing through Bedfordshire and Herts.

On route the campaigners collected signatures for yet another petition. "Women in the ranks wore serviceable dresses of russet brown and a light wagon with the great petition brought up the rear," reported the Express. Lanterns were carried as night fell. In July 1913 the law-abiding suffragists organised a march to Hyde Park with supporters coming from the length and breadth of England.

On route they stopped at every town they could manage and, coming along the Great North Road, called at Baldock, Letchworth, Hitchin, Wymondley, Stevenage, Knebworth and Welwyn.

The local committee of the National Union of Women's Suffrage Societies appealed for all men and women who valued their political freedom to support the women in their lawful endeavour to secure their enfranchisement.

*Baldock as it appeared in about 1870*

*Howard Park, Letchworth, pictured in the early years of the garden city*

The march of the Pilgrims, as it was called, reached Baldock on Saturday, July 19. As they arrived in North Herts, Mr Samuel of the Anti-Suffrage Union held an impromptu meeting in Hitchin Market Place.

The crux of his argument was that the vote was demanded by only a few women and, if it was won, it would not be used. Women were already represented on local bodies and they were not well equipped for national bodies nor was the hurly-burly of political life well suited to them.

As he spoke the suffragists were arriving in Baldock by bicycle, very tanned and dusty after their long journey. However, the good residents of Baldock had no intention of welcoming their visitors cordially.

One pub landlord refused refreshment and admission to the premises, becoming abusive as he swore they would not step inside his door. In the ensuing struggle a woman was pushed off her bike into the dust. Another publican followed suit and it was only after the police had been called that the women were allowed to go inside.

As evening approached they arranged for a lorry to be set up outside the Wesleyan Church and formed a platform. They got little response for their trouble – the people of Baldock who weren't hostile to the cause seemed completely apathetic.

Exasperated, speaker Miss Meekly declared that she and her companions had, during their pilgrimage, had experiences that were far from comfortable. At every town they had been roughly handled and abused. She demanded:

*"Why should we endure such things if we are not convinced women want and ought to have the vote?"*

On Sunday afternoon the women rallied at Howard Park in Letchworth, drawing a large crowd. Mrs Beaver, who had marched from Newcastle, replied to Mr Samuel's comments. It was not true, she said, that only a small section of women asked for the vote – more than one million were organised for it. Anyway the question was not whether they wanted it or not, but was it just?

Her companion Mrs Gordon was even more forthright. "Women always have to take second place, at school, at the very beginning of life, at work and afterwards," she told the crowd.

*"Why should she, who was equal to man, and in fact had a sphere of her own which needed representation as much as any man's, be debarred from equal privileges?"*

Her comments were supported by Mr Bruce Wallace, who gave a religious address at the Howard Hall on Sunday morning. "The logical outcome of Christianity was the full recognition of women in all spheres of political, religious and social life," he told the audience.

*"Justice necessitates that women's half of humanity should be fully recognised."*

By Monday morning the women were in Hitchin, swelled by supporters who included Ebenezer Howard, to number 70 strong. They staged their meeting near the railway station but Mr Samuel had no intention of letting them address the crowds quietly.

He was already there, and "things assumed a somewhat lively aspect on the appearance of the Pilgrims," stated the Express. Mrs Taylor took the stage and declared the Pilgrims came:

*"As an expression of the spirit of our age, which showed by this means the desire of multitudes of women to share in righting the wrongs from which our sisters suffer. This was not a sex war, they did not wish to stir up strife with the men, from whom they looked for and obtained help and companionship."*

Mr Samuel heard none of this, he was too busy entertaining a splinter group with a voluminous speech, mainly consisting of jokes and anecdotes.

But this irritation was nothing compared to the problems the Pilgrims faced when they reached Stevenage later that afternoon.

They were greeted by local members of the National Union of Women's Suffrage Societies only to find the town plastered with anti-suffrage posters. In an effort to foil Mr Samuel, the women set up two meetings near the ESA factory and spoke where the opposition was quietest. An attempt to overturn one wagon platform was frustrated by the police.

It was difficult to make themselves heard above the constant noise, the badly-sung music hall ballads and voices yelling witticisms along the lines of one reported jest against a male supporter: "That man is under his wife's thumb."

When singing failed the men hissed, shouted the national anthem and launched another assault on the second platform.

Undaunted the women marched to the Bowling Green and then set off for Knebworth where a welcome message of support was read out. It came from Sir Robert Cecil, who had won strong praise from Miss Meekly at Hitchin.

She told the few people who could hear that there was no man in the House of Commons whom she admired more. "In our most arduous work he has always stood by us. He has the making of a true statesman and therefore stands by that which he believes to be true."

The treatment of the women brought severe censure from Mr W E Burke, writing in the Express the following week.

What impression would they have of the chivalry and gallantry of Stevenage residents, he asked?

*"When the writer arrived at the meeting he found the place in a state of noise and ferment, the children being helped on by laughter and encouragement to insult those whom proper training and teaching should have taught to respect; for whatever one may think of the views of these ladies as to votes, they were ladies – and God help Stevenage, or any other place, when it is considered fine form for children to insult and badger a woman. What of the young men who tried to upset the waggonette and with it the ladies, to their intense bodily risk and hurt? Fine sport and pluck is not it, to insult and assault a woman?"*

The issue dominated the letters page a fortnight later, after a report by the Rev H Colony, Rector of Stevenage, who told parishioners: "I like to think that the intrusion of women into the labour market and man's sphere is a passing and unhappy phase.

"Woman is on an equal, but on a different pedestal, which is meant to supplement what is lacking in the other.

*"I take it that women's highest privilege is to be a mother of children."*

He came up with a very original idea for extending suffrage.

"Were the vote granted to women – I hope it never will be – I would make the qualification, not a rate paying one, or any subservient copy of men's suffrage, but a maternal qualification, a vote granted to every married woman who is the mother of four children.

*"A woman best serves the state, not by her labour, but by rearing future citizens."*

He continued his bizarre train of thought onto equal pay, a newly voiced idea.

The rector reasoned that if you give women the same money as men, who are more selfish than women, the inevitable result would be that women would become the wage earner and men would live on their wives' earnings. This provoked a stream of letters.

One clerical correspondent asked if the rector would prefer the doll-type woman of the Victorian age to return, an animated pin cushion, a material parasite often compelled to remain at home where poverty and pseudo-responsibility went hand-in-hand for the sake of that which was deemed proper.

Another correspondent had a chastening story to tell in reply to the rector's view of motherhood.

One suffrage campaigner was told by a sentimental mother, embracing her child, "I don't want the vote. I have got my baby."

"He is not your baby, he is your husband's," was the quiet reply.

The law did indeed give custody of children to fathers whenever it was in dispute.

Suffragists from Letchworth travelled to Bedford in October 1913 to lobby Lloyd George, but they were met by 'hobbledehoys' yelling, singing, letting off crackers and disrupting them every time they tried to speak. Finally they were forced to escape the furious mob by climbing over the railings of St Paul's Churchyard, which were pulled down during the fracas.

The women had to be taken to the police station for their own safety. One commented:

*"The police were fine sturdy yeomen and they unceremoniously but very kindly and capably helped the ladies over the rails into the churchyard and out of harm's way."*

The women, used to forceful opposition, had a very jolly journey home in a brake.

Lady Betty Balfour, the sister of Lady Constance Lytton, spoke at a meeting of the Conservative and Unionist Women's Suffrage Association at Stevenage Public Hall late in 1913.

*"Women are being put to work in so many departments and yet they are denied the vote. I have realised that I cannot stand aloof from the movement any longer."*

She began to argue her case. Florence Nightingale had been called an immodest hussy in the House of Commons when she started work in the Crimea but: "Now they bless her name and

*Bancroft, Hitchin, between 1885 and 1900*

*A recruiting meeting held in Hitchin Market Place in June, 1915, with F P Delmé-Radcliffe addressing the large crowd*

know that no more worthy work could have been done. To serve the country to the best of our ability, we need the vote."

A telegram was read out at the meeting from Sir Robert Cecil. It said:

*"Best wishes for a successful meeting tonight on behalf of the cause of liberty and justice."*

The suffragettes, realising they were getting nowhere, began to widen their base and campaign against the white slave trade – prostitution. The country was whipped into a fervour of panic with every town on the alert for smart women procuring young girls for immoral purposes.

Mrs Nott Bower, speaking at Hitchin, said the trade was carefully organised under syndicates with large numbers of agents on the Continent and in Asia and South America.

An article in the Express claimed that 55 girls aged between 16 and 22 had gone missing in just three months of 1912. Women, it advised, would win their case:

*"Not by hysteria and hooliganism, energies squandered on militarist campaigns, hunger strikes and the like, but by rousing the conscience and chivalry of England on the purity question."*

Lectures were held on the subject in Hitchin.

Women might be tempted into the white slave trade by poverty. A meeting at Knebworth in November 1912 heard that fallen women were forced by scandalously low wages to add to their income as well as they could. "Traps and devices of several kinds decoyed innocent young girls," added the speaker.

At the end of 1913 a meeting in Letchworth was told: "Prevention is our first concern and parents should teach their boys and girls to beware of the very great dangers they might have to face."

Letchworth, always at the forefront of liberal thinking, discussed the issue of equal pay for equal work at its Literary and Debating Society meeting in 1913.

The injustice of the system where a female teacher might earn £60 a year less than her male colleague so moved the members that they agreed to equal pay by a large majority.

Although they did not realise it, the endless debating, the marches, the militancy, the rhetoric and the action, were all about to become superfluous.

On August 4, 1914, war started, a war that changed Western society and killed two million British men – one in every 10 up to the age of 45. One in five was injured.

The Express newspaper abandoned its quirky humour, lost its idiosyncrasy and became a remorseless list of the slain and wounded.

"Hero" became a euphemism for "dead."

The suffragettes took only days to respond. Emily Pankhurst ordered the cessation of activities in the Women's Social and Political Union; the Express reported the suspension of the ordinary work of the National Union of Women's Suffrage on August 15, 1914.

Instead the women, united at last, would fight the Germans. With their efficient organisation and their zeal, the suffragettes were able to mobilise women to take over men's jobs when they left for the front. Enemies were now firm allies.

By March 1917 it was clear that the barriers to suffrage were as flimsy as any muslin. On December 14, 1918, women went to the polls for the first time.

They turned out in force in North Herts, women of all political persuasions and temperaments, some wanting their husband's guidance, others willing to guide him.

As one woman left the polling station a bystander commented: "She's done three years driving a steam plough." The Express reporter wrote:
*"Who would suggest that the full rights of citizenship have not been earned by this sort of war work? A firm decisive manner of approach to the polling booth is acceptable and justified."*

But the story was not yet over and, in its last flurry, a second Hitchin MP was to rise to national prominence following in the footsteps of Julius Bertram.

Under the new law women were disenfranchised until the age of 30, although men could vote at 21. Such an anomaly could not endure and in 1927 the Government decided the day of universal suffrage had come, and proposed lowering the voting age of women to 21.

The measure became known, often with derision, as "the flappers' vote."

One advertisement in the Express went so far as to declare: "Vote for Flappers is giving rise to a difference of opinion but there's only one opinion with regard to the claim of the London Central Meat Company to supply the best Canterbury lamb."

The Representation of the People (Equal Franchise) Bill was not unopposed though – even some of the government's own members were prepared to vote against it. One of the 10 Tory rebels was Major Guy Kindersley, MP for the Hitchin/Stevenage/Letchworth area.

*MP Guy Kindersley*

In March 1927 he explained his reasons at length to a meeting at Stevenage Public Hall. His main objection was that, following the slaughter in the Great War, female voters would decisively outweigh male.

The rebels proposed an amendment to the bill:
*"That until the views of the present electorate have been ascertained on so grave a constitutional change, this house declines to accord a second reading of the Franchise Bill which, purporting to put both sexes on an equal footing, would endow women with permanent political supremacy."*

"The flappers' vote" was a foolish phrase, thought the Major. Nor, he declared, was he against votes for women, stating with great perspicacity: "That issue has been settled."

He did not even think men greatly superior to their sisters at the age of 21, but he went on: "I do say that you can't give votes to men and women on the same terms with regard to age without making a vast and fundamental and permanent constitutional change on which the electorate have never been properly consulted.

"Hitherto and for centuries in this country, men have had political supremacy and the responsibility which that supremacy carries with it."

The bill would shift the balance and women would have the whip hand – not a prospect Major Kindersley favoured. "The sex who perforce, and through no fault of their own, must be the least politically educated, is made the most politically responsible," he thundered.

It would be the female view which always took precedent.

Often there may be no conflict between what the sexes want, he continued, but "on certain questions there is definitely a man's view and a woman's view. The woman's view should have expression but under this Bill the woman's view is to prevail."

The Major moved on to even more tricky ground. "There are also fundamental reasons against this measure based upon the facts of nature," he asserted. Laws were no use unless they could be enforced. If women drew up regulations that men did not want to obey, who would make them?

"I have been accused of encouraging the sex war," he thundered. "Believe me, if you want to avoid it, don't disregard the facts of life as they are disregarded in this measure. For this reason, whether it be in family life or national life, the ultimate responsibility must rest with men, and so rests by nature.

"I believe that to evade or give up responsibility which is laid upon my sex is to be false to my manhood."

He had a simple solution. More women could be given the vote, but only to an age ( which must be known to the government, he asserted confidently) which would give them the same number of votes as men.

That could be done at once, he conceded, and then the electorate could be asked at the next election if they wanted all women to have the vote at 21. The result, he believed, was a foregone conclusion. "I don't believe that women want that responsibility nor have they asked for it," he ended.

He sat down to tumultuous applause. Julius Bertram would have been proud of him.

The major's resistance was even more futile than Mr Bertram's. In May 1928 women finally won the vote on equal terms with men.

*Women found new skills and resources during the First World War – this group were working at Kryn and Lahy, set up in Letchworth as a munitions steel foundry in 1915*

# Favourite Express-ions – 1910

✸ George Malkin was a disreputable character, appearing in the pages of the Express on several occasions. He caused particular problems at elections, when he liked to get involved in proceedings.

Early in 1910 Mr Malkin, of Queen Street, Hitchin, campaigned on behalf of the Unionist candidate, Dr Alfred Hillier. The Express reported, with weary resignation: "That man Malkin led a band of about 100 urchins provided with Unionist cards and games together with horns, bugles etc all around town.

"He carried a pole to which was fastened a large board bearing the legend 'Vote for Hillier.' Surmounting this was a small loaf!" This referred to one of the main issues of the day.

His ministrations may have had some effect, for Hillier won by 5,761 votes to 3,877.

✸ Hitchin Debating Society discussed the merits and needs of Hitchin in January, insulting Letchworth along the way. More residents were needed in the town, asserted Mr Lygo, but "Garden City freaks were not wanted." He added: "It was detestable to see the Garden City absorbing people from all over England. Hitchin could knock spots off the miserable place."

Hitchin was not perfect however and needed a proper town centre lavatory, playing grounds for children to keep them out of the way of their mothers and a public swimming pool and properly organised skating at Walsworth.

The Express newspaper came in for high praise from Mr Crosoer, who said it was one of the best things in Hitchin, with a very high tone of scrupulous independence and providing a model for other districts.

*Workers at the Russell tannery in Bancroft, pictured in 1910*

✶ Hitchin Board of Guardians were asked to provide a donkey to take washing from Letchworth to the workhouse but, after some discussion, decided it would be better to employ an extra man instead.

✶ Women's hats were still causing problems at public shows, including the town hall, by blocking visibility. Under the heading The Matinee Hat Question, Frank Curzon, manager of the Prince of Wales Theatre, wrote to the Express suggesting women wore small toques instead of huge fashionable hats.

✶ The American Spirella company announced it was building a factory in Letchworth. Bosses had chosen the garden city because of its healthful location and beautiful surroundings. Maybe they were influenced by the first arbor day in March, when trees were planted and a procession took place from the Skittles Inn.

✶ A labourer and his wife from Biggleswade were sent to prison for two months for neglecting their six children, aged from 13 to one year old. The children were covered in vermin and lice, sleeping in bedrooms that smelt abominably and looked half starved.

✶ A white goods sale was advertised in the Express – but this one did not include any electrical goods. Instead it consisted of beautifully worked examples of dainty underwear and dresses.

✶ Hitchin was shaken by news that a body had been recovered from the River Hiz in the grounds of the Priory. It proved to be that of Mr Delmé-Radcliffe's head gardener Frederick Brandon, who had committed suicide while under notice to quit.

"The foreman of the inquest jury said they were very sorry this had happened on Mr Delmé-Radcliffe's premises as he had been a kind master to Brandon." reported the Express.

His death was followed within days by that of a gamekeeper at Benington, who killed himself because he was worried about losing birds.

✶ In June General Sir R S Baden-Powell, 'the hero of Mafeking and the idol of every Boy Scout in England' came to Ickleford Manor for a rally.

The Union Jack was raised and war songs chanted while the youngsters put up tents, made camp fires, and demonstrated drill and signalling.

Baden-Powell walked into the crowd where he "cheerily advised the boys to become recruits."

Scoutmaster Hollis then called for three Scout cheers for the Chief Scout. "The singing of God Save the King was followed by ringing cheers for His Majesty."

✶ Eager readers were promised a treat in October's Express – a special agricultural article entitled "high class pig breeding."

✶ "A practical attempt" was made at Letchworth in November to solve the domestic servant problem. The Countess of Aberdeen opened Homesgarth, a block of 32 houses to be run on co-operative principles with a central administration building, a dining hall, washing and smoking rooms and a manageress responsible for catering and overseeing the servants, who would work in the attached houses.

If this middle class model worked it was proposed to set up something similar for artisans, to relieve their wives of some of their daily toil.

The servants benefitted by not having to live in their employers' house, having regular hours and easy work due to modern labour-saving devices said Ebenezer Howard.

✶ Mr E Daniell of Hatfield disinherited his eldest son Edward because he had become a Roman Catholic. He: "Had caused great sorrow to his parents," reported the Express.

*A humorous look at the Garden City freaks who were not wanted in Hitchin. Among the comments in the cartoon are: "Single life hotel, French polished rice always ready," "Visitors are requested not to teaze the citizens," This way to the non-tox pub," "Danger here without a guide," "To the hairy-headed banana munchers," "Nuts are sold here for the bald-headed nut-peckers," "To the non-tox birds at Birds Hill," and "To the long nebbed sandle footed raisin snifters." A boy demands: "Daddy, I want to see them feed."*

# Bigamy and two claimants to a will

The respectable widow who walked into Kensington police station was immediately rushed and gushed over. But within moments she was being passed along to a senior officer – bigamy, a doubtful will and a husband pretending to be a brother-in-law were too much for a constable to handle.

Dorothy Josephine Wagstaff had come to confess, to make an end to blackmail and threats. "I gave myself up because I have been terrorised so much by the other side," she explained. "It's a perfect worry to me and makes me quite ill."

Within weeks, in January 1907, she was seated in the dock, admitting bigamy and displaying considerable emotion as her story unfolded.

Twenty-three years earlier, while a young nurse, she had married medical student Alfred Jalland. But on the very night of the wedding he had vanished and, after a few worried weeks, she reverted to her maiden name and went back to work. She heard of her errant husband from time to time and the news was not good.

He was scraping a living as a medical assistant, dabbling in drink and drugs when he had the money. In contrast his wife did well and rose to be the matron of an asylum.

By 1892 she had more than one admirer. The most persistent was a catch indeed, a high sheriff and deputy lieutenant of Bedfordshire, the owner of a London house and Manor Park at Potton. James Poole Wagstaff's fortune was valued at £180,000, he boasted a startling set of whiskers, a profligate past and a reputation as "a character." Now he wanted to settle down and had fallen head over heels in love with the comely matron.

He was quite undeterred by her unconsummated marriage and not even the surprise appearance of the missing husband, Alfred Jalland, put him off.

Jalland was now sick and in need of nursing after swallowing a dose of strychnine that left him with a form of paralysis of the spinal cord.

*Manor Park, Potton, the home of the Wagstaffs*

Who better to help him in his hour of need than his spouse, a qualified nurse and a matron? He sent word he needed her.

The forgiving wife went, cared for him assiduously and even slept at his lodgings. While she was tending her unsatisfactory spouse, Mr Wagstaff made frequent visits to the house and, for a fancy never explained, called himself Dr Fitzjames and claimed to be Mr Jalland's doctor.

He made no secret of his affection for Dorothy Josephine and his concern for her welfare, telling Jalland: "What a pity that a splendid woman like your wife should go out in the world as a single woman and take up these positions."

Mr Jalland was certainly not going to keep her – in fact it was the other way about as Mr Wagstaff gave him several gifts of money to help him out.

By January 1893, Mr Wagstaff was determined to settle everything and have Mrs Jalland for himself. He met her husband at Charing Cross and, in the station restaurant, told him his true name and revealed his intentions.

Mr Ogden Lawrence KC, cross questioning Mr Jalland later, was brutal. "I think the bargain was made that you should sell your wife for £25," he declared. Angrily Mr Jalland denied it. "I certainly did not sell my wife," he cried. "He gave me £25 as a present."

Mr Wagstaff, discussing the situation over luncheon, had asked Mr Jalland if he could provide a home for his wife because:

"*It was a pity so fine a woman should have to knock about the world; it was a cruel thing for her.*"

Pity or not, Mr Jalland had no way of supporting his wife and said so. Mr Wagstaff looked him straight in the eye and dropped his bombshell. "In this situation I am going to ask you to allow her to become my wife," he explained to the shocked husband. "I can make her happy until the end of my days." Mr Jalland choked over his drink. "I have been very unfair to her I know," he cried. "But it would certainly be bigamy!" His companion was quite calm and merely said: "Oh, my dear fellow, that will be all right.

"You have never supported her or been a husband to her. I am a JP and know about the law. All you have to do is hold your tongue and say nothing."

Mr Jalland was not reassured – he admitted in court he knew it was wrong, "absolutely wrong," although he denied conniving at his wife's bigamy.

> '*A bargain was made you should sell your wife*'

Mrs Jalland was persuaded to give up her life in London and come to Potton as Mr Wagstaff's housekeeper, claiming to be the widow of a Mr Gibson Jalland. She even had visiting cards printed in that name to give to new friends and acquaintances.

From March until December, 1893, she lived as Mr Wagstaff's platonic companion, telling the court "there was never intimacy between them before the marriage ceremony."

No doubt this was a major factor in Mr Wagstaff's decision to break the law and marry his love. Another motive, conjectured in court, may have been "to put himself right in the eyes of the county he was living in."

Whatever the reason, they were married late in the year, announcing the fact through the pages of the Hertfordshire Express, and they went on a honeymoon tour of Italy.

Their married life seemed a contented affair, although marred by the death of their only child, Dorothy, at nine months. But in 1903 Mr Wagstaff died and his widow's troubles began in earnest.

Hearing all the particulars of the case, seeing Mrs Jalland/Wagstaff before him, the judge sentenced her to three days' imprisonment. Since she had already served that long on remand, she was immediately free.

It was far from the end of the story though. Mrs Wagstaff had not confessed to salve a guilty conscience but because of pressure from her in-laws, clamouring for their share from the will.

Two legal battles ensued, at which her reputation and that of both her husbands were dragged through the Edwardian mud.

As a fascinating aside, two cousins were also locked in legal dispute as to which of them was left a revisionary interest in Mr Wagstaff's will, as the eldest surviving son of "my cousin John."

Unfortunately for legal clarity, Mr Wagstaff had two.

In the blue corner, meet Mr Berners Shelley Wagstaff of Middlesex, the eldest surviving son of Mr Wagstaff's cousin John.

In the red corner stands John Wagstaff, the eldest surviving son of another John Wagstaff, also cousin to the bigamous but rich and dead old man.

At centre stage, fighting all the way, is Mrs Jalland/Wagstaff, intending to keep her life interest in the £180,000 estate, worth £5,000 a year, as bequeathed to her with the words "to my wife as long as she remains a widow."

The cousins John were united on one point – Mrs Wagstaff could not be the heir to the fortune because she had not been a wife and therefore could not be a widow.

Her argument was equally simple – since her husband knew she was already married, indeed prompted the bigamy, he obviously meant her to inherit. Mr Rufus Isaacs, appearing for one John's son, said the truth about the bigamy rested on her word alone and called her:

"A clever, astute woman who did not possess moral sense in any great degree."

He was even harder on Mr Jalland, as: "On his own confession, drink and drugs had effectively dulled any moral sense he ever possessed." He found the decisive luncheon at Charing Cross an amazing affair.

"There was no bargaining, no haggling about price, apparently, but the wife passed to Mr Wagstaff and some of Mr Wagstaff's money passed to Mr Jalland." Witnesses began to appear. One, the coachman/butler, handyman Thomas Hill, was compared to Sam Weller from *Pickwick Papers* by the judge. Mr Hill told the court Mrs Wagstaff's state was no secret.

"She was a woman posing as a widow and he heard Mr Wagstaff say to Mr Jalland, what a fine woman I have made of your wife. Look what gold can do."

Jalland, it appeared had become a regular visitor at Potton, passing himself off as Mrs Jalland/Wagstaff's brother in law. So close had this odd couple become that he was installed at Manor Park in 1907, living in one of the attic rooms.

The cook Mary Wakes knew the truth too – Mrs Wagstaff had told her the truth and Mr Wagstaff paid her £10 to keep it a secret. He made her promise on the Bible not to tell.

The cousins argued about which of them sat more often on the Wagstaff knee, what the old man had told their fathers and which one was meant to be the favoured John. It was all in vain, that issue was left unresolved.

There was no doubt who was the victor of the day though – Mrs Wagstaff, totally vindicated by Mr Justice Kekewich.

Mr Wagstaff, he said, was eccentric and his wife/widow had been through a painful ordeal.

"I have come to the conclusion she was telling the truth," he said, dismissing the legal wrangling over the word "widow."

Mr Wagstaff was determined to brave it out even after death, acting the part of a married man taking care of his dear wife. It was foolish, but if he had meant widow in its strict sense, it would have been "a cruel mockery and something worse" – the judge found it difficult to put his horror into words.

He was sure Mr Wagstaff meant to provide for his "wife." Mrs Jalland, he concluded, was entitled to a life interest in the estate until she contracted a marriage subsequent to the death of Mr Wagstaff.

The relieved wife/widow went straight home, to Manor Park at Potton, to celebrate the end of her terrible ordeal. She was greeted with joy and fanfares.

She arrived at Biggleswade Station at 5.30pm, and travelled on in a coach and pair. At Potton the fire brigade, spruce and trim in their uniforms, were waiting to meet her. They stopped the coach, removed the horses from the shafts and pulled the carriage up to Manor Park themselves.

There a great crowd of people was assembled, cheering enthusiastically as she approached. The brass band struck up "See the conquering hero comes" and "Home sweet home."

The local police sergeant tried to keep the crowd from going up the drive but they took no notice at all, pushing past and gathering in front of the mansion. As Mrs Wagstaff alighted from the coach they broke into three tremendous cheers.

Mrs Wagstaff was overwhelmed. She spoke briefly, thanking them for their kindness and saying she had not expected such an enthusiastic reception.

"I will not forget it," she told the crowd, looking from them to the bright flags flying in front of the house and over her gates.

She hoped to return their kindness by giving them a dinner, she added, turning towards the door. But they would not let her go yet – again and again and again there were cheers, the band repeated "Home sweet home" and finally, amazed by the reception and the warmth from the crowd, Mrs Wagstaff walked back into the house.

The cousins John and Berners Shelley did not give up so easily. In November, 1907, they appealed, and their case was heard before the Master of the Rolls and two Lords Justice.

The three eminent men agreed with their colleague, Mr Justice Kekewich.

The Master of the Rolls was impressed that Mrs Wagstaff's testimony had been unshaken by the severe cross examination. It was evident, he added, that Mr Wagstaff was seized with a great passion to make Mrs Jalland his wife and that he was willing to face and risk anything to accomplish his desire and to persuade her that the marriage would not be bigamous.

His eminent friends agreed and once again Mrs Wagstaff left the court, a free and a rich woman, while the sons of the cousins John gnashed their teeth and disputed their claims.

> **'I will not forget it,' she told the crowd**

# The angry vicar who followed Christ

THE Rev Robert Charles Fillingham, low church vicar of Hexton, was an extraordinary character, fearless in pursuit of what he deemed right.

When he stood in front of a crowd he mesmerised them, adjusting his pince-nez and moving his body from side to side, enunciating like an actor. One observer, who heard the vicar address a meeting in Letchworth in August 1907, wrote:

*"Words fall from his mouth like a torrent. He flings himself about in the desk and now and again turns round and tries to look at his back."*

He found the Rev Fillingham compulsive, although he was not physically arresting, being under medium height, with a substantial figure, mobile features and a nervous manner.

He snapped his mouth defiantly shut, glared scornfully around him and was not to be deflected from his purpose. His forceful and vigorous personality was made a little more approachable by a sense of humour and an unexpected interest in the good things of life.

The vicar's character appeared to be a mass of contradictions. The observer went on:

*"Here is a man who baffles all our inquiry, not to be included in any category known to us, a man who is alone and apart."*

He was "eternally right in an eternally wrong way." and "A man with the soul of a poet and the tricks of an acrobat, a man who preaches non-resistance at the point of a sword...a good man pretending to be a bad one."

He was also certain he was utterly right and loved to face rebellion with "rare and unparalleled courage."

Adjectives drop like grains of sand from the observer's lips – tremendous force of character, boundless energy, restlessness, sceptical, revolutionary.

*"It is impossible to sum him up in words. He reverses all formula and contradicts all experience."*

*Bancroft, Hitchin, pictured in about 1920*

Having admitted defeat, immediately the observer starts trying to pin the vicar down again. *"He has a passion for truth and a sublime disregard of persons and consequences. He cares nothing about hurting our feelings; he would indeed as soon hurt them as not. He seems to delight in causing aggravation and is happy when he can rub us up the wrong way."*

But the observer is won over, as so many were. "He has a message for our times and most of us are in sore need of the rough handling he can give us."

The Anglican church was not always so sympathetic and the Rev Fillingham was involved in numerous altercations with parishioners, fellow priests and the hierarchy after arriving at Hexton in 1891.

By 1900 he had fallen out badly with the leading member of his congregation, Mr Torr of Hexton House, over some box trees in the churchyard and the vicar's Protestant campaign.

Mr Torr took to walking out during the service to show his disapproval, departing by the chancel door during the hymn before the sermon. But one Sunday night the wily vicar locked the door quietly and then watched with considerable amusement as Mr Torr struggled to get out.

As he pulled on the handle the vicar announced the title of the next hymn: "Knocking, knocking, who is there?" Finally Mr Torr was forced to walk the length of the nave followed by barely suppressed laughter from the congregation, who generally thought their eccentric vicar rather a good chap.

They approved of the way he attracted publicity and brought a stream of visitors into services to hear him preach. But he was a man who could go too far and he became the centre of another notorious incident in January 1900, when he was charged with indecent behaviour in a packed church at Kettlebaston, Suffolk.

He could not get a seat in the pews and stood ostentatiously by the door jotting down points in a notebook. He was accompanied by 54 followers, some his parishioners, who stood up as one during the prayer of consecration and chanted: "This is idolatry Protestants. Leave this house of Baal."

*Rev Fillingham's grave at Hexton Church*

Rev Fillingham appeared in court in March, where Mr Dibdin KC, for the prosecution, accused him of a very gross act and "a most impudent interpretation of divine service by a gentleman who was himself a beneficed clergyman, who ought to have known better." He was fined.

In October 1901, the Express reported that the fiery reverend was in trouble for preaching at a Baptist church in Maida Vale. He was quite unrepentant despite rumours of a church inhibition after allowing a Noncon-formist to preach at Hexton. "I mean to go on with it," he said.

He incurred the disgust of many Americans in November, after writing to the president of the United States asking him to stop the Boer War: "Prompted by the single desire to see the end of this awful and useless bloodshed."

He told President Theodore Roosevelt: "Nearly half of the people of England have from the first felt this war to be unnecessary, disgraceful and unjust. These feelings have been intensified by the methods pursued by our government – farm burnings, concentration camps, savage proclamations contrary to the usages of warfare. We feel as patriots that these things are bringing an indelible disgrace on the English name."

He asked the president to intervene, adding: "The continuance of the struggle is to us ruinous and disastrous and we shall not be long able to endure the strain in men and money."

The president made it clear he was strictly neutral on the matter but an article in a Yankee paper was, reported the Express, full of condemnation for Rev Fillingham.

"For an Englishman to almost ask for an armed intervention seems to me disgraceful and deserving to be the subject of a trial for treason," ran the article, adding it was "exaggeration without excuse."

Such antics soon made the Rev Fillingham well known locally, but he rose to national prominence after founding the Church of the Literal Obedience to the Sermon on the Mount in 1902.

It was in response, he said, to the corruption of the existing church and its failure to take Jesus as the Master as well as the Saviour. "The church was not doing what it could, it did not testify for righteousness or against injustice or poverty or inequality. It was permeated with worldliness." One specific fault was that it did not testify against war. But the new church would be different, and would consist of people pledged to peace, righteousness and equality. It would take Christ at his word.

In 1905 the Rev Fillingham announced he was going to ordain a Mr White to serve as Presbyter in the Church of Jesus Christ, after the manner of the early church.

Mr White was, he said, "a young man of exceptional talents and blameless life." Be that as it may, a furious Bishop of St Albans forbade the ceremony, to be held in Southend in April.

He declared that Rev Fillingham was not qualified to ordain other people but the outspoken vicar announced he would be a coward to draw back. The bishop must be ignorant of early history he said, adding that he was a vindictive and unfair man.

Not everyone agreed with the vicar. At the ordination someone shouted from the congregation: "Fillingham, you are a disgrace to your King and the Church of England.

"I pity poor little White who has fallen into your hands." There was loud applause from part of the church, which worried the Rev Fillingham not at all.

A few days later he announced that they might get him out of the Church of England but "as far as God gives me health and strength I will make things hot for the bishops."

The confrontation was not long delayed, and early in April, 1906, Rev Fillingham was summoned to the ecclesiastical courts. He appeared before the Bishop of St Albans at the Court of Arches, charged with preaching and administering the sacraments in Nonconformist chapels, disobeying a bishop and ordaining a Nonconformist minister in a chapel at Southend.

He turned on the attack, reviling the bishop as a successor, not to the Apostles, but to the high priests who persecuted Christ and who knowingly opposed the truth.

"We who started this little church at Southend the other day were guilty of a literal obedience to Christ's command.

*"If I am a criminal because I try to start such a movement as that, if I am a criminal because I tried to follow in the light of Christ's teaching, then I glory in my crime."*

The bishop remained unimpressed and suspended the Rev Fillingham for two years.

He was already in contention with the criminal courts, for non-payment of a portion of the poor rate due to the parish of Hexton. But in this he had plenty of support from fellow priests and ministers.

Their strong views on Roman Catholics united them into staunch supporters of the passive resistance movement, refusing to pay the educational portion of the poor rate.

The crisis was triggered by the abolition of the school boards, which had financed education in a variable manner round the country. By 1903 every ratepayer had to contribute to the costs of elementary and secondary schools, run by county councils. For the first time a statutory system of secondary education was created.

Wrath and fury scarcely described the reaction of many non conformists, who dubbed the bill "Rome on the rates" because Catholic schools would get funding from the new local education authorities. A passive resistance league was established and its local activities filled the Express newspaper throughout late 1903 and 1904, only tailing off gradually over several years. An early public meeting slammed the iniquitous education act as a violation of civil and religious rights.

Many people seemed to regard Roman Catholics as direct disciples of the devil.

A public meeting in Hitchin's Market Place "certainly did not err on the side of charity," reported the Express, in 1905. "Among the statements were that Catholics filled our prisons and our lunatic asylums, kept the police going and were responsible for half the poor rate. The confessional was said to be a direct incentive to sin."

In July several lectures entitled *Know Popery* were held under the auspices of the Protestant Alliance. Mr J Caplin contrasted the Catholic's degrading and worldly worship and the unholiness of the confessional with the Protestant's beautiful simplicity and belief in forgiveness by atonement.

At the second meeting the audience had been infiltrated by Catholics, who put up a heated defence of their faith and almost came to blows with their hosts.

The Rev Clement Bryer, pastor at Hitchin Congregational Church, preached a furious anti-Catholic sermon on the anniversary of the Gunpowder plot the same year.

The Reformation, he declared, had revived true Christianity but today they stood in danger of again losing it. He urged the congregation to do all in their power to prevent this by remaining true to the teaching of Christ.

The Rev Fillingham was a strong supporter, declaring the times were dangerous and the episcopal church was at risk from the high church movement. He condemned the government for helping Catholics to capture the schools.

*"That made the danger 10 times more serious and more necessary that Protestants of all denominations should fight together."*

As early as the summer of 1902 meetings were held protesting at the education bill. After one at Baldock Town Hall a resolution was sent to the MP declaring: "That the prevalence of the Romish heresy among a large section of the clergy of the established church makes them unfit and untrustworthy guardians of religious education in the schools of the nation."

If they got their hands on the young, the resolution went on: "The purity and the faith and the freedom of the English people" would be in danger. A few weeks later, at a meeting in Hitchin, the Rev Bryer declared the education bill was unjust and unfair.

The crisis came in Hitchin in January 1904, when 25 passive resistors prepared to go to jail for their beliefs. Instead their debts were paid anonymously through Messrs Hawkins and Co – much to their chagrin. Charles Messent, of Little Belville, said:

*"They dare not suffer us to appear in the police court to expose its injustice."*

A meeting was held at the Primitive Methodist Church Hall to protest. The Rev Bryer said he had not thought anyone in Hitchin capable of such a mean and underhand thing.

It was well known they were of the opinion that the education act inflicted a serious injury on the Free Churches of this country and they were prepared to go to prison to resist this iniquitous act.

As free churchmen they could not pay for the teaching of doctrines which they solemnly believed were contrary to the New Testament.

If they sat still and made no protest the effect in 15 or 20 years' time would be that a whole generation would be infected.

The Express took a more cynical view, reporting that an increased number of conscientious objectors, real or pretended, were expected to register when the new rate comes to be paid: "Since there are no doubt many quite willing to have the educational portion paid for them on any pretext whatever."

No one stepped in to help the passive resistors in Stevenage and nine appeared in court in February, 1904. They included the Rev Vernon Bird, pastor of Bunyan Baptist Church and Mr Sloan of the China Inland Mission, represented by his wife. Mrs Sloan told the magistrates she could only feel:

*"It was a privilege to have had the opportunity of taking up the position for the Lord. The Church of Rome is determined to have the children."*

Mr Bird declared: "If people do not make a bold stand and keep it, we shall be ruined by Romanism and mammon worship."

The Rev Fillingham told the Express he was being persecuted.

*"I must pay for children to be taught to worship an idol; I must pay for children to be taught to invoke the Virgin Mary; I must pay for children to be taught that to be Nonconformist is to be guilty of mortal sin; or else my property must be seized or I must go to gaol."*

He said he was fighting for liberty of conscience and to prevent the sham priests of ritualism from undoing the work of the Reformation. The act would, he believed, bring the nation into danger "for our greatness is bound up in Protestantism."

When the half-yearly rate payment became due in July 1904, 21 ratepayers in Hitchin refused to settle in full. Only one, Ebenezer Housden of Ellenslie, York Road, actually went to prison, for a month. "The sentence caused a great stir among the Nonconformists of the town," reported the Express – it also attracted attention nationally. Mr Housden, a young man living at home with his mother, was singled out because of poverty – the bailiffs could not find enough goods to pay what he owed.

After 16 days in prison he was unexpectedly released from St Albans jail. At first he had no idea why, but it emerged that the debt had been paid anonymously.

## 'They were called to fight, not to rest'

He became a 15-minute hero, feted by the mayor of St Albans, and told Express readers he had chopped wood in prison, had two hours exercise a day and read a lot.

The issue would not go away and the Express letters page was full of comments and reports. In October, 1904, a public meeting was held at Hitchin Town Hall. The audience heard that nationally 34,910 summonses had been issued, 1,305 forced sales taken place and 49 people had gone to jail – seven of them twice.

James Everett, secretary of the national Passive Resistance League, said: "We are trying to save the children from having their souls soiled and from having them taught doctrines which we as Free Churchman regard as rank blasphemy."

The Rev Fillingham was summonsed yet again in August 1905 but refused to come to court, sending a message that "if I appeared I would be recognising you as a court of justice."

Since the magistrates were enforcing the teaching of idolatry and superstition, their court was a court of injustice. "I regard the educational act as unconstitutional," he added.

The magistrates disregarded his letter and issued a distress warrant to confiscate goods to the value of the debt. Bailiffs seized his gold watch in September.

Shortly afterwards the vicar laid out his philosophy in a letter to the London papers.

"The churches preach dogmas Christ never dreamed of. Christ – who was, whether intentional or not, the greatest social reformer that ever lived – laid down certain laws, which if obeyed would have regenerated humanity. There was to be no war, no law court, no prosecutors, no poverty. The world would have became paradise. But Christians soon became corrupt."

He filled in the two years of his church suspension by preaching in Nonconformist pulpits around the country, bringing yet more criticism on his head.

He treated the accusation of schism with contempt and sneered: "The man who thought the infinite God was confined to a certain body of men was on the level of an African savage in the primeval forest, who thought his god belonged to his tribe alone."

He stimulated some lively debate in the Express in 1907, when he wrote a pamphlet on the Short Life of the Blessed Virgin Mary, dismissing the virgin birth as simply legend. In the end the editor called a halt to the correspondence.

Trouble followed the bold vicar wherever he went. In September 1907 he visited Tuam in Ireland, leaving religious tracts in the cathedral and various shops.

It was not long before someone realised how inflammatory they were and a crowd formed, intent on driving the Rev Fillingham out of town.

As he walked to the railway station, the mob seized him and threw him to the ground, leaving him unconscious by the side of the road.

The vicar was puzzled. His tracts: "Were not attacking Roman Catholics in any way, but explaining some of the new theology, and showing how it makes it possible to believe old dogmas when interpreted in a rational fashion."

So did his parishioners, who welcomed him back with open arms in March, 1908. "His reception by the villagers was extremely hearty," reported the Express. A banner was stretched across the road, reading 'Welcome' and the vicarage was gaily decorated with flags and bunting.

"The parishioners vied with each other in congratulating him and the church bells rang merrily." In his first sermon he told them: "In the spiritual life they could not have peace, they were called to fight, not to rest."

But the struggle was almost over for the Rev Fillingham. On December 8, while travelling from Rome to England on the *train de luxe*, he was taken ill. As the train pulled into Dijon station at 2.35pm his manservant leapt out to summon help. The vicar was carried to a first aid station and then to hospital, where he died at 5.30 that afternoon, of a heart attack. He was just 48 years old.

Shock and consternation greeted the news in Hexton, where a large crowd gathered for the funeral. The vicar, perhaps with a strange premonition, had recently told his mother he did not want to be buried in the family vault, but in the village churchyard: "Where the happiest period of my life had been spent."

The congregation returned his gratitude: "Showing all tenderness to one who would himself say he had many faults," as Canon Griffiths put it at the funeral.

The old cliché beloved for eulogies was indeed true – they would not see his like again. As the Express commented:
*"He held very strong views and he was absolutely fierce in his mode of expressing them."*

The affection for this wild, wayward, controversial spirit could not be denied.

> 'There was to have been no war, no law court, no prosecutors, no poverty'

# It was Christmas Day at the workhouse

Miss Gates was hysterical by the time she reached the workhouse. She had got into the cart without a qualm, believing she was going for a drive with that nice Mr Prater, and there was nothing odd about travelling from her Codicote home towards Hitchin. But when she arrived at Chalkdell and saw the fearsome buildings, she knew.

The staff at the workhouse were in a quandary. Miss Gates was remonstrating loudly about being taken in, getting very upset and excited, but it was late at night and no-one was prepared to drive her home.

Finally they admitted her but they were so worried about her state that the doctor arranged for an attendant to sit with her through the night. The next day, March 23, 1911, Miss Gates applied for her discharge and in late April the guardians found themselves discussing her case.

It was obvious her brother-in-law wanted to be rid of her. He had already written to the guardians saying she was not capable of self-protection and persuaded the relieving officer Mr Prater that she needed care, but the doctor would not sign a detention order.

Miss Gates had cooled down now and was quite calm, although adamant she did not want to stay.

The workhouse master Mr Knight told the guardians he could not keep Miss Gates against her will. It would be different if one of her relatives could persuade her to stay. Her home was still intact – Mr Knight had sent word to her relatives not to dispose of anything or get rid of her cottage until the issue was settled.

The family were still anxious for her to live in the workhouse but, if necessary, Mr Knight would turn her onto the streets and force them to take her home.

At the workhouse Miss Gates, unloved and unwanted, prepared to leave. Sad as her plight was, at least she would be free.

The poor "would only approach the workhouse as a rule when they were on the borders of starvation and the brink of despair," declared The Hon Mrs Ernest Fordham, of Odsey, in April, 1907.

One of her in-laws, Edward Snow Fordham of Ashwell Bury, presided at the North London Police Court and his cases were regularly reported in the Express. A man described as "a poor old worn-out circus performer" applied to him for assistance in October 1900.

*The Hitchin workhouse band*

Mr Fordham described his case as one of chronic distress but told him there was no choice but to go to the workhouse. The poor man broke down, crying: "I can't."

But for others the workhouse did offer welcome relief and they were prepared to cheat to get in. In 1902 James Dunham appeared before Hitchin Magistrates after trying to gain admission by professing to be destitute when he actually had 4s 6d cash on him.

It proved a bad move – he ended up in prison instead, sentenced to seven days' hard labour.

Dunham was one of the "undeserving poor" who caused such headaches to the guardians, responsible for administering a system dating back to 1834. Along with the mass of respectable, labouring folk who fell on hard times, Dunham and his like were a major issue in Edwardian times.

There was a pauper to every 35 inhabitants in Hitchin in 1903, with a ratio of one to 21 in Royston and one to 42 in Welwyn.

Keeping them cost money and the guardians were, first and foremost, cost conscious. Some had more compassion than others, but they were always keen to spend as little as possible.

Conditions at Hitchin workhouse became a matter of national controversy when the Daily Mail smuggled in a reporter, pretending he was a tramp. The article, under the byline Bart Kennedy, caused an enormous row in North Herts in 1904.

Mr Kennedy claimed the treatment he had received was excessively rough and inhuman. He arrived at the workhouse in Chalkdell after walking 26 miles (or at least claiming to) and was immediately searched.

His supper was one piece of dry bread and he was put to sleep on a stone floor in a room crowded with others. In the corner was a bath half full of dirty water, already used by 13 men.

*The odour was not good or, as Mr Kennedy put it: "In that room was the curious, lowering, sickening smell of low lodging houses."*

His only covering were two vermin-infested blankets. Things did not improve in the morning, when he was given dry bread for breakfast and had to drink water from a bucket shared with everyone else. Then he was set to work, as payment for his night's lodging and food and as a deterrent to coming back.

The tramps had to unpick four pounds of unbeaten oakum, a rope which had been soaked in tar, separating it into strips six to nine inches long.

It was a dreadful task as the rope was very hard and Mr Kennedy did not take kindly to it.

Fortunately for him, because he had been given the floor to sleep on, he was allowed to go at 10.30am, but the men who arrived in time for a bed had to stay at their task all day.

Mr Kennedy declared this work was "a last torture" and ranted against: "The cruel and damnable workhouse system that disgraces England." The guardians were furious when the Daily Mail article appeared and immediately issued a long statement refuting the allegations.

*West Alley, pictured between 1880 and 1900*

Referring to Mr Kennedy's arrival they stated:
*"It is not needful for casuals of the common type that at their journey's end they should be ushered into richly furnished apartments, there to be treated as honoured guests and finally invited to lay their weary limbs on beds of swansdown."*

His ideas were "sentimentalism gone mad."

They accused him of grossly exaggerating his descriptions of the home and the way it dealt with casual paupers. No man living, they declared, could pick four pounds of unbeaten oakum in a day.

Half that was reckoned to be a good day's work in prison, where they were used to it. The bath water in the dormitory had been changed five times for 10 men and the blankets had just been fumigated.

*Patients at Hitchin Infirmary in Bedford Road, pictured outside in 1897*

Not everyone was convinced by the guardians' protests. One Hitchin resident wrote to the Express saying it was ironic that a Utopian city (Letchworth) was being created on the edge of Hitchin, where the workhouse meted out "treatment that was not fit for a dog."

This was not the impression taken away by a party of Americans visiting the workhouse in 1913. They were very impressed. They met the oldest inhabitant, 94-year-old Ann Chalkley, who told them she darned all the workhouse stockings.

*She turned to the old lady sitting next to her and remarked:*
*"She's 87 and she threads my needle."*
*The Express reporter commented:*
*"Although 94, Ann is said to have never found a sweetheart."*

Among the bedridden patients, the Americans met a crippled girl engaged in some beautiful crochet work and a girl with a withered hand whose knitting was admired. There were also several blind people.

The Americans envied the conditions and the way different needs were catered for. At home, they said, the feeble-minded, ordinary invalids and epileptics were all put in the same ward.

They were also taken with the same tramp wards that had so appalled Bart Kennedy. One commented: "I had worse accommodation in steerage once."

Interest was keen in the tramps' task of pounding stones and the Americans asked if it wouldn't be better for them to chop wood. "Mr Armstrong explained that this task was more congenial to the old men of the house," reported the Express.

In Belgium experts had come up with an idea they much admired. If a man was found with no fixed abode and insufficient money to keep himself for more than two days, he was immediately sent to prison for up to five years.

There he was forced to learn a trade and, on his release, he was an asset to the community instead of a burden. This scheme apparently helped all with few exceptions – those of bad habits, mental deficiency or with hereditary problems.

Old age pensions came into force in January

1909. By 1913 the number of elderly people who were claiming out-relief had plummeted since so many were receiving a pension instead. An editorial in the Express was enthusiastic about the result. Out-relief was capricious and inadequate and hurt people's pride, the writer commented.

"Under the old system aged persons who had worked and striven all their lives on wages which presented no margin for thrift were confronted when, at last age compelled a relaxation of labour, with the alternative "of the house" or a miserable pittance paid grudgingly and carrying with it what to simple homely minds meant shame and degradation and bitter thought."

As far as the elderly were concerned: "The workhouse was now a home of rest, where those who have few ties and would be a burden to themselves, could find a refuge."

This really was sentimentalism gone mad. It was a place of last resort, and the guardians often had only one object in mind – economy. Early in 1903 a bricklayer, born and bred in Hitchin, asked for a shilling to pay the cemetery fee for burying his stillborn child.

Hearing that he had not been able to work for eight weeks one guardian muttered: "He didn't want to do any," and the appeal was dismissed unanimously.

Lavinia Day applied for an increase in her out relief allowance in October 1902. The Board of Guardians were told that she rented a room which she kept clean and neat and made some money sewing. "She is very respectable and much respected," explained the clerk. But her eyesight was failing and she needed a larger allowance from the guardians.

They agreed but one commented: "The woman would be much better off in the workhouse than paying 3/6d a week for rent."

But a second similar case was immediately rejected when the clerk commented that the applicant was not clean and not in good surroundings.

A widow from Kimpton did not get much sympathy either when she asked for out relief in May 1903. The story was reported under the headline: "A striking case of thriftlessness."

Her husband had been a bricklayer earning good money and should have been able to "lay up enough for their old age. But he spent all the money in the pub and his wife encouraged him to it."

The guardians told her she must either manage on her own or come into the workhouse to live.

There was no such thing as a free dinner at the workhouse and casual tramps, if lucky enough to escape unpicking oakum, had to break stones instead. The new master of the workhouse in 1903 was Mr W Cook, who had a reputation for being hard on tramps.

At Buntingford, where he had been in charge, he reduced the numbers calling in for a bed from 10 a day to just one. He told the Hitchin guardians: "I made them do their work and detained them if they did not.

> 'The woman would be much better off in the workhouse'

"I made the distinction between honest work seekers and tramps but there were not many of the former class."

Hitchin proved a tough nut to crack and the number of tramps rose during his first few months in post. In November he increased their work to four pounds of oakum a day but sometimes they managed to slip out before the task was completed.

Old hands used a boot tip to help with the unpicking – a fiddle not allowed in prison, apparently. Mr Cook was urged by the guardians to enforce the regulations more stringently.

They were in a more compassionate mood by January 1905, when the tramps were being asked to break stones as their allotted task.

Although they could legally demand tramps to tackle 13cwt of stones a day, the guardians decided to set the figure at eight. Even that was too much for chairman William Hill, who commented: "It is almost impossible for anyone to do it." The Rev Mr Jowitt suggested that Mr Cook be asked to incline on the side of mercy.

The secrets of a tramp's tricks were revealed to Express readers in late January, 1912. The writer had gained admission to Hitchin casual ward to talk to the "Weary Willies" staying there but they certainly hadn't won him over to their way of life.

"The roadster of today is virtually as cunning as the proverbial heathen Chinee. From being a pariah he has cultivated a low standard of artfulness," he commented.

He was also, asserted the writer, likely to be

bordering on imbecility in one form or another "and, as is well-known, there is no more cunning person than an imbecile."

One trick concerned tobacco. "Weary Willie dearly loves his little dirty clay pipe," stated the writer. Mostly he smoked HHU or hand picked, hard-up, meaning fag ends taken from the gutter.

As tobacco was banned at Hitchin Workhouse the tramps would smuggle it in, sometimes in their boots or on a string round their neck. Some had hair so straggly they could conceal threads of tobacco in their beards or on their heads.

Weary Willies would do anything to avoid working, declared the writer, and were adept at feigning illness to get out of stone breaking. "I have known a tramp open an old wound in his leg to obtain respite from work and a few days in the workhouse infirmary."

They also liked to scribble doggerel high up on the walls and could wax poetical. One wrote:

*"When I was young and in my prime,*
*I could break the stones by half past nine.*
*But now I am old and going grey,*
*It takes me nearly all the day."*

A tramp who refused to break up 56lbs of stones at Hitchin Workhouse was brought into court in January 1911, accused of refusing to perform his allotted task while a casual pauper and assaulting William Elliott, labour master.

Charles Smith had caused a scene because he had been fed nothing but bread and water. He started brawling with Elliott, each claiming they had been hit by the other, and Smith ended up needing two stitches in a cut over his eye. Elliott testified:

*"In trying to keep the defendant in his cell Smith's head came into contact with the door.*
*I used no unnecessary force."*

Smith protested loudly. "You kicked me on the head," he yelled, adding: "I'm a working man and I don't want to work on bread and water."

The court believed Elliott and Smith departed for 14 days in the even harsher environment of St Albans jail.

Six male inmates staged a strike at the workhouse in November 1907, refusing to pick oakum because they were cold from lying on the floor all night. They said there was no hot water and their window was broken – apparently it had been smashed by Jane Whiskin, a destitute wayfarer.

Herbert May got an unusually sympathetic hearing when he appeared before Hitchin magistrates in October, 1907, charged with destroying his own clothing while an inmate at Hitchin Union. Described as a refractory tramp, he had been admitted to the casual ward one evening at 6pm and next morning his trousers were found torn up beside him.

Mr May told the magistrates he was ashamed to walk about in the trousers. A sawyer by trade, he had been invalided out of the Navy and was making his way north to get work on a ship. The magistrates ordered him to be imprisoned only until the rising of the court.

The new garden city of Letchworth provided work for numerous labourers and encouraged a variety of unemployed men to pour into the area from all over the country – often to be disappointed.

In October 1905 Hitchin guardians heard that 185 casual paupers had been relieved in one recent week

*Hitchin slums at Thorpe's Yard off Queen Street in the late 1920s*

– 153 seeking work, 14 habitual vagrants, and 14 women and children. Mr Cook was instructed to write to national papers pointing out that the rumoured work in Letchworth was a myth.

Meanwhile tramps at Luton were being asked to pound stones instead of just breaking them, which needed much more skill.

Sixteen special cells had been set up for the job and a hundredweight of flints had to be reduced to dust by moving a special pestle and mortar apparatus.

The final powder had to be fine enough to pass through a sieve and was used for making bricks.

"The mighty thudding of the stone pounders as they crush the flints into countless atoms is liable to supply a splitting headache to the novice," declared the Express.

Each tramp at Luton was given a hot bath when he arrived, supplied with a clean cotton night shirt and served with eight ounces of bread and a pint of hot or cold water. Women got less bread but gruel or tea to drink. There was bread and cheese for dinner and small babies were given milk and sugar.

Not every tramp was keen on the compulsory bath – one was caught, wearing very little superfluous clothing, climbing out of a window.

In the morning the tramps, who slept in hammocks, were woken at 7am and given a frugal breakfast of bread and water. Many finished work at about 3pm and were allowed to occupy themselves as they liked until their release the following morning.

No one picked oakum at Luton by 1905 and older or sickly tramps were asked to clean and scrub instead.

Harsh as this regime was, it did not equal that of the Dutch, who would put recalcitrant tramps into a cistern and turn on a stream of water. To avoid being drowned the tramp had to operate a pump vigorously. "The discomfort of the method is so extreme that the tramp soon decides he would rather work," commented the Express, with evident relish.

Tramps were only one category of inmates at the workhouse. Another large section were children and orphans. Typical were four youngsters being discussed by Hitchin guardians in April, 1912. Their mother had left them to run off with an organ-grinder and was rather slow to contribute to their upkeep in Hitchin workhouse. Should she be forced to take the children away?

*Kind-hearted Canon Jones thought the best thing for the children was to keep them in the cottage home where they could be well looked after.*

But Mr Dalton thought it would be opening the floodgates if they did that – Hitchin was full of people who would be only too glad to get rid of their children, he said. Fortunately for the youngsters, Canon Jones won the day.

## 'Women got less bread but gruel or tea to drink'

The same argument had been discussed in June 1904, when children from two families had been admitted to the workhouse because their parents were incapable of looking after them.

There was great reluctance to accept them however, one guardian commenting that parents: "should not be relieved of their responsibilities at the expense of the ratepayers."

The case of "the man Alderman" from Codicote occupied the guardians early in the same year.

*His house had been certified as unfit for human habitation, he had been evicted, his wife and five children (one only 18 days old) had been taken into the workhouse – but if he hoped for any sympathy, he was on a sticky wicket.*

Instead the guardians agreed to charge him with neglecting to find any house for his family and allowing them to be chargeable to the rates. But before the proceedings could go through the guardians discovered that Richard Alderman had been jailed for 14 days for being drunk and disorderly.

Guardian A A Armstrong was furious – this was the undeserving poor in all its sordid mendacity, draining resources from the hard-working, ratepaying middle classes.

It was not only the poor who caused problems for the guardians though – so did the staff. A suitable master and matron must be appointed to run the workhouse and only married couples were considered for the posts.

The nervous exhaustion of the matron Mrs

Fowler in 1902 was disastrous news for her husband – when her health completely broke down and she had to leave, so did he.

There was fierce competition for the jobs, with 97 couples applying before Mr and Mrs Cook were appointed from Buntingford.

The nurses were causing a headache too, with the situation reaching a crisis at Hitchin Infirmary in April 1902, as they left in droves. The Board of Guardians were told:

> *"The living was rough, the bedroom accommodation was bad, food was indifferently served. The living at the infirmary was so rough that no refined woman could stand a place like that."*

The vice chairman was confident the problem could be solved. In his experience, he confidently asserted, untidiness often took away a young woman's appetite.

Flowers and clean cloths on the table would bring about a great change.

Christmas was a special time even at the workhouse and the holiday in 1903 was "one of the happiest days they had spent in the institution," reported the Express.

The 192 inmates were given additional food to eat , starting with extra sweet strong tea at breakfast. For lunch they tucked into roast pork, parsnips and plum pudding while the patients in the infirmary could have rabbit if they preferred.

Every man was given tobacco and a pint of beer or, if teetotal, mineral water, while the women had extra tea with sugar. Oranges were distributed to everybody.

Tea included half a pound of cake each, followed by entertainment as matron kindly played the piano for the older inmates, who apparently retired to bed well pleased.

Prominent families in the town sent evergreens for decorations and supplied toys and oranges. Some took their philanthropy very seriously and called in to see the inmates in person during the afternoon.

In Henlow bread was distributed to the poor.

During Christmas 1908 there were 224 people in Hitchin workhouse. "One little privilege that was greatly appreciated was when the old people in the infirmary of both sexes were allowed to dine together, a thing they had never done before," reported the Express.

The children, who were given their presents from the tree on New Year's Eve, were taken to a pantomime in the town and, at Hitchin Hospital, Santa brought five bundles of clothes on Christmas Eve along with toys for the children.

Almost 150 people visited a soup kitchen set up in Bancroft.

The girls from Scott House invited 30 workhouse children to tea. The table looked very pretty, laden with cakes, fruit and crackers. After tea at 4pm the children enjoyed a play, games

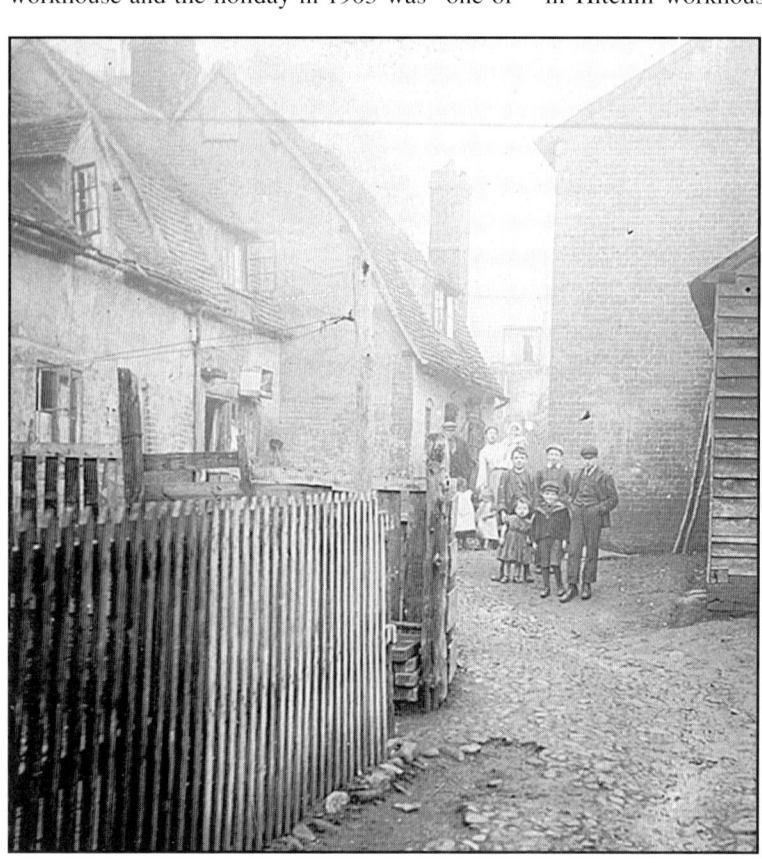

*Thorpe's Yard, Hitchin, pictured in 1911*

music, singing and dancing. Every girl was given a doll nicely dressed with garments to take on and off, while the boys went back with trumpets.

"One little fellow asked if he might take a cracker home for his brother so a parcel was made of the things left over from the tea and given him to take back to those who were prevented from coming."

In 1909 the old chestnut of whether the inmates should be allowed beer for Christmas surfaced again. The Board of Guardians discussed the dilemma in Hitchin, and Canon Jones proposed that no intoxicants should be provided.

He talked about the evils of intemperance and said there might be people in the workhouse trying to resist the lure of alcohol. "Are the guardians going to take responsibility for sending them down the road to ruin?" he thundered.

Mr Dalton was more pragmatic, pointing out that everyone on out relief was getting an extra shilling for Christmas. Much of that would be spent on drink, he was sure.

It was rather illogical to stop the inmates having a beer with their festive lunch.

Rev J W Tilt felt very differently to Canon Jones, warning against treating the inmates as children and denying a small treat to some because one or two may have been drunk on occasion. He won the day and, as always, the beer treat went ahead.

# The poor 'would only approach the workhouse as a rule when they were on the borders of starvation and the brink of despair'

*Almhouses helped the poor – top Skynner's Almhouses in Bancroft in about 1900 and, above, the Biggin in 1907*

# Favourite Express-ions – 1911

★ Farm labourers were being intimidated into voting Conservative, declared Hitchin Liberal MP Julius Bertram in January. Although the ballot was secret, farmers would dismiss their men if they suspected them of not voting Tory. "The employer often stands at the polling station and as the voter comes out demands of him point blank if he voted for the Conservative candidate," said Sir Julius. He condemned the practice as "vilest terrorism."

It was not all bad news for the Liberals though – party members in North Beds were celebrating the recent election victory of Mr Black, known to be a ladies' man. There was no shortage of female fans and several wished to kiss the member, reported the Express.

★ A letter to the Express from someone entitled *Philanthropist* protested at placards advertising an objectionable cinematograph exhibition in Hitchin, showing the latest tragedy in the East End. Such dubious entertainment should not allowed in the Town Hall, he wrote, adding sadly that he expected the shows would be packed.

The audience would need warm coats however. The recent change from gas to electric lighting at Hitchin's Town Hall had not been compensated for by turning up the heating and women in evening dress were especially feeling the chill.

★ The death of an unnamed 72-year-old patient at Three Counties Asylum was worth a few paragraphs in the paper only because she had been a certified lunatic for 63 years, being admitted in July 1848 to Bedford Asylum when she was just nine years old.

She was transferred to Arlesey 12 years later. The case, apparently, "was one of arrested mental development and the deceased retained the childish habit of nursing a doll almost up until the day of her death."

The Express added idly: "To some readers it may prove an interesting arithmetical exercise to calculate the total cost of this patient's maintenance during all these years."

*Staff at Hitchin's Post Office in Brand Street pose for a picture in front of their building*

*The village of Charlton, near Hitchin*

✯ A farmer who didn't report a case of anthrax at Upper Stondon was in trouble in February. Robert Long convinced the magistrates he never thought the cow, sickly for several months, had died of such a serious disease until a second one keeled over. By that time meat from the first had been fed to dogs, a badger (which died) and to a man, who not only ate it with relish but said he wished there was more.

✯ A persistent black and tan collie won approval from staff at Hitchin Hospital in March. He refused to be shooed away until he was finally made a fuss of and fed in the kitchen. When the doctor Mr J Gilbertson arrived he realised the collie had come to his house in Walsworth Road that morning and been turned away. "The dog's perseverance at last met with reward and he received attention," said the Express. His injured foot was also bathed.

✯ When a butcher's assistant, who had worked for six years without any wages, left his job, he was sued by his boss for the return of a £1 loan. John Saunders of Stotfold had been given tobacco and beer and fed puddings by the butcher's wife, but never given cash, while living at home with his father. He was ordered to pay the pound back to his boss over 10 weeks.

✯ Kind Mr Goimbault wrote to the Express in July criticising the practice of docking horses' tails, meaning they could not brush off flies. "To realise only in part their sufferings one would need to spend but a very short time in a field on a hot day without a hat and with one's hands tied behind one," he said.

Eager sightseers left Hitchin at 2.20am one Monday in July to catch a glimpse of competitors in the 1,000-mile air race. At 3.30am they were walking up Offley Hill towards Luton and at 4.15am they saw their first biplane, using a telescope and binoculars, quickly followed by another two. The planes: "Were like great swifts, but unwheeling and unswerving in their flight...quick and undeviating above the dull south horizon."

✯ Letchworthians were as earnest at their summer school as in other areas of their life. In August Mrs Colby lectured on the redemption of the body. Man, she declared, is a thinking animal and should free himself from all sickness, misery, loss and death caused by the failure to perfect his bodily conditions, and the unity of body and mind.

# The plane that dropped like a bird

FEW watched the fatal fall of the Deperdussin monoplane as it seared through the sky. It was early in the morning and most people were in bed or busy in their homes. But there were witnesses who saw the machine drop for 100 feet, turn on its back, then drop again as if to make a final descent.

Some said they saw a body fall from the air, tracking a vertical line to the earth as the plane careered downwards, crashing with a noise that echoed from Willian across to Graveley and beyond.

News of the Deperdussin's fatal last flight – ironically one of its first – spread quickly. The narrow road beyond Letchworth became congested with vehicles and people running to the scene. Many were desperate to help but others, knowing there was no help to be given, came out of idle curiousity.

They found both bodies pinioned under the shattered machine, with one pair of legs visible beyond the carcass. Parts of the fuselage had broken off and were discovered later in the surrounding fields.

The men were smashed beyond recognition but there was no doubt of their identity or purpose. The Deperdussin, piloted by Captain Patrick Hamilton, was part of a huge Army exercise carried out across East Anglia in September 1912, involving an invasion by the Redland Army, to be repulsed by the Blue.

Captain Hamilton, along with his observer Lieutenant Athole Wyness Stuart, was heading for a temporary alighting camp set up at Willian near Letchworth. Eye witness accounts of the crash varied and there were several theories about its cause.

One account read: "I was watching the machine come along, then it seemed to shudder as if it was being stopped; then it dropped like a bird and again righted itself.

"All at once the left wing collapsed, hanging helplessly on its side, and the whole thing fluttered to the ground, just like a bird which had been shot in the wing."

*Crowds gather to watch the funeral procession of Captain Hamilton and Lt Wyness Stuart as it passes along Walsworth Road, Hitchin*

Another was equally graphic. "We were watching the monoplane flying across the village when suddenly there was a loud crash and a report and I thought the machine had exploded. I saw several pieces of stick and spar fall out from the aeroplane which dashed to the ground like a dart. We knew then that an accident had happened and that nothing could prevent those in the machine being dashed to death."

The bodies were taken from the scene in a horse-drawn ambulance, accompanied by an escort of Army officers and police. The melancholy procession moved along the road from Letchworth to Hitchin, where the officers were laid in the mortuary at St Saviour's Church.

A special service was held for them on Sunday morning. The Rev J Williams told the large congregation: "These two soldiers gave their lives for our sakes," and praised their work in defending the realm against a future enemy. They were "courageous and intrepid men," he stated.

Thousands of sightseers poured into the fields around Graveley at the weekend. Many found pieces of debris, thrown from the plane as it broke up during its horrendous descent.

The police later asked for a look at these fragments, along with a note of where they had been found, and promised to return them.

The most poignant souvenir was Captain Hamilton's map, bearing his name, found half a mile away.

The inquest was heard at St Saviour's School in Hitchin. The £1,000 Deperdussin had been bought by the Army only a week earlier and had flown a total of just 12 hours when the accident happened, probably because, said an expert witness, something had broken in the engine.

Walter Brett, landlord of the George and Dragon at Graveley, had seen the plane wobbling in the air, going up and down. He saw it tip and then "came a report like a gun."

"It seemed to collapse altogether and I was too horrified to look at it any more. It fell in the end of my meadow, about 100 yards from the house," he told the coroner.

Villager John Alldritt described the plane giving a quiver and then righting itself. "It then gave a dip but recovered again and then suddenly seemed to turn turtle." He was one of the first to reach the scene and tried to lift the plane off the bodies "but it was too heavy."

The jury returned a verdict of accidental death, offering their sympathy to the families. Juror Mr G Moulden, organist at St Mary's Church in Hitchin, said: "The sympathy not only of ourselves but of the whole nation would be extended to the relatives of those brave officers who had made brave deaths.

*"We hope their untimely end will not deter others from following their brave example for their king and country."*

Captain Hamilton's mother was so moved by the jurors' regard that she wrote to thank them and Lt Stuart's brother Albert sent a letter via the council to the kind hearted inhabitants of Hitchin, expressing the family's "heartfelt appreciation and sincere thanks for all the kind sympathy shown at this darkened hour attending the tragic loss."

*The memorial to the airmen*

A few days after the inquest a large crowd watched the funeral cortege pass from the church to Hitchin Station. Each oak coffin bore a simple wooden cross at the head and a bunch of flowers.

The lilies-of-the-valley on Captain Hamilton's were tied with white satin ribbon and bore the message "From Derryle" – his American fiancée, Miss Law.

Lt Stuart's coffin carried amber and red chrysanthemums with the words "In heartbroken remembrance: his wife."

The procession moved slowly along Walsworth Road, watched by large crowds. Two gun carriages bore the coffins, accompanied by police, soldiers and surpliced clergymen. Among the 50 floral tributes for each officer were two declaring: "With sincere sympathy from the inhabitants of Hitchin" and "In loving sympathy from the congregation and Church of Holy Saviour, Hitchin, a small token for the privilege of caring for the bodies of the brave men, September 6 to 11, 1912. Dulce et decorum est pro patria mori."

As the crowds watched, the coffins were carefully loaded onto the train to begin their journey to their graves – Captain Hamilton at Hythe and Lt Stuart near Frome. Both men were just 30 years old.

In May, 1914, Capt Hamilton again made news headlines when his fiancée, who had started an action for breach of promise shortly before his death, won a £600 personal settlement. She told the High Court that Captain Hamilton had promised her the money if she postponed the wedding. He felt a marriage would injure his chances of promotion.

The Army manoeuvres caused great interest and diversion in North Herts, lasting from September 2 for more than two weeks.

The Redland Army crossed the frontier and moved towards London, while the Blueland forces repelled them. A total of 75,000 men were involved in an operation that stretched from the Wash down to the capital and covered all East Anglia.

King George V travelled to Cambridge to watch the battlefield and special programmes were printed, giving details of events.

A camp was set up for 10 days at Baldock with 1,800 men and 1,500 horses. Residents were in a fever of excitement.

Lt Fox of the Royal Flying Corps became a celebrity after an emergency landing at Wilbury Hills, watched by hundreds of people who had come out of their houses to see the plane pass over. He was aiming for the temporary Willian air shed but ran into trouble in bad weather as he passed Hitchin.

"When the squalls caught me I looked up and saw a very big cloud coming towards me and glanced round for a fairly big field to land in," he told enthralled Express readers. "I tried to get the machine round and then she began to dive. I missed the telegraph wires and dropped like a stone." He landed successfully without damaging himself or his machine and, demonstrating enviable bravura, ate a packet of biscuits with relish before being driven off to Willian.

In the days that followed Lt Fox and his colleague Lt de Havilland put on impromptu displays for the crowds who walked and cycled out to Willian, thrilled at the idea of seeing planes for the first time.

On one occasion they had their machines wheeled from the sheds and took quickly to

> 'It seemed to collapse altogether and I was too horrified to look'

> 'I missed the telegraph wires and dropped like a stone'

the air, attracting even more people who came rushing out to watch. Lt Fox had problems with his engine and was forced to land again but de Havilland stayed in the air for nearly one and a half hours "giving a splendid exhibition," declared the Express enthusiastically.

This excited more interest than ever and "morning, noon and night the roads reaching Willian were crowded with people walking, cycling and driving."

It was not until late afternoon on the next day that the stalwarts who had stayed near the camp since dawn were rewarded for their patience. "Lt Fox's engine having been taken to pieces, cleaned and replaced, both aviators were in the air for some time to test the engine."

Next day many of the visitors were back. About 5.30pm the two big planes were brought out of the sheds. Lt Fox, smoking a cigarette, set his engine in motion.

"With a rush the machine, looking like a huge beetle, with its fish-shaped nose covering the Gnome engine, raced across the field, turned and halfway on the return journey gradually left the earth and passed over the spectators' heads. Lt de Havilland quickly followed." He was, reported the Express with awe, the holder of the record for the highest flight, achieved in that very machine.

The planes – "two unwieldy looking structures when on earth but entrancing and picturesque machines in the air" – turned one last time and flew to the north, away from Willian and the ecstatic crowds for new adventures.

*St Saviour's Church, pictured at about the time of the air accident*

Captain Hamilton and Lieutenant Stuart were not forgotten. Very soon after their death a memorial was proposed to honour their courage. It stands now on the road from Willian to Wymondley, at the site of the temporary airstrip, commemorating their valour.

Hundreds once again came to the site to take part in a simple and impressive ceremony in late November, 1912, including friends, relatives, brother officers and members of the public. The memorial reads:

*"In memory of Captain Hamilton and Lieut Wyness Stuart of the Royal Flying Corps who lost their lives whilst serving their country as aviators Sep 6th 1912.*
*Erected by local subscription."*

King George V's equerry wrote to Captain Hamilton's mother and his letter was printed in the Hythe Parish Magazine of October, 1912.

"Though the King felt very keenly for you in the loss which you sustained by the death of your son, Captain Hamilton, through the recent terrible flying disaster at Hitchin, His Majesty was, until a few days ago, unaware that three other of your sons had served in the South African war; that two of them had lost their lives on service, while the third had been killed by lightning within a few months of resigning his commission.

"The King now realises what must be the increased bitterness of your fresh sorrow, and I am commanded to assure you of His Majesty's heartfelt sympathy. His Majesty can only hope that you may find some consolation in the thought that the dear ones who have been taken from you gave their services and sacrificed their lives for Sovereign and country."

In St Leonard's Church in Hythe, high above the sea, Mrs Hamilton erected a brass plaque in memory of her husband and four dead sons, all Army men. The catalogue of grief starts with the father, Major Thomas Bramston Hamilton, who died when he was only 47 years old, in 1884.

The first son to die was Kenneth, overwhelmed by fever in Bloemfontein, South Africa, on May 13, 1900, aged 24.

Just 17 days later his younger brother Ernest was killed in action at Sleepers Nek in a Boer War conflict.

In December 1902 Alastair, aged 28, was struck by lightning at Machadodorp.

Finally the grieving mother heard that Patrick had perished during manoeuvres. At the end of the plain and unsentimental memorial, she put:

*"They counted not their lives dear*
*unto themselves."*

Outside the wind howls through a myriad of gravestones, raddled and weary with age.

*Lt Fox is pictured preparing to fly from Willian in 1912*

# The Sherlock Holmes detectives

IT was hard to get away with a crime in Edwardian times – it was an age where everyone knew everybody else and their business, even in a town as big as Hitchin (11,905 residents, according to the 1911 census.)

In August 1904 two men and a woman appeared in court charged with stealing three packets of postcards from Walter Smith's shop in Hitchin High Street. Mr Smith realised the packets were missing after they left the shop and called the police, who mounted a search for the villains.

They were found at 5.25am, sleeping against a stack of sanfoin on Pirton Road. Sgt Birch woke them up, reportedly saying: "I have come to search your property as there is some property missing from a shop you were seen to enter."

The stolen cards were found hidden in the corn near where the trio had been sleeping. As they were arrested one of the men turned to the woman, muttering: "It is you that have led us into this!"

Shortly afterwards an alert Pc Clay caught a clothing criminal. A coat had been stolen from a tailors in Watton at Stone on a Tuesday.

The following day Pc Clay saw a stranger in Hitchin Market Place wearing a similar coat and, after making enquiries, arrested him. The man, William Millar, was sent to prison for three weeks.

In January 1909 an eagle-eyed officer apprehended two naval deserters at Starlings Bridge, Hitchin. Pc Clark noticed that one of the men was wearing naval trousers and he stopped and questioned them both.

Under his piercing scrutiny they soon revealed they had absconded from HMS Nelson at Portsmouth. The miscreants were sent back to port the very next day.

It wasn't only Hertfordshire police who were so resourceful – they could be rather canny over the Bedfordshire border too.

In June, 1906, Dc Chamberlain and Sgt James were told about two men who had stolen a small sum of money from a shop in Hitchin Road, Luton, and been seen escaping towards Offley.

The detectives were not daunted by the lateness of the hour but set off in pursuit, going steadily on until they reached Hitchin in the early hours of the morning.

*Keen motorist Mr Fred Carling, pictured in 1905*

Knocking on lodging house doors, they found the two men they were looking for, arrested them and had taken them back to Luton police station by 3am.

But sometimes the police could be a little too clever for their own good. Pc Lea came a cropper at Royston in June, 1906.

He told magistrates about the night he listened outside the White Bear pub, as landlord Frederick Greenhill appeared on a charge of allowing gambling on licensed premises during prohibited hours. Pc Lea listened at the window after seeing lights on in the bar.

He said: "I heard the voices of several men and the rattle of cards being shuffled. I went close to the window and listened for about 15 minutes to the conversation going on.

"During that time I thought I heard one person using an oath."

The reporter added: "The witness saw three mugs on the table, one containing beer, which he tasted." Mr Greenhill was full of injured innocence.

The men were friends, he said, and there was no money about. The one pack of cards found by Pc Lea was used for whist. The case was dismissed.

Conjuror Horace Kreutz of Islington fell foul of the widespread suspicion of any stranger. He wrote a letter to the Express in July 1904, full of sarcastic praise for Hitchin policemen.

On one short visit to the town he was twice stopped and asked where he was going and why. The second time, in Bancroft, he was told: "You don't live in Hitchin and when people report a strange man going about, we are obliged just to inquire into the matter."

Mr Kreutz wrote: "I then satisfied him that I was not a burglar, house breaker, pickpocket, murderer nor even a swindler and the diligent officer left me with half an apology." A frequent traveller, he had not been questioned in this way elsewhere, he said. "Is it police zealousness or the potential influence of snobs and nouveaux riches in Hitchin?" he asked.

Car drivers might have thought they were exempt from speeding byelaws – after all there was no way of measuring velocity.

But the wily police soon devised a strategy, as in a case which came to court in May 1905. A motorist was seen passing through Ware and the time noted down before the officer telegraphed a colleague further along the road.

He wrote down the time the car passed him and simple mathematics gave an answer of 29mph – way above the permitted 20 for that stretch of road.

Getting on a bike was no guarantee of evading capture either. A Bygrave man reported that his cycle had been stolen from outside a house in Church Street, Baldock, early in 1901. The thief was seen pedalling in the direction of Royston, so the police telephoned their colleagues further east, who simply waited by the side of the road until the thief cycled into view.

A smart capture was effected by Detective Marks of the GNR Company's force in October 1905.

He noted two suspicious characters in Walsworth Road, Hitchin, followed them to the station and got on the same train, to Hatfield.

One of the men became suspicious and bolted but, with the help of the Hatfield police, Det Marks managed to capture both men. When searched they were found to be in possession of house-breaking implements.

*Bancroft, Hitchin, between 1885 and 1900*

# Favourite Express-ions – 1912

Mary Clark might have earned herself a place in the Guinness Book of Records as the oldest pickpocket in the world if their sleuths had been in court in January 1912. For Mary, who gave her profession as a hawker and pleaded guilty to stealing a purse in Hitchin Market Place, was 92 years of age.

She had 45 previous convictions dating from 1868. Judge Sir Alfred Reynolds was perplexed. "It is impossible to do anything with a prisoner of your age and with such a record," he told her.

*"I have no doubt in the world that you have had plenty of chances to be a better woman and lead a better life. It is perfectly absurd to give you a long sentence at your age. But for your own sake and the sake of the people upon whom you preyed, I must give you a fairly long sentence."*

Mary left court to spend a year in prison, without hard labour.

The vogue for the Russian ballet was influencing women's fashion, declared the *Women's Realm* columnist in the Express. Some of the newest and loveliest dresses had become very short, merely to the ankles, diaphanous and light as thistledown.

The vexed question of working women was discussed by Hitchin Debating Society in the middle of January. "The invasion of the commercial and industrial markets by women is deplorable in that it creates an economic peril by the cheapening and displacement of men's labour, is a deterrent to matrimony and is conducive to the deterioration of the race by neglect of the responsibilities of motherhood," was the resolution before them.

Supporting it, Mr T J Faulkner declared that women were prepared to work for lower wages than men, "depriving them of their very existence," and making it impossible for them to marry.

"Men gained in value as they grew older and became more experienced but women of 40 were not wanted in the industrial world," he said, adding:

*"Many girls simply endeavour to earn money in order to satisfy their craving for dress."*

Mr C Crosoer, speaking against the resolution, said poverty had not increased since women began to work and how was a single woman supposed to survive? "All women could not be married because there are not enough men to go round." (laughter)

Despite their frivolity the audience appreciated his argument and the resolution was lost.

The Rev E F Tallents was concerned with another form of immorality and thundered from the pulpit at St Mary's Church, Hitchin, against the results of the 1857 divorce act. It had opened the floodgates of immorality and infidelity, he declared.

The falling birth rate was threatening the nation with race suicide.

"If life was regarded as something to have a good time in, what wonder that so many grew up indifferent to duty, unpatriotic and shirkers of responsibility?" he proclaimed.

One can imagine what the Rev Tallents would have thought of Alfred Richardson's new form of spelling, which he introduced to bemused Express subscribers in March – or NYU speling, as he put it. He had rather a rose-tinted view of children.

"Through the happy golden days of six long years they have rolled on the lawn and sported in the shade," he wrote.

*"The voice of the streams has been in their ears. A summer sun has browned their chubby cheeks and limbs, they have skipped with the lambs, whistled to the birds. They have filled their baby laps with buttercups and daisies. We now call them from all this; we beckon them from the sunshine, shut them in a closed room, pluck the buttercups from their tiny hands, and place the spelling book there."*

The solution, to save the sanity of the poor darlings, was a phonetic system. Mr Richardson finished his article in grand style.

"I doo not supoez yu wil at furst liec the looc ov theez cloezing wurdz," he wrote with admirable perspicacity.

✵ A son dropped dead in a Luton thoroughfare while making arrangements for his mother's funeral. Mrs Ellen Ellingham, of Chapel Street, had died in her bed of a heart attack in September, aged 75. Her son George, who was only 54, succumbed to a blood clot on the brain. The inquest found the double death was pure chance and coroner G Whyley remarked that it was an extraordinary co-incidence – a domestic tragedy as it were.

✵ The curious career of James Rennie, colporteur, (a hawker of books, particularly Bibles) was outlined in the Express as tribute was paid to his 40 years of work, tramping the streets of Bedfordshire and Herts.

Mr Rennie, now aged 61 and of Scottish blood, had grown up in the Australian bush and served four years as an apprentice to a blacksmith.

He then opted for a total change of direction and started selling door-to-door for the Scottish Tract and Book Society.

He came to Hitchin after working in Biggleswade and only called into the town while waiting for a train connection. He was so successful there and so taken with the town that he made it his base for the next 38 years.

In that time he sold 48,000 Bibles, 22,000 prayer and hymn books, 827,000 volumes of standard works, more than a million periodicals and booklets and 3,164 tracts. Every single page had been carried on his back.

He started work at 8am, taking about half a hundredweight of books in a knapsack and covering three or four villages as well as farms and workshops.

He travelled up to 20 miles a day. He loved his job although he been forced to use a tricycle for the last 10 years following a bad ankle injury.

But he wasn't entirely happy with the way the world was changing. "One of the things I detest at the present time is the increase in the circulation of small literature of the novel kind," he said.

*Above: Mr Rennie the colporteur, pictured selling his religious books and tracts in Hitchin Market Place in 1900.*

*Right: Mr Rennie and his wife celebrating their golden wedding anniversary in 1926. Mr Rennie died the following year, aged 74*

★ Mr Rennie would no doubt have been appalled at a one-day play showing in Hitchin after a successful London run – Bunty Pulls The Strings.

★ Fate was cruel to 25-year-old Robert Smith, a street musician with only one arm. He appeared before Hitchin magistrates charged with attempting to kill himself by jumping off the railway bridge over the Stotfold Road on April 16.

He was stopped by a passer-by who said Smith looked very strange, was on the point of collapse and half starved. He was poorly clad with no soles on his boots. The magistrates kept him in custody for observation, instructing the police to "look after him and feed him." When Smith was brought back to court a few days later the charge had been changed to "wandering abroad in an insane condition" and he was sent to an asylum.

★ Figures were produced in May to prove that motor vehicles were five times more dangerous than horses. A R Butterworth of the Highways Protection League thought the problem lay in unnecessary journeys made at an unnecessary speed. Motors were being used for the mere pleasure of racing through the air, he said. "It is the pace that kills and injures."

★ A baby's body was sent through the post from Fulham, being delivered to a house in Woburn. Police were investigating the death of the newborn girl and how she had been sent, apparently from a woman in hospital.

★ Rebecca Millard had the strangest story to tell when she appeared at Bedford Magistrates court in September – she claimed her husband Henry had sold her. Rebecca was applying for an order under the Summary Jurisdiction Married Women's Act, claiming persistent cruelty and asking for maintenance.

Henry, a silver plater, of Bower Street, Bedford, said she had run off with another man 10 years earlier but Rebecca alleged he had sold her for one shilling (5p) and Henry's own mother backed her up. But the magistrates decided in Henry's favour and no order was made.

★ An even odder case followed. Robert and George Allen of the Live and Let Live pub at Pegsdon were charged with stealing a hive of bees from a field in Lilley.

Sergeant Birch told the court he found the hive in the Allens' garden and put it in a cart with the brothers, to take it over to Lilley for identification. As they were travelling along, George Allen pulled the top off and 300 to 400 bees flew out. The owner was horrified, telling the sergeant that if it had been a warm night they would all have been killed. The brothers were fined.

★ Hitchin was in the grip of measles that autumn, with schools closed and hundreds of cases reported, spreading from the younger children up to the older. The epidemic lasted several weeks and it was only late in October that the Express reported the monster measles outbreak was finally subsiding.

★ Poor Edgar Hewitt was found naked and exhausted in a wood near Broom in September. A Swaffham man, he had been sent to Stotfold by anxious relatives because they thought the change of air might boost his frail health.

Bedfordshire failed to have the desired effect and he vanished, triggering a two-day search. Pc Vincent, who found him in the wood hungry, scratched and suffering from exposure, procured clothes for him and took him to Biggleswade Police Station where he ate and drank ravenously.

He was certified as insane and taken to the Three Counties Asylum. His boots were later found in Shefford and his clothing strewn over two roads.

★ An Anti-Socialist Union meeting went awry in Letchworth in October when the speaker was too ill to attend. Seeing a crowd gathered and waiting, the Socialists seized the opportunity to tell them about the movement.

★ Were whist drives illegal? That was the vexed question facing local fund raisers after a national decision threw the issue into doubt. But many decided the question was ridiculous and went ahead with events anyway.

★ A letter writer to the Express recalled an old custom of hanging nettles and branches of may blossom on the knockers of Hitchin domiciles, as a mark of unpopularity or respect, depending on which plant was used.

★ Three boys appeared at the children's court in December, and were bound over for malicious damage. They had broken windows and the headline reporting the story in the Express read "Imitating the Suffragettes."

# The battered boy left for dead

Young Frederick Primmett was only found because he moaned. He lay unconscious in a clump of stinging nettles, his head terribly battered and his body covered in blood. He was perilously close to the edge of a chalk pit, in danger of rolling over and tumbling into the abyss below.

His parents were already concerned and searching for him. He was only just 12 and always home soon after Welwyn church choir on Sundays. Why should this night, in April 1912, be any different?

Freddie's father William, a caretaker and gardener, soon discovered the reason.

Freddie had been seen by some of his friends, walking with a man they knew a little, called Day. By 9pm they were in a village shop and Day was buying the lad sweets. Then the pair had vanished.

Thoroughly alarmed, Mr Primmett went straight to the police.

As Pc Briden prepared to organise a search, a message arrived to say Freddie had been found, but in a pitiful condition.

Near his body was a blood-stained hedge mallet with hairs embedded in the gore. Carefully Freddie was lifted up and carried home, where a doctor stitched his wounds and made sure he was warm in bed, surrounded with hot water bottles.

The doctor returned the next morning at 7.45 and, finding no improvement, transferred Freddie to the cottage hospital where he hovered between life and death for more than a week. Police began a serious manhunt for the attacker, aware that the charge might soon be one of murder.

They found their quarry at Ayot St Peter, where Supt Pear interviewed 21-year-old George Day after a tip-off.

His clothes were enough to confirm any suspicions on their own, being filthy, splattered with dirt and covered in spots of blood.

Day's coat also had blood on it and was smeared with green slime as though it had been dredged through a pond.

When Supt Pear arrested Day he confessed, saying:

*"I clumped him over the head with a club, the one my father used when he was hedging. I did not do it for spite.*

"It was the whisky that made me do it and no one would have stopped me from doing it at the time.

"I like the boy very much and he will follow me anywhere.

"I hope the boy is not dead."

At his committal Day declared he remembered nothing after drinking a couple of beers and a quarter bottle of whisky, only coming to himself the next morning. He told the court:

*"I was very fond of the boy and the boy was very fond of me."*

His trial for feloniously and maliciously wounding Frederick Primmett with intent to murder took place in late June. Despite his earlier confession, Day pleaded not guilty.

Freddie was well enough to give evidence himself, telling the jury he had met Day after church, went with him to buy sweets, and then walked at his side towards the chalk pits.

"Day said there was a duck's nest there," he explained.

*"While we were looking for it, Day hit me. I don't remember anymore."*

The doctor's evidence caused ripples of excitement. Not only did he set out the extent of Freddie's injuries but he added that the boy had been knelt on and hit at least three times while stretched out on the ground.

Day's counsel Mr Graeme mounted a novel defence. He thought it very much in his client's favour that the boy was found on a spot close to a high precipice, which Day could have thrown him down "and no one known he had been attacked." Mr Graeme then added: "It was the act of a madman frenzied with drink to have done such a thing."

The jury found Day guilty of unlawfully wounding with intent to cause grievous bodily harm. Before sentence was passed Sgt Wood gave a summary of Day's character, based on an acquaintance of three years. Day, he declared, was idle but had not been in trouble before.

"If he could get any little boy to kick a ball about with him or shoot a catapult, it was his heart's delight," he told the court. His father had been in an asylum for 10 years.

Judge Forest Falton was in a quandary. "I feel great difficulty as to how to punish you," he said. "It was a wicked crime. It is fortunate that the boy is still alive – thanks to the extraordinary skills of medical men."

After a little more thought he sentenced Day to five years' penal servitude.

*Right: The sons of Francis Ransom, one of Hitchin's most prominent families, pictured in 1901.*

*Below: nurses from Hitchin Hospital in 1912, the year Frederick Primmett was almost killed in an unprovoked attack*

"It was a wicked crime. It is fortunate that the boy is still alive – thanks to the extraordinary skills of medical men."

# The neighbour from Hell

LEONARD Bell was weeding his potato patch. He had been out in the garden for two hours and was crouched on his knees, while his wife Emily and daughter Dorothy worked in the house. It was just after midday and he was enjoying a day off from his job as a clerk at the Royal Assurance Company in London.

He did not hear the footsteps approaching until the last moment. It is doubtful whether Dorothy's voice drifted down the garden to him, calling to her mother in alarm: "There's Smith at Dad again," or that he was ever aware of Emily moving anxiously towards him. He could not have known because, long before his wife reached him, Smith took out a revolver and shot him three times, through the arm, the shoulder and the head.

Henry Smith had led a varied and interesting life. While young he worked in the cotton trade, then became a teacher before enlisting in the Scots Guards in 1883. After 18 months he transferred to the Royal Engineers as a quarter master sergeant, serving in the Far East, including postings in India, China, Hong Kong and Singapore. He left in 1905 with a good character, a long service medal and a pension of £50 a year. But even in his Army days he earned a reputation as an eccentric.

On one occasion he decided to get rid of his moustache, but regulations forbade shaving it. Instead Smith pulled every hair out one by one until his upper lip was smooth.

He settled at number 201 Baldock Road, Letchworth, in 1906, becoming one of the garden city's pioneer smallholders with an acre of land. He had no friends, did his own housework and lived with only the company of a mastiff dog.

Those who knew him described him as powerfully built, blunt, eccentric and excitable. His passion was breeding Minoca chickens which, as the years passed, became an overwhelming obsession.

*Baldock Road, Letchworth, pictured in about 1914*

Neighbour Alfred Prince, a retired Metropolitan police inspector, told the judge at Smith's trial: "Apart from the question of the fowls, which the prisoner frequently talked about, he was a perfectly sensible man on every other subject."

"It would appear that brooding introspection has produced a species of melancholia," asserted the Hertfordshire Express newspaper soon after the killing.

Leonard Bell was very different. Aged 47, he was happily married with two children approaching adulthood and still living at home. "He was well known and had many friends, to whom the news conveyed to them in the City by the early morning papers and posters came as a great shock," reported the Express.

*"He had a rare gift of humour with a Yankee twang about it and the gift also of telling the most absurd and outlandish yarns in the most solemn and circumstantial way."*

A keen politician, he was a member of the Independent Labour Party.

The Bell family were thrilled when they moved to their new home in 1909, next to Mr Smith. Like him they kept chickens and they grew many of their own vegetables. At first they got on well, in a distant way, with the taciturn Mr Smith. But after a year everything changed. Mr Smith's fowl grew sickly and some died. There could have been a variety of reasons but in his mind there was just one possibility, and the suspicion immediately became fact. Leonard Bell had poisoned them.

Smith was a man of action. He challenged Bell, who denied the charge vehemently. Smith, quite unconvinced, complained to the police. He pestered Supt Reed at Hitchin with such frequency and eloquence that a constable was sent to watch over Smith's garden.

But although Pc Bowman lurked in the bushes for several nights, he saw nothing at all. Supt Reed made more enquiries, visited Smith in his home for almost two hours, and gave him some advice on feeding his fowls. Smith was not pacified.

## Smith kept a secret diary as he spied on the family

*When Supt Reed returned a month later to see how the situation was progressing he was told in no uncertain terms that the "dosing" was still going on, that he was being ruined and that Bell was responsible for it.*

The casual atmosphere at numbers 199 and 201 Baldock Road would never return. Smith, feeling himself persecuted, retaliated in kind.

He threatened Mr Bell, punched his son and wrote malicious letters. In desperation Mrs Bell went to the police herself, asking for help from the urbane Supt Reed.

"On his advice she made an opportunity of speaking to Smith and said: 'It is a nice day'," reported the Express. Mrs Bell's olive branch was not a success.

Smith growled: 'Do you have any respect for yourself?' and, stung, Mrs Bell snapped: 'Do you?'

"Nothing else was said. When she tried again later he 'made use of hostile language'."

However bad things seemed, the Bells had no idea of Smith's real state of mind or the lengths his obsession was driving him to. They did not know about the diary, in which he recorded, sometimes several times a day, minute observations about them and the condition of his fowl.

They were unaware that Smith was sending his dead birds away for chemical analysis. And they had no suspicion that he had set up a telescope to spy on them.

At his trial Mr Gill, for the prosecution, told the jury that from 1910 until July 13, 1913, Mr Smith: "Seems to have directed the whole of his attention to the conduct of the members of Mr Bell's family and to have anticipated that trouble was likely to arise."

He repeated his problems to anyone who would listen. Neighbour Albert Parker, a market gardener, heard it all many times.

"I said his suspicions were entirely unfounded," he told the court, but added that he could not take Smith's mind off "such an unpleasant subject." On June 28, 1913, only two weeks before he killed Mr Bell, Smith wrote in his diary: "Boy at home? B just done 15 minutes' weeding. The wind is fairly strong. For a couple of nights B has been burning weeds long after sunset."

The entries revealed an obsessed man reaching breaking point as night after sleepless night passed. He was racked by deep fatigue, both mental and bodily.

Almost every entry in the diary detailed a grievance against the Bell family, events and motives that Smith imagined and how he felt about them.

They showed, said the prosecution: "The extraordinary interest that occupied the prisoner's mind in reference to his and Bell's property."

"Smith's complaints were absolute delusion," Supt Reed told the court. "But he believed them, very strongly."

By July 1913 the situation was at crisis point. Mr Bell wrote to Smith, threatening legal action for slander.

"Ever since I have had the misfortune to be afflicted with your presence as a neighbour I have had ample opportunity of realising the truth of that old adage which asserts 'His satanic majesty will suggest nefarious employment to the idler.'

"So in your case; having no business in which to occupy your mind, you have for the past 12 months or longer ill-spent your spare time in wilfully circulating reports concerning myself and members of my family of a malicious and lying description.

"I have treated your despicable conduct with the contempt which it deserves, always having in mind the fact that your character is so well known in Letchworth, but matters have reached a crisis and I hereby give you notice that unless you tender me an unqualified public apology in the columns of the local Letchworth paper in the issue of the 11th inst, withdrawing absolutely all your accusations and stating the same all have been falsely made, I will immediately instruct my solicitor to institute proceedings for an action for slander against you."

It was a threat Mr Bell would never carry out, for he was shot before he could see a lawyer. In court both his wife and his daughter described the scene as he lay dying in his garden. Mrs Bell sobbed as she gave evidence at the inquest.

Smith, she said, had deliberately shot her husband three times. As she screamed hysterically Dorothy ran towards Smith and hurled the first thing she could find at him – a lump of earth.

He looked at her for a moment, said nothing and calmly turned away towards his house.

Very deliberately, only his white face betraying any emotion, he laid the gun on the table, made sure the dog was inside and then left, locking the door behind him. He fetched his bike and rode away, in the direction of Hitchin.

He left a chaotic scene in the garden of number 199.

Mr Parker, who had heard three shots followed by screams from his nearby orchard, came running up followed by another neighbour. At first they assumed there had been an accident, as they bent over the unconscious figure of Mr Bell, bleeding profusely from three separate wounds. They soon realised the truth.

Mr Parker took charge, sending Mrs Bell for

> 'I have treated your despicable conduct with the contempt it deserves'

> 'You will have to see me. I have done it this time. I have done for him.'

a pillow and running for his bike to fetch help. It was then he saw Mr Smith riding down the road. "I went after him and followed him to Hitchin police station," said Mr Parker, in evidence.

"He knocked on the door and then came down to me and asked me if I wanted to speak to him. I said: 'It doesn't matter now'. He went back and went in," – to the police station.

A sigh of exasperation must have escaped Supt Reed when he heard that Smith was demanding to see him again. Smith must have known this for his first words were: "You will have to see me this time. I have done it this time, I have done for him."

When he was charged later, he simply said: "Well I will take the consequences, but I only want satisfaction."

As the dreadful truth unfolded, Supt Reed rushed out of the station to see the situation for himself. In the garden he found poor Bell, still unconscious and on the point of death. He went straight to Smith's house next door, where the mastiff was growling and pacing from room to room. Supt Reed broke the window and, avoiding the angry dog, managed to get in. On the table he found a small automatic magazine pistol of French make.

Supt Reed believed he knew something about guns, having used them in the past. There were three bullets in Bell's body and three live cartridges in the magazine.

He took them out and put them in his pocket, confident the pistol was now empty. "Supt Reed held it in his left hand while he drove the empty magazine home with his right," stated the Express. "Instantly there was a report."

A bullet passed through his left hand, chipped the window and entered the right hand and abdomen of Mr Shaw, who was standing in the garden." Poor Alan Shaw, a newsagent from Nightingale Road, Hitchin, paid a heavy price for his curiosity.

He was taken off to Hitchin Hospital in the Letchworth ambulance, where the bullet had to be removed from the top of his leg. Supt Reed fared better, only needing to have his hand dressed.

He was able to appear at Bell's inquest the next day and hear the jury return a verdict of wilful murder against Smith, adding the rider that he was suffering from mental derangement.

*The junction of Hermitage Road and Bancroft, pictured about 1900*

The mystery of the six-bullet gun that had seven cartridges was soon cleared up – there had been six in the magazine and one in the chamber.

A few days after Bell died, his funeral was held at Letchworth churchyard. "A few subdued and markedly sympathetic groups of residents waited for the remains of one who had been to some of them a respected and genial neighbour, to others a chatty and agreeable companion of many railway journeys to and from London, and to still others a pleasantly remembered acquaintance," reported the Express.

"At the graveside afterwards it was not only the relatives of the departed but many others who were very deeply affected."

Smith was held in jail for several months, not standing trial until the end of October. The hearing was short, with the whole defence strategy depending on an insanity plea. Dr Sidney Dyer, chief medical officer at Brixton Prison, testified that Smith was now insane, suffering from a very marked delusion and had been unable to judge what he was doing when he shot Mr Bell. It was the most marked case that he had ever known, he told the court.

Summing up Mr Justice Bucknill told the jury to consider whether Smith was so far overcome by this terrible delusion that he thought his act was not wrong but right.

The evidence all pointed one way, he said. The jury needed no more prompting and did not even bother to retire, giving a verdict of guilty but insane within three minutes.

*Above: Nightingale Road, Hitchin*
*Right: A couple pictured beside a carriage in 1910 in Hitchin*

# How to get a drink in a teetotal town

Contrary to popular belief, Ebenezer Howard did not want to create a teetotal town when he established Letchworth, calling it "a coward's policy."

In July 1906 he declared: "They must not drive the evil into neighbouring towns and villages but deal with it themselves," and advocated opening one public house in the town.

He believed, with charming innocence, that residents of his ideal city would spurn a pub in favour of gardening, debating and family life. The licensed premises would be forced to close, through lack of custom. However, other Garden City pioneers were more realistic and voted against allowing public houses.

There were occasions when Ebenezer's faith must have been sorely tested. Early in 1911, Customs and Excise brought their first case of selling beer without a licence in Letchworth. "Excise Officers' Clever Ruse," trumpeted the headlines in the Express. "Remarkable Allegations, The Young lady at the Piano, A Conversation Concerning Crippen."

Two families stood accused, the Crowthers and the Stokes, who both lived in Moira Cottages and made ends meet by taking in lodgers.

One Friday night a polite young man knocked at Mrs Stokes' door, asking for a room. He said he was a stone mason and carried a bag with his tools inside. Mrs Stokes had no room but, anxious to oblige, took the man to her neighbour, where she knew there was a space.

The man said his name was James Lessopps and he seemed very pleased with his billet. He settled down to an evening meal with the other lodgers and then asked, conversationally, whether there was any beer. Maria Crowther told the court there was not and said she gave him none.

Mr Lessopps claimed she served him generously from one of several crates in the passage, charging 4d a glass.

*Passengers pour off a train at Letchworth's first railway station*

This was hotly denied by Mrs Crowther who explained the procedure for getting alcohol in the new town. "I told him he had to send a postcard ordering it or walk to Baldock or Willian to fetch some," she testified.

Mr Lessopps, already half drunk according to her, was too lazy go out and asked for a postcard. He filled it in, embellished with a picture (she didn't have any plain cards, she said) and her daughter posted it. The only beer ever served in her house, she swore, was for lodgers who bought it themselves.

Mr Lessopps took his new undercover role seriously. He went to a football match at Hitchin on Saturday afternoon, with another lodger, and then accompanied Mr Crowther into Baldock on Saturday night for a legal pint. He came home so drunk, allegedly, that he lay down on the garden path and had to be helped to bed, with rather a struggle.

The job was obviously an onerous one, for next morning reinforcements arrived to help him. Mr Lessopps went to Letchworth station to meet another officer, Arthur Baker. They walked back to Moira Cottages in the late October sun and, tired and thirsty, sat down outside the Crowther's house and ordered a couple of beers.

After drinking a total of four – obviously just to make sure they were on sale – "We were sober the whole time," Mr Lessopps told the court – the pair of spies moved next door to the Stokes' cottage where, said Baker, they wandered about the garden for a while and saw five men go inside and come out again. When another two approached, Lessopps and Baker decided to join the party and went inside.

Perhaps it was the four beers they had already had, or maybe the Stokes were just more cheerful people than the Crowthers, but it was a lively lunchtime whichever account you believe.

Even Mr Baker admitted sitting next to the young lady at the piano and turning the pages of her music – but he vehemently denied trying to kiss her.

He also had a conversation with Mrs Stokes about Crippen, on trial for murdering his wife. But no, Baker told the court, he certainly didn't try to bet five shillings that he would not be hanged.

"I was quite sober when I left," he testified. "I have visited similar premises and clubs and I have no taste for beer." Mr Lessopps was clear headed too, he added. The Crowthers and the Stokes produced lodgers who said they had spent years under their roof and never seen a bottle of beer sold.

They told the court Lessopps was drunk from the moment he arrived until he left, on Monday. Mrs Crowther howled: "Why did he single out me!" It was all to no avail.

Both families were found guilty and the magistrate at Hitchin, Francis Delmé-Radcliffe, said they would deal leniently with them because it was the first offence in the Garden City. He fined them £2 each and added: "If any further cases are brought before us they will be considered in a very severe manner."

*The non alcoholic bar at the Skittles Inn*

An easier way to foil prohibition was to go outside the town. As early as October 1905, pubs in Baldock were reported to be flourishing as visitors to the Garden City Cottages exhibition went east for a drink.

Others headed west – the Drunkards' train back from Hitchin was mentioned nationally in March 1908, with a picture painted of Hitchin landlords rubbing their hands with glee as they plied their new customers with intoxicating liquors.

"What could be the scene when they arrived home!" asked Percival Grundy of Whitbread and Co, who thought there would be more temperance in Letchworth if pubs were allowed there.

The Herts Express commented. "The matter has been a topic of conversation in the district for sometime past." No one should be allowed on the train if they were drunk, went on the article.

There had been a scene on Saturday with four men lying on the platform and another two "in a condition which overtakes bad sailors on rough sea."

"An Adam's ale drinker," writing to the Express, said the situation was a disgrace to the police and the publicans of Hitchin.

*"Even if the publicans are allowed
to make people worse than beasts,
they ought not to be allowed to turn them
into the streets to be a nuisance
to the public. They ought to provide
lodgings for them."*

He suggested stables or pigsties with clean straw. Alternatively they could walk home, clearing their heads and thinking of how foolishly they had behaved.

The Drunkards' train was causing trouble again in May, 1912, when Reginald Ohlson of Gernon Road, Letchworth, appeared in court charged with being drunk and disorderly, and obstructing the ticket collector at Hitchin station.

He and his friends had frightened some passengers and, when thrown off the train, rushed at the carriages again. A policeman had to be called but when he tried to arrest the drunken party, the others ran off. The story was headlined "Another scene at Hitchin station."

The question of a licence for Letchworth would not die, but a referendum in 1907 won a clear vote for staying teetotal. Meanwhile the Skittles Inn, set up to provide gentle refreshment to the working man, was having its own problems.

"Some exhilaration has been derived from a nut brown barley beer which has been regarded as non-alcoholic," reported the Express, in July 1907.

It was rich and frothy, looked and smelt like beer and "titillated the nerves." But not everyone was convinced it was entirely innocent and it was ruthlessly banished, although later reintroduced.

A temperance cider remained banned, after excise officers suggested it was not as harmless as it appeared and may have been above two per cent in strength. The Drunkards' train looked set to roll on.

*The non alcoholic Skittles Inn, Nevells Road, Letchworth, is now the Settlement*

# Favourite Express-ions – 1913

✴ A "man of the road" made an eloquent appeal to Hitchin Board of Guardians in January, asking for his fare to Bedford. "I met with a misfortune on Friday and no human being can help misfortune," he told them.

"In consequence I am unable to walk as well as I can usually. I am anything but strong in my constitution. I am passing through on my way to Bedford to look for work, having lost all I had in a speculation.

"I have sustained two fractured ankles and have no ligament to bind them. Please take a merciful view of my case. Kind I have always been to the poor and I hope you will now be kind to me, my money having become exhausted."

He had a friend in Bedford who would help give him work, he explained. The guardians were unimpressed and refused. "Then I think I shall have to return to your house," he murmured sadly, referring to the workhouse.

✴ Hitchin Town Hall was turned into a Normandy fishing village in February, for a bazaar. Visitors could see half timbered "houses" with lattice windows and curious carvings, along with stone cottages, well furnished shops and a 16th Century chateau. At the end of the village was the sea shore. The effect was completed with tableau vivant.

✴ Marital problems came up in court early in the year. Lydia Hollis, a confectioner from Codicote, asked for a separation order from her husband Charles.

She said he was drunk, absconded with women, including one known as the Merry Widow, and had beaten her for years. He had even threatened to kill her.

Mr Justice Bucknill refused to consider evidence about misconduct as Hollis had never been seen in a compromising act but found the cruelty proved and granted the judicial separation.

*Old Park Road, pictured by the now-demolished Horse and Jockey Pub, between 1900 and 1920*

✷ Mr Edward Snow Fordham, of Ashwell, presiding at the West London police court, was not sympathetic to the plight of another wife with a drunken husband, who applied for a separation order at West London police court in March. Mr Snow Fordham lost all sympathy when he heard that the husband still kept his business going although he stayed out until 3am. "I cannot help you there," he told the unhappy wife. "Many men, I believe, stay out all night playing bridge but the law cannot correct that."

"I have a very unhappy life at home," complained the woman. Mr Snow Fordham was firm. "I dare say. Many married women are miserable, and all woman who are not married are miserable," he said.

✷ A strange case in Saffron Walden so intrigued the editor of the Express that he included the item although it was out of his area. It concerned a two-year-old girl who was in the care of the police there.

She had been handed to a guard by a young woman at Liverpool Street station, with a half ticket and a label pinned to her clothing. The woman asked the guard to put the little girl out at Audley End, where she would be collected.

He did as he was asked, but there was no one to take the child away. When the station closed, Porter Fitness (who had five children of his own) took the girl to his wife, who looked after her for the night.

In the morning there was still no sign of anyone asking for the child, so the porter cycled over to the address on the label, where he had to wait till nightfall for the lady of the house to return.

It was a wasted journey, she announced firmly that she would have nothing to do with the girl, and the porter was forced to return to the station with the child still in tow. The station master took the child to the police and she was being cared for in the workhouse. A lady had offered to adopt her but there was no explanation for her plight.

✷ The Cock Inn, Hitchin, spearheaded a move into the modern age by becoming the first hotel in Hitchin to hire out a car. The "very fine landaulette" held five passengers and was upholstered in deep crimson with thin white stripes. Mr Alfred Doughty, proprietor of the Cock, said he had no intention of reducing his stable of open horse-drawn carriages but he had acquired the car for speedier journeys.

✷ Hertfordshire police officers were celebrating after being granted one day off in 14. But there was a little grumbling over one superintendent's order that any policeman leaving his house should not only say he was going out but where and why. Another officer caused widespread merriment when he resigned – because he was afraid of the dark.

✷ Letchworth held an Esperanto lantern lecture in March and Baldock announced the building of a cinematagraph theatre for 800 people. Hitchin's NSPCC met with the motto: "Every child has a right to an endurable life."

✷ In June there was a serious accident when the brakes failed on an an omnibus travelling between Hitchin and Luton. "The vehicle proceeded at an alarming rate down the hill and the occupants, consisting mainly of ladies, became considerably excited."

The conductor urged people to jump and a couple of men did so, injuring themselves quite badly in the process. The ladies, surrendering themselves to the driver, fared better as he "remained pluckily at his post and eventually brought the vehicle to a standstill."

✷ A former prison governor at St Albans was convicted of burglary at a house where he was employed to water the plants. Henry Wood told the police court at Marylebone that he was very ashamed.

"I was hard up. My child was dead and my wife was ill."

He had only been a few months away from getting a pension at St Albans prison when he committed "an indiscretion" and was sentenced to three years' penal servitude. His wife had lost her reason and he found she had built up numerous debts. His plight failed to move the magistrates, who gave him six months' hard labour. The "indiscretion" was apparently embezzling £250 from the Prison Commissioners in 1906.

✷ The Rev E Tallents of St Mary's Church in Hitchin decided to deliver a sermon on the subject of holidays in August. Overall he thought them a good thing but he was full of dire warnings.

People often showed their worse self on holidays, he said, and this could create serious problems – spiritual degradation of young people, disgusting familiarity between the sexes, disregard for decency and self respect, outrage of public modesty, foul language, intemperance and – goodness – an impudent swagger. The awful pity of it! The vicar added, just in passing, that he regretted that there was so little love of poetry among the population at the present time.

He would no doubt have appreciated the work of a poet from Gravenhurst who rose to prominence, not surprisingly with verses such as:

*"The gin shops they will all be closed,*
*But they'll burst themselves with tea."*

Another gem ran:

*"Blessed little rain drops,*
*Falling all the day;*
*Come and fill the water butts,*
*For our washing day."*

★ An increase in lunacy was attributed by experts to the growing stress of modern business life.

★ A terrible bus smash at Amwell led to the deaths of four men and 26 injured. They were returning in the evening from a works outing at Cambridge when the driver swerved to avoid a young girl on a bicycle and the coach overturned. The passengers were flung to the ground.

In the dark the less seriously injured were stumbling about trying to help their friends, many of whom were unconscious. Others were moaning and sobbing. The Express reported:

*"Cyclists were the first to carry the news to Ware and Hoddesdon and when the doctors and conveyances began to arrive they were faced with a distressing spectacle.*
*"A few candles had been obtained from outlying cottages and by the aid of the flickering light men suffering from severe wounds in their heads and arms were trying to assist those more seriously injured than themselves."*

The rescuers commandeered any vehicle they could to carry the injured to hospital, including an ice cart and private cars. News of the accident reached Waltham Cross, where the men lived, and anxious wives and families remained in the streets until the early hours of the morning.

★ There was a move to extend Sunday trading in Letchworth but not everyone was in favour. One businessman wrote in protest to the Express:

*"I think it is an unfair business competition and desecration of the Sabbath and should be dealt with by the strongest means and ways in our power."*

Who could need to go shopping on a Sunday, he asked rhetorically, but some persons who are so busy:

*"On Saturday evenings either listening to or expounding a lot of high flown Socialistic ideas that they are unable to get their shopping done."*

★ Was Phoebe Harvey fit to care for children? That was the question Biggleswade magistrates had to consider in October when she was charged with cruelty to a six-year-old boy and wilfully neglecting a girl of 11.

Mrs Harvey, a 50 year old with a laundry business in Arlesey, supplemented her income in the summer by taking in children from London.

In August 1913 she had 12 in her house, with eight sleeping in one room and four in another. She was accused of thrashing a boy with a horse whip but, despite claiming another child had done it, she was convicted and fined.

The neglect case concerned Florence Green, who was sent to Mrs Harvey because the country air would be good for her weak heart. She stayed for eight months, being used, said the prosecution, as a drudge. When she returned home her hair was so matted and thick with lice it could not be combed and had to be cut off. She was covered in sores that ran down her head, neck and back.

The magistrates, after hearing very conflicting evidence, decided there had been neglect but not enough to convict.

The chairman, Sir John Burgoyne, said he hoped the press would see that the case was reported in London so that no more children would be sent to Mrs Harvey who was "perfectly unfit to conduct a house of that sort."

★ Paranoia about the white slave traffic gripped Letchworth in the autumn, following reports of a phantom motor car and a female agent of the trade with a commanding appearance and ingratiating manner.

The woman was supposed to be scouring Letchworth looking for prepossessing girls of 16 to 18 years old "whom she has entertained with lavish hospitality" at her new garden city home.

The Express reporting staff decided to investigate the rumours, scouring estate agents and talking to a wide range of citizens. They drew a total blank, even from the Vigilance Committee.

The story might have been false but it was salutary, they concluded.

If it brought home to parents and guardians (and girls) the necessity for watchfulness and the straight line in moral matters, the panic would not have been in vain.

✴ The shortage of suitable accommodation for labourers was still causing problems. The Marquis of Salisbury gave a speech saying that, although homes should be built to certain standards, the price could be kept down by not giving families things they didn't want, such as bathrooms and a parlour in addition to a kitchen.

A leading Liberal campaigner Harold Spencer thought this a niggardly viewpoint, replying:

*"I really do not think God would like us any better if we got up there unwashed."*

He had nothing but contempt for a working man who didn't want a bath and a parlour, he declared. "When housing was put on a proper level, houses would not be built for any man, either duke or workman, without a bath."

The shortage of rural cottages was being made worse by rich folk buying up two, knocking them together, and using them for weekends. Clerks were also living further from their work now they could travel to their jobs on a bicycle.

Fabian Mrs Pember Reeves was concerned with the plight of the poor, pointing out that most children never saw milk and that many poor babies weighed less than 14lbs when they were a year old.

*"No wonder the children suffer from malnutrition – a clever word (instead of starvation) carrying with it the false implication that ignorance on the parents' part was responsible. The conditions under which the poor live are horrible and overwhelming."*

✴ The year ended with a consideration of what presents would be suitable for Christmas. The debutante could always be given a dainty little fan of lace sewn with gold and silver spangles. An odd novelty recommended by the Express was a pair of sugar tongs in the form of a Dutch doll, with the straight legs acting as the tongs.

Men, as much of a headache in 1913 as they are now, would be pleased with a new can for their shaving water or something to furnish their den, such as a down cushion.

It must not be covered in some delicate brocade but in serviceable tapestry or even leather.

The Express went on to suggest:

*"A good idea is a contrivance which holds the newspaper up in position so that it may be easily scanned while breakfast is being eaten."*

*Bancroft junction with High Street, pictured between 1899 and 1923.*

# God punishes Man with *Titanic* disaster

North Herts is almost as far from the sea as any place in England. But land locked and parochial as it was, the news of the sinking of the *Titanic* in April 1912 shook residents to their core.

No one could believe the scale of the tragedy. The Express reported: "The Great White Star liner *Titanic*, hailed not many days ago as the greatest, safest, staunchest and most luxurious ship that ever took to the water, collided with an iceberg in the darkness of Sunday night when off the dread Newfoundland banks and sank less than four hours later taking with her 'to sleep in the noiseless bed of rest' some 1,500 of her passengers and crew."

But even in the midst of the terrible news, the patriotic spirit was stirred. "A thrill of pride touches even the wounded heart, when reading down the too short list of survivors one realises the meaning of the fact that they are nearly all women and children. As the Prime Minister said in his impressive reference to the catastrophe in the House of Commons, the finest traditions of the sea have been preserved.

"Our duty now is to join in the expressions of sympathy which are echoing through the world over the storm-swept graves of the helpless voyagers who have gone down with the stricken leviathan. The English and American people gather in spirit united by a common grief."

*Water caused a smaller disaster for residents when Bridge Street flooded in 1912*

Every church offered prayers and hymns to the dead on the Sunday after the news broke and the pulpits echoed with varied attempts to make sense of the tragedy.

Some vicars were not as charitable as others. The Rev J Williams of St Saviour's in Hitchin didn't think the disaster was "mere fate and destiny. It was not just a huge and regrettable accident."

No, God was speaking to a world which had pushed him into the background, taking from his hands all the blessings of modern science and engineering but grown too proud and self confident.

"By one swift stroke He has arrested the triumphal march of man as conqueror of sea and air. He has called a halt and made us think." It was not a judgment but a warning that man was going too far, believed the Rev Williams.

Pastor J Harris at Tilehouse Street Baptist Church dwelt more on the nobility of the dead. "I cannot think without a thrill of the quiet dauntless heroism of men who in that supreme crisis obeyed orders with perfect discipline and made the safety of the weakest their first care.

*"Who that saw the mammoth vessel proudly sail from Southampton on her maiden voyage amid the cheers of a great host of onlookers, could have imagined that within a few days she would be lying in the depths of the Atlantic Ocean, carrying down with her lives more precious than all the ships of the fleet?"*

Rev R Jackson at the Free Church in Letchworth gave an eloquent and striking address on: "The impartial, democratic death that had claimed millionaires and poor men alike. Two miles below the passionless waters the great liner lay, a gigantic coffin. A great hush had fallen upon their noisy politics, their business activities and human cries. It was like a rending of the veil of eternity."

There was no sympathy however from Mr Bruce Wallace, speaking at the Howard Hall Worship meeting. The *Titanic*: "Was obviously built for the indulgence of members of the class that must carry their luxuries with them," he thundered.

*"The palm garden, the swimming bath and the promenade were not for all the passengers of the best ship ever made. All had been devised for boundless self indulgence.*

*"They had thought they were safe – that they had bought all that wealth could give of science, luxury and safety. But a voice said: 'This night your soul is required of you! And all the mass of science and skill went out with them."*

There was a silver lining, however. "The poor bodies have gone down but the souls have fallen into the boundless sea of God's grace," he stated magnanimously.

The people of North Herts were more generous than Mr Wallace. They responded with enthusiasm to helping the disaster fund, staging concerts, football matches and other activities to help the survivors and the families of the dead.

In May the Express reported that some people were now so afraid to sail across the Atlantic that a method was being devised to get to America by railway. The paper thought it "surely most impractical."

It involved sinking a tunnel under the Bering Straits, which connect Alaska to Russia, at a cost (in 1912 terms) of £50million. A railway line would then be laid across 4,000 miles of swamp in Arctic Siberia, which could only be crossed when it was frozen.

The journey from England to New York would take six weeks: "With the off chance of death from cold or starvation during the last third of the journey." Every summer the railway line would sink into the Siberian swamp and need to be rebuilt.

Not surprisingly the idea didn't catch on.

Visitors to a lecture at Hitchin in November, 1907, would have already been familiar with the principle. Harry de Windt described his 18-month overland journey from Paris to New York, which cost him £11,000 and almost ended his life.

He assured the audience that no-one had ever done the journey before and it was unlikely to be accomplished again. After he described the thousands of miles travelled at 78 degrees below zero, the 80 dead dogs, and the general exhaustion and distress involved, they could only agree.

*"There was no silence like the silence of the Siberian wilds. The Arctic silence was nothing to it. It was awful; it pressed down on one's brain and sent people mad."*

# The patient no-one cared about

Nobody cared about the man with smallpox. The Board of Guardians were angry at the extra expense incurred. The caretaker at the isolation hospital was so scared he ran away. The doctor wanted his fees increased for visiting the patient and the contacts, who might be incubating the infection, were furious at being isolated in the house and watched all the time. It was a bad business all round.

The first hint of problems came with the news that a mother and two children had been diagnosed with smallpox, at Benson's Row, Biggleswade in the summer of 1902. An isolation camp was set up in a meadow, residents vaccinated and the Sunday school closed. The town reeked of disinfectant.

The patients, kept alone in a small hospital, responded well to treatment. Their rooms were sealed and watchers placed to make sure they did not attempt to leave.

Two weeks later another case of smallpox was reported, at Titmore Green. Hitchin Board of Guardians, with a stoical grimace, swung into action.

The sick man was taken to the isolation hospital at Langley. The old wagonette used to carry him there was left in the grounds.

As no nurse could be found who would agree to come, Dr Day, the medical officer of health, stayed at the hospital himself for the first night, only leaving at 1pm the next day when relief arrived.

*Women pictured strawplaiting at Titmore Green between 1880 and 1910*

The patient was very ill. As he drifted in and out of consciousness a flurry of activity centred on his bed, spreading across the area with expensive vigour and efficiency.

A replacement had to be found for the cowardly caretaker, who had broken his contract when he ran away. Mr Hawkins was appointed to act as a go-between, carrying messages from the hospital to the town "in cases of great urgency only" and a tent was put up for him to live in.

Nurses were found at the huge fee of three guineas a week. Like Mr Hawkins, they were revaccinated. Hitchin tradesmen arranged to call with goods and leave them to be collected by Mr Hawkins when they had gone.

Mr Underwood, the sick man, had shared a house with two other men from Pirton. Fortunately for them they had been away for a few days before he fell ill, but his father and brother had to be put into quarantine. They were allowed to stay in their home but watched for 16 days by men who stayed outside, until it was calculated there was no chance of infection.

The watchers were paid six shillings a day but were baking in the hot sun and asked the guardians for some kind of covering.

Dr Tarbet was now attending Mr Underwood at the isolation hospital and sent word to the board of guardians that he was not happy with the scale of fees. He could not see other patients while he was visiting the isolation hospital so often, he declared.

*"When he considered the distance to be travelled, the risk of infection, the professional ability to be exercised and the fact that as a precaution he had renounced the rest of his work, 7/6d must seem inadequate."*

The guardians were lucky – Mr Underwood recovered and there were no more cases of infection. At the end of August they counted the cost of this one small outbreak of Britain's most feared disease.

The nurses had been paid £30 12 shillings and guarding the contacts had added another £15. There were bills for two suits – Mr Underwood's, which had been destroyed and Nurse Turner's, ruined by disinfectant. The total costs of caring for Mr Underwood came to £80.

Dr Tarbet's plea for extra money was rejected – the doctors had agreed the fees themselves, after all, and the guardians didn't think he needed to stop seeing other patients during the outbreak.

Poor Mr Hawkins came out of the experience very badly. He caught pneumonia, had to be replaced by a woman, and was still seriously ill when Mr Underwood was settled back in his home, a well man again.

Sickness preoccupied the Edwardian age. Noxious smells were a constant problem, with farmers pulling manure through the streets and slaughterhouses in every town.

Dr Day, Hitchin Medical Officer of Health, reported on March 2, 1901, that pauper sickness had been very great in the first part of the year and there had been 30 notifiable cases of diptheria, croup, scarlet fever, enterics and erysipelas.

Only 220 babies had been born in Hitchin, the lowest number on record, and there had been 157 deaths including 10 from whooping cough, two from diarrhoea, 15 from TB and four from influenza. The deaths included 38 babies under a year old and 17 children between one and five.

Three children in Whitwell caught diptheria from standing over "some very foul drains which were being unblocked."

In Hexton villagers "derived their drinking water from dipping holes in the course of a roadside ditch" and in Breachwood Green rain water collected in underground tanks poisoned about 60 people. Eight died of dysentery and only those who boiled their water escaped.

In Pirton the school had been closed for six weeks following an outbreak of scarlet fever. The Medical Officer of Health's report was scathing:

"The epidemic was mild in character and much difficulty was experienced in checking its spread on account of gross carelessness of many parents, and it was only by threats of legal action that obedience to directions could be enforced," he said.

One local man had caught typhoid from London manure (decomposing waste from butchers) that he was taking in his cart:

*"The smell of which he described as very offensive."*

The situation did not improve and the compassionate Dr Day worried endlessly about the poor and their plight. In 1904 he reported on the housing situation, saying: "Many parts of the district contain much wretched cottage property which must soon be dealt with.

"There is a great dearth of cottages for a man earning 12 shillings to 15 shillings a week, especially if he has a large family."

# Dates and details to decode the Edwardian age

**1901:** Boer War was continuing (started 1899) as Britain tried to gain control of the Transvaal and Orange Free State. Tories in power after winning 1900 khaki election.
Population of Britain, 37million.
January 22: Queen Victoria died and Edward VII became King.
**1902:** May, end of Boer War, leaving 40,000 dead and large rise in income tax to pay costs.
Education Act abolished elected school boards and brought schools under county control, including voluntary church schools. It led to protests and partial non-payment of rates by protesters, especially non-conformists.
**1903**: First Garden City set up in Letchworth.
Joseph Chamberlain split the Tory party with his policy of trade tariffs rather than free trade.
Anxiety began over German military intentions and rearmament.
**1904:** France and Britain agree an entente cordiale to settle outstanding colonial disputes.
**1905:** Foundation of Sinn Fein.
WSPU began policy of agitation and heckling at public meetings.
**1906:** Landslide Liberal election victory. They stayed in office until the outbreak of war in 1914, with two elections in 1910 and 1911, introducing a wide range of social measures which required finance to be raised in new ways – it was the start of a redistribution of wealth.
**1907:** Unearned income taxed at higher rate than earned.
Probation introduced at courts.
Boy Scout movement started.
**1908**: Lloyd George appointed Chancellor of the Exchequer. Old age pensions introduced for people over 70 on a means-tested basis.
Increasing friction with workers and strikes eg in cotton, engineering and shipbuilding industries.
**1909:** Lloyd George's People's Budget rejected by Lords, leading to long parliamentary crisis.
Labour exchanges set up.
Rearmament continued to be a major issue as German power grew leading to the call for more dreadnought battleships.
Indians were allowed to take part in provincial councils in India, the first step towards regaining control of their own country.
**1910:** Edward VII died in May to be succeeded by George V.
**1911:** National Insurance Act gave sickness and unemployment cover for workers.
Payment for MPs.
Population reaches 40.9million.
Parliament Bill introduced to reduce power of the Lords.
A series of strikes lasting until the 1914 war brought civil unrest eg London dockers and printers.
Prospect of war with Germany looks increasingly likely.
Half-day for shop workers introduced.
**1912:** The government announces Home Rule Bill for Ireland, bitterly opposed by Unionists.
Miners strike followed by a dockers strike.
**1913:** Home rule Bill was thrown out by the Lords in January and again in July.
**1914:** Violent disagreement over the Home Rule Bill for Ireland led to violent clashes between Protestants and Catholics with a threat of civil war.
Miners and railway and transport workers form the Triple Alliance.
August 1914: First World War declared.

*Hitchin High Street at the turn of the century, preoccupied with its own concerns and with limited interest in national issues*

# Countdown to Women Winning the Vote

**1832:** First Reform Act gave vote to many middle class men but, for the first time, excluded women by describing a voter as a "male person."

**1867:** Second Reform Act gave the vote to about 2.5 million men – about a tenth of the total population. MP John Stuart Mill spoke up in favour of women's suffrage in Parliament

**1884:** Third Reform Act extended the vote to about five million men, almost two thirds of adult males. The poorest, many servants, criminals and lunatics were excluded.

**1897:** National Union of Women's Suffrage Societies founded. It waged a generally law-abiding campaign and supporters were often known as suffragists.

**1903:** Mrs Pankhurst founded the Women's Social and Political Union, known as the WSPU. Members became increasingly militant.

**1905:** Liberals won a landslide election victory and many women hoped they would introduce votes for women.

**October 1905:** Christobel Pankhurst and Annie Kenney of the WSPU were arrested for protesting at a Liberal meeting and sent to prison.

**1906:** The Daily Mail coined the term suffragette to describe militant women campaigners for the vote.

**1907:** NUWSS organised the first London procession with more than 3,000 women attending.

**1908:** The National League for Opposing Women's Suffrage was founded.

**Spring 1908:** The WSPU adopted its purple, white and green trademark colours – purple for dignity, white for purity and green for fertility and hope.

**April 1908:** PM Sir Henry Campbell Bannerman died and Herbert Asquith took his place. He was totally opposed to votes for women.

**June 1908:** More than 10,000 women took part in a NUWSS march.

A week later the WSPU held a Women's Sunday in Hyde Park, attracting at least 250,000 to a demonstration, dressed in purple, white and green. Shortly afterwards a demonstration in Parliament Square was attended by 5,000 police, who were accused of brutality to the women. Twenty-seven were arrested and sent to prison.

**Summer 1908:** The suffragettes increased their profile and their activities as their frustration grew at the lack of progress.

**October 1908:** 60,000 people converged on Parliament Square for a rush – to try and enter the House of Commons. Twenty-four women and 13 men were arrested and 10 protesters needed hospital treatment. Mrs Pankhurst, Christobel and Flora Drummond were sent to prison.

**June 1909:** 108 women were arrested and 14 window smashers were sent to Holloway during an attempt to talk to Asquith.

The women went on hunger strike, asking for political status, and the Government ordered them to be force fed.

**1910:** The Conciliation Bill led to a truce from the WSPU while it was going through. It was hoped it would lead to votes for women but as the year progressed these hopes fades.

**November 1910:** Black Friday demonstration ended in a pitched battle with more than 150 women injured.

**1911:** For much of the year the truce was renewed. The WSPU organised a peaceful women's Coronation procession in June, featuring more than 1,000 banners.

**November 21, 1911:** The WSPU lost faith in the Conciliation Bill and attacked commercial property for the first time. More than 200 women were arrested.

**1912:** New Reform Bill was postponed. The window smashing campaign was increased.

Mass hunger strikes among women prisoners.

**1913-1914:** Violence increased. Greenhouses at Kew Gardens were attacked, chemicals poured into letter boxes and Lloyd George's home was bombed, along with other homes and public buildings.

The Cat and Mouse measure was introduced to stop criticism over force feeding, Women were released on special licence when they were weak and rearrested as they got stronger.

**June 4, 1913:** Emily Wilding Davison threw herself in front of the King's horse and died. The funeral was attended by 2,000 people.

**June-July 1913:** NUWSS organised a Women's Pilgrimage, a peaceful march to London where 50,000 met at Hyde Park.

**March 1, 1914:** Mary Richardson slashed the Rokeby Venus at the National Gallery. The Tate and Royal Academy were closed.

**August 1914:** War declared, women stopped campaigning. Millicent Garrett Fawcett of the NUWSS said: "Woman your country needs you. Let us show ourselves worthy of citizenship, whether our claim to it be recognised or not."

**February 1918:** Representation of the People Act. Women over the age of 30 were given the vote and women could stand as MPs.

**1928:** Women aged 21 and over got the vote on the same terms as men.

**1970:** the Equal Pay Act was introduced.

# Remember the bulldozers, dirt and hurt

*In August 1956 the Angel Inn, in Sun Street, Hitchin, was demolished within days of a structural survey revealing serious problems. The building, pictured above, was considered too expensive to repair. Henry VIII had stayed there in the 16th century and the inn was at least 500 years old.*

# Index

Page numbers in *italic* and **bold** refer to illustrations

Aberdeen Countess of, 136
Adam and Eve Alley, Hitchin, 103
Albone Dan, 28
Alderman, Richard, 153
Aldgate Street Railway Station, 93
Aldritt John, 159
Alexandra, Queen, 43
Alexis-Coventry, Lady, 58
All, Mark, 70
Allen, Robert and George, 167
Alverstone, Lord Ch Justice, 95, 97
Amalgamated Society of Railway Servants, 111
America, 64, 73, 150
Ampthill, 127
Amwell, 180
Angel Inn, Hitchin, **188**
Anti-Socialist Union, 167
Anti-Suffrage Union, 129
Arlesey, 21, 24, 28, *55* - *59*, 79, 100, 156, 180
Armstrong Mr A A, 150, 153
Army, 158, 159, 160, 162
Arnold Arthur, 98
Ashwell, 19, 41, *77*, 148, 179
Atkins, Ryland, 102
Aubrey, Mr, 58
Aubrey, Mr W B. 101
Australia, 72, 78, 166
Austria, 20
Automobile Club, N Herts, 85
Aylott Arthur, 48
Ayot St Lawrence, 71, 123
Ayot St Peter, 168
Ayres, George, 42

Bacon, Miss Gertrude, 120
Baden-Powell, Cln, 24, 136
Bakers and Confectioners Exhibition, 111
Baker Arthur, 176, R H, 31
Baldock, 19, 28, 32, *35*, 38, 40, 46, 50, 54, 71, 85, 86, 98, 99, 103, 106, 115, 118, 125, ***128***, 129, 145, 160, 161, 164, 176, 179
Baldock, Minnie, 121; Pc, 31
Balfour, Lady Betty, 124, 131
Bancroft, *6*, 10, 11, 31, ***34***, ***41***, *70*, 71, 115, 135, ***142***, 154, ***155***, ***164***, ***173***, ***181***
Barker, Elizabeth, 104
Barnardo, Dr, 69
Barnes, Sir Gorrell, 32
Barnes T W, 110
Barrett, Mr J, 86
Baylis, Mr, 114
Beard, Walter 103
Bearton Road, Hitchin, 115
Beaver, Mrs, 129
Bedford, 30, 36, 50, 55, 61, 88, 131, 167, 178
Bedford Prison, 72
Bedford Road, Hitchin, 69, 106, 115, ***150***

Bedfordshire, 100
Bedfordshire Imperial Yeomanry, 31
Bedfordshire Times, 57, 58
Beecham's Pills, 23
Beeton, Frederick, 91-97
Bell family, 170 - 174
Bellward, Mr and Fred, 31
Belmont, Battle, 21
Bendish, 105
Benington, 136
Benslow Lane, Hitchin, 32, 98, 119
Bertram, Julius, MP, 119, ***120***, 121, 122, 133, 134, 156
Biggen Lane, Hitchin, ***106***
Biggen The, Hitchin, ***155***
Biggleswade, 19, 22, 28, 31, 38, 57, 58, 74, 101, 102, 103, 104, 136, 141, 166, 167, 180, 184
Bile Beans, 87
Birch Sgt, 163, 167; Mr W, 85
Bird, Rev Vernon, 146
Birrell, Mrs, 89
Black, MP, 156
Black Horse Lane, Hitchin, 50
Blake, Harry, 123
Bloemfontein, 24
Blondin, 49
Blood A T, Hitchin Inspector of Nuisances, 39, 70, 71, 117
Blue Cross Temperance Brigade, 108, 110, 113, ***114***
Board of Guardians, 31, 53, 54, 114, 151, 153, 154, 155, 184
Boddy, Mary and Thomas, 31
Boer War, 21-28 (*21, 23, 26*) 143, 162, 186
Bowman, Pc, 171
Boys Grammar School, Hitchin, 111
Boxing Day, 25
Bradley, Mr, 113; William, 86
Brand Street, Hitchin, 19, ***46***, 108, ***109***, 115, ***156***
Brandon Frederick, 136
Breachwood Green, 185
Brett Walter, 159
Brice, Sgt, 43
Briden PC, 168
Bridge Street, Hitchin, ***53***, 90, 111, ***182***
British Queen, Meldreth, 80-83 (***81***)
Brixton Prison, 174
Brookers, 88, 90
Broom, Beds, 16, 116, 167
Brown, Ambrose, 40; Clarence, 79; Eliza, 115; George, 115; James, 71; Joseph, 115; Private, 22; Thomas, 36
Bryer Rev Clement, 145, 146
Bucklersbury, Hitchin, ***25***
Bucknill, Mr Justice, 174
Budd & Co, Hitchin, 90
Buffalo Bill, 53
Bulton Inspector, NSPCC, 115
Buntingford, 31, 108, 151, 154

Bunyan Baptist Church, 146
Bunyard, Miss Emily, 89
Burbridge, Martha, 55, 58, 59
Burke, Mr W E, 130
Burrows, Pc, 69
Burtons, Hitchin, 112
Bushey, 41
Butterworth A R, 167
Butts Close, Hitchin, 31, 44, 53
Bygrave, 164
Bygrave George, 57
Bysouth, Frederick, 123

Cabmen's shelter, Hitchin, ***38***
Cactus, 121
Cadwell, Hitchin, 55, 56
Cambridge, 47, 82, 84, 160
Canada, 42, 43, 52, 90, 100
Caplin, Mr J, 145
Carling, Fred ***163***, William, ***113***
Carpenter, George, 104
Castle, Miss, 18
Catchpole, George, 104
Cecil, Robert, MP, ***126***, 127, 130, 132
Cemetery Road, Hitchin, 69
Chalkdell, Hitchin, 18, 148, 149
Chalkley, Ann, 150
Chamberlain, Dc, 163
Chapman's Yard, Hitchin, ***10***
Charlton, ***13***, 18, ***157***
Chesterton GK, 100
Chiltern Road, Hitchin, 116
China, 65, 100, 110, 151
Christmas, 22, 23, 25, 70, 100, 104, 111, 113, 117, 154, 155, 181
Church Lads' Brigade, Hitchin, 27
Church of the Literal Obedience to the Sermon on the Mount, 144
Church of Jesus Christ, 144
Churchyard, Hitchin, ***1***, 10
Circus, 31, 53, 109, 110
Clark, Dr, 39; John, 31; Mary, 165; Pc, 163
Clay Pc, 163
Clifton, 22, 29
Clothall, 33, 34, 36, 69
Cock Hotel, Hitchin, ***11***, 12, 85, 179
Codicote, 24, 98, 114, 148, 153, 178
Colby, Mrs, 157
Cold Harbour, 41
Cole Frederick, 32, 33, 35;
Cole Sgt Major W, 87
Colney, Rev H, 130
Congregational Church, Hitchin, 145
Cook Mr, 53, 151, 153, 154
Corn Exchange, Hitchin, 118
Cotton Lt, 27
Craig, Gordon, 85; Martha, 111
Crawley, Florence and Violet, 105
Crimea, 87, 131
Crippen, Dr, 175, 176

Crosoer, Mr C, 120, 135, 165
Crowther family, 175, 176
Cutlack, Alfred, *80, 89, 90*

Dacre Road, Hitchin, 20
Dalley Lucy C, 119
Dalton, Mr, 153, 155
Daniell, Mr E and Edward, 136
Davies, Emily, 119
Day, Dr, Frontispiece, 10, 98, 184; George, 168, 169; Mr J, 88; Lavinia, 151; Thomas, 38
Deacon George, 30
de Havilland Lt, 160, 161
Delmé-Radcliffe, Francis, 103, 105, 115, *132,* 136, 176
Dering George, 49, 50
Derryle Law, 160
Despard, Mrs, 118
Digby, Captain John, 78
Dimmock Emily, William, 50
Doan James, *87,* 88
Doughty, Alfred, 179
Dressler Rev Paul, 69
Drummond Flora, 121, 187
Drunkards Train, 176, 177
Ducklands, Hitchin, 48
Dumb Creatures Xmas League, 117
Dunham James, 149
Dunstable, 22, 41
Dyer, Dr Sidney, 174

Economic Funeral company, 51
Edgeware, 103
Edward VII, 7, 19, 30, *42* 43-46, 52, 108, 186
Electricity, 71, 79
Elizabeth I, 9
Ellingham, Ellen, George, 166
Ellis Miss, 61; Mrs Arthur, 85; Percy, 54
Elliott, William, 152
Ely, 143
English Pc, 106
Ennion Dr Octavius, 82, 83
ESA factory, Stevenage, 130
Essex, 71, 98
Everett James, 146
Exchange Yard, Hitchin, 78, 113

Farrar William and family, 72-74
Farrow, Herbert, Marie, Alfred, 48
Faulkner, Mr T J, 165
Ffolliatt Rev F. 57, 58
Field, Henry, 106
Fillingham Rev Robert, 142-147
First World War, 112
Fitzjohn, Peter and Alfred, 32-35
Flanders, GC, 24, *89, 108*
Flappers Vote, 133, 134
Flinders Petrie, Professor, 111
Fordham Snow Edward, 19, 148, 149, 179; The Hon Mrs Ernest (Mary) 121, 128, 148
Foster, Mr; 57; Miss, *63*
Fowler, Mr and Mrs, 154
Fox Lt, 160, 161, *162*
Franklin, Albert, 116; Mr, 39

Friends Adult School, 111
Frome Wilkinson Rev, 121

Gainsford, Rev, 85, 113; Mrs, *113*
Gamlingay, 74
Garden City Freaks, *137*
Garden City Press, 119
Garley, Annie, 30
Garratt and Cannon, Hitchin, 10
Garratt, Leonard, 111
Gaskell Percival, 111
Gates, Miss, 148
Gatward Frederick, 104; John, *90*
Gawthorpe, Mary, 118, 122, 123
Gelbflaum, Rev Isidor, 39
George III. 72
George V, 45, 46, 160, 162, 186
German Hospital, Hitchin, *98, 99*
Gernon Robert, 122
Gibson, Pc, 116
Gilbertson, Mr J, 157
Gill, Mr, 171
Goimbault, Mr, 157
Goodwin, Arthur, 85; Tommy, 21
Gordon Mrs, 129
Gosling, Lt, 27
Graveley, 89, 104, 158, 159
Gravenhurst, 180
Graves, William, 55, 56, 57
Gray, Mrs, 88; Police Sgt, 115; William, 105
Grays Lane, Hitchin, *17*
Great North Road, 104
Great Northern Railway, 51, 55, 58, 59, 78, 91, 164
Green, Florence, 180
Greenhill, Frederick, 164
Greenwood, Nurse, 87
Grellet, Dr 57; M H R, 117; William, 13, 17, 40, 48, 103, 105
Griffiths, Canon, 147
Grundy Percival, 177
Guilden Morden, 19

Halsey, Arthur, 11
Hamilton Cpt, 158-162, 161
Hare, William Loftus, 111; William, Emma and Arthur, 48
Harley, Minnie, 30
Harmsworth, Mr, 78
Harris, Major, 25; Pastor J, 183
Harrison, Jack & T Fenwick, 68
Hart Pc, 104
Harvey, Phoebe, 180
Hatfield, 31, 39, 55, 78, 124, 136, 164
Hawkins and Co, Hitchin, 145
Hawkins, Mr, 185
Hayles, Mrs, 86
Henlow, 48, 154
Hepworth, Ella, 122
Hermitage Road, Hitchin, *173*
Hertford, 14, 18, 95, 97
Herts County Council, 52, 114
Hewitt, Edgar, 167
Hexton, 42, 142-147, 185
High Street, Hitchin, 12, *29, 49, 51, 131,* 163, *181, 186*

Highbury Road, Hitchin, 88
Highlander pub, Hitchin, *17*
Hill, Ralph, 48; Thomas, 140; William, 151
Hillier, Dr Alfred, 135
Hills, Clarence, 50; John, 50
Hine, NJ, 40; Reginald, *8,* 119
Hitchin Carriage Works, *90*
Hitchin Debating Society, 84, 117, 120, 135, 165
Hitchin Fire Brigade, 38, 39, 44, *52*
Hitchin Football Club, 109, 110
Hitchin Hill, *20,* 30, 38, 51, 69
Hitchin Hospital, 115, 157, *169,* 173
Hitchin Infirmary, 56, *150*
Hitchin Liberal Association, 122
Hitchin Market, 71, *166*
Hitchin Museum, 7
Hitchin Musical Society, 109, 111
Hitchin Post Office, 19, *156*
Hitchin Railway Station, 31, *38, 84, 94,* 95, 107, 160
Hitchin Soc of Arts & Letters, 111
Hitchin Swimming Pool, 100
Hitchin Total Abstinence Soc, 110
Hitchin Town Hall, 29, 39, 40, 48, 69, 108-111, 115, 116, 121, 122, 125, 146, 156
Hiz River, 136
Hoddesdon, 180
Holland Mr W, 117
Hollis, Scoutmaster, 136; Lydia, 58
Hollow Lane, Hitchin, *70*
Holloway Prison, 122, 124, 125
Holloway, Rachel, 50
Horse and Jockey, Hitchin, 178
Hoskins, Mr J, 86
Housden, Ebenezer, 146
Howard Ebenezer, 40, 130, 136, 175
Hugget, Mrs, 21
Hull Dr, 78
Hunt, AW, 108; James Terry, 32, 34, 35; Bruce, 35; James, 37
Hunt's Temperance Hotel, Hitchin, *34,* 35, 37
Hutchinson, Dr, 61

Ickleford, 41, 98, 104, 136
Ickleford Road, Hitchin, 112, 115
Impey, Elizabeth, 122, 124
Independent Labour Party, 99, 171
Innes Taylor, Mr RD, 29

Jackson, Rev R, 183
Jackson's Yard, 54
Jaggers Matilda, 69
Jalland Dorothy Josephine, 138-141
James Sgt, 163
Japan, 42, 53, bazaar *110*
Johnson, Arthur, 96; Miss, 111
Jones, Rev H E, 14, *16,* 18, 48, 99, 114, 153, 155; Mr and Mrs, 15, 18; William, 98
Jowitt Rev, 151

Kelley Mr, 41
Kennedy Bart, 149, 150
Kiddle Kate, 101, 102

Kimpton, 151
Kindersley, Guy, MP, *133*, 134
King, George, 105; Mary J, 14
King's Cross, 27, 108
Kings Road, Hitchin, 35, 88
Kings Walden Bury, 68
Knebworth, 27, 45, 128, 130, 132
Knebworth House, 124, 128
Knight, Pc 103; Police Sgt, 17
Knott, Walter, 104
Kryn and Lahy, *134*

Ladysmith, 22. 24
Lancaster Road, Hitchin, 48
Lane, Nellie, 101
Langford, Mr W F, 84, 117
Langley, 184
Latchmore, Arthur, 113, 114
Lawrence, Annie, 78; Mr Ogden 139
Lea, Pc, 164
Lee Mr, 78
Leggatt, Bertie, 53
Lessopps, James, 175, 176
Letchworth, 40, 46, 67, 70, 78, 91-97 *(97)* 100, 111, 114, 118, 122, 123, 125 -137, *(129, 134, 137)* 142, 150, 152, 153, 157-159, 167, 170-180 *(170, 175, 176, 177)* 183, 186
Lewin, Sophie, 48
Lilley, 36, 110, 167
Little Berkhamsted, 29
Live and Let Live, Pegsdon, 167
Livingstone Dr, 75
Lloyd George, 114, 122, 131, 186
Locke, Dorothy, Phoebe, 93
Lockleys, 49
Logsdon, Cpt Edwin, 38, *39*
London, 19, 24, 27, 31, 38, 40, 51, 78, 85, 92, 93, 99, 108, 109, 111, 147, 174, 185
Long, Robert, 157
Longstaff, Abigail, 58
Lord, Edward, 93
Lorna, 65, 66, 67, 122
Lovet, Fireman, 56, 57
Lucas, Miss May, 69; W Tindall, 105
Luton, 13, 15, 16, 18, 29, 30, 36, 39, 42, 51, 153, 157, 163, 164, 166, 179
Lygo Mr, 135
Lytton, Lady Constance, *124*, 125, 131; Lord Victor, 124. *125*

McClean, George, 73, 74
McClelland, Elspeth, 70
McConnell, Primrose, 54
McKay, 20
McKenna Reginald, Home Sec, 126
MacKenzie Rev, 75, 76
Macpherson Dr Robert, 115
Madden Rev A C, 39, 43
Mafeking, 24, 25, 38, 109, 136
Malkin, George, 39, 135
Manasomba, Chief, 75-77
Manley Mrs E, 88
Market Place, Hitchin, *7, 9, 12*, 19, 24, 27, *28, 30*, 42, 43, *44, 45, 79*, 85, 89, 90, 99, *112, 118*, 121, *123*,

129, *132*, 145, 163, 165
Marks Detective, 164
Marsh, Mabel, 32
Martel, Mrs Nellie, 122
Martin John, 56
Martindale, Mrs Rose, 51
Mary, Queen, 46
May Herbert, 104
Maylin Charles, 115, 116
Maynard Samuel, 103
Meekly, Miss, 129, 130
Melbourn 47, 80, 82
Melbourne, Australia, 51, 73
Meldreth, 80-83
Men's League for Woman's Suffrage, 125
Merchant C H, 88
Merrimac, 117
Messant, Charles, 145
Michael Maurice, 58
Midland Cottages, Hitchin, 85
Miles, Walter, 104
Millar William, 163
Millard, Henry & Rebecca, 167
Millbrook, 72
Miller, Irene, 120; J J W, 118
Modder River, 22, *23*, 24
Monk Alice, 30; Pte, 22
Moss, Cllr W B. 12; Edith, 47
Moulden, Henry George, *14*, 16, 159
Murphy, Mr, 15-18
Musgrave Arms, Hitchin, 25

National Union of Women's Suffrage Socs, 124, 127, 128, 133
New York, 37, 64, 122
Newmarket, 31, 70, 85
Newton, Mr F, 27, 39
Nicholls, Mr, 48
Nightingale Road, Hitchin, 69, 117, 173, *174*
North Beds, 156
Norton 50; Common, 54
Norton, Rev W, 68
Nott Bower, Mrs, 132
NSPCC, 115, 179
Nuns Close, Hitchin, 115
NYE spelling, 165

Odell, Beatrice, 30
Oldfield, Josiah, 117
Offley, *13*, 16, 27, 74, 163
Offley Hill, 27, 157
Ohlson Reginald, 177
Old Age Pensions, 150, 151
Old Park Road, Hitchin, 98, 115, *178*
Oldfield, Josiah, 117
Olive, 23, 24, 26, 43, 60-65
Olley G A, 85
Orange River Hospital, *21*
Otter houndsmen, 71

Page, Alice, 105
Pallett, Alice & Frederick, 106
Pankhurst, Christobel, 120, 122, 187; Emily, 118, 119, 120, 122, 133,

187
Paris, 49, 62, 90, 107
Park Street, Hitchin, 90, 115
Parker, Albert, 171-173; Alfred & Frederick, 104; Mrs Barry, 128
Pass, Mrs, 18
Paternoster & Hales, 42
Pauling George, 68
Payne, C, 105
Paynes Park, Hitchin, 42, *52, 54,* 69
Peace, Rachael, 126
Pear Supt, 168
Pease, Mrs J A, 121
Pegsdon, *40,* 167
Pember Reeves, Mrs, 181
Pepper, Thomas, 55, 56, 58
Periera Nurse, 85
Perks & Llewellyn, Hitchin, *51, 105*
Pestell, family, 103
Peterborough, 51, 57, 93
Pethick-Lawrence, Emily, 118, 126
Philanthropist, 156
Phillimore Mr Justice, 83
Pilgrims March, 129, 130
Pirton, 20, 40, 78, 84, 106, 121, 185
Pirton Road, Hitchin, 163
Playhouse, Hitchin, *112*
Porter, Henry, *38*
Potton, 108, 138-141 *(138)*
Prater, Mr, 92, 148
Press Association, 27
Preston, 48
Primitive Methodist Church, 146
Primmett, Frederick, 168, 169
Prince, Alfred, 171
Prior Dr John, 105
Priory, Hitchin, 103, 105, 136
Procter Rev Lowell J, 75-77
Protestant Alliance, 145
Pryor, Alfred, 106
Puckeridge, 108
Purser, Mrs, 22
Purwell, Hitchin, 110

Queen Street, Hitchin, 10, 31, *53,* 70, 71, *100,* 110, 115, 135, 152

Rabley Heath, 78
Radcliffe Road, Hitchin, 123
Radlett, 10
Radwell, 75-77
Ransom family, 11, *32,* 38, 116, *169*
Reed, Supt, 171-173
Rennie, James, 166, 167
Renwick, G H B, 15, 18
Reynolds, Peter, 40; Sir Arthur J, 37, 165; Supt John, *103,* 105
Richardson, Alfred, 165; Mary, 126, 187
Ripley, E & Sons, 31
Rodgers family, 80-83 *(80, 81)*
Rowley, Miss, 89
Royston, 19, 24, 29, 50, 103, 149, 164
Rudge Whitworth bike, 85, *89*
Russell's Slip, Hitchin, *18*
Russell's Tannery, Hitchin, *135*

St Albans, 18, 30, 71, 99, 115, 144, 146, 152, 179
St Andrew's St, Hitchin, 10, 105, 115
St Mary's Church, Hitchin, 14, 19, 43, 85, 99, 156, 165, 179; School, 20, 50
St Saviour's Church, Hitchin, 59, 85, 159 - *161*, 183; School, 159; Working Men's Club, 110
Salisbury, Marquis, 124, 181
Salt, Emily & Walter, 106
Salusbury,-Hughes, Mr, 105
Sanders R E, **90,** *107*
Sandy, 21, 105
Sartoris, Mr & Mrs, 101
Saunders, John, 157
Scott House, Hitchin, 154
Scott, William, 31
See, Fred, 28
Seebohm family, 45
Sharman, P A, 85
Sharpe, Samuel, 52
Sharpe, Charles, 29
Shaw, Alan, 173; Bertram, 50; George Bernard, 71, 123
Shefford, 167
Shepherd, Walter, 29
Shillington, 85, 106
Shillitoe, Francis, 16, 57; Richard, 100
Short, Jane, 125, 126
Shuttleworth, Cln and Mrs, 31
Silsby, William, 22
Silsoe, 104
Simkins, Annie, 106
Simmonds, Alice, 105
Simpson, Jane, 101
Sisserman, Charles, 104
Skittles Inn, Letchworth, *176, 177*
Skynners Almshouses, Hitchin, *155*
Sloan, Mr, 146
Smith Bosanquet, G, 115
Smith, Charles, 152; George, 56, 58; Henry, 170-174; Mr & Mrs, 35; Robert, 167; Seth, 117; Walter, 163; W H, 91
Smithson, Sarah, 119
Smythe, Dr Ethel, 128
Solomon, Miss, 116
Somerset, Lady Henry, 37
South Africa, 21-26, 162
Spectator, 30, 52, 53, 61
Spicer, Mrs, 105
Spirella Co, 136; Dancers, *67*
Spriggs, Insp, 106
Spurrs, Hitchin, 85, 89, 90, 117
Squibb, Rev George Meyler, 69
Stapleton, Jesse, Lydia, 48
Starlings Bridge, Hitchin, 163
Startup, Ernest, 106
Steggles, Mr & Mrs, 20
Sterry, David, SPCC, 103
Stevenage, 21, 24, 35, 38-40 **(37)** 42, 43, 45, 53, 54, 68-71, 84, 85, 88, 100, 103, 104, 118, 119, 128, 130, 131, 133, 146
Stevens, Mrs, 29; Thomas, 85

Stimson, Charles, 102
Stockall, Thomas, 93-97
Stokes family, 175
Stone, Elizabeth & Helen, 114
Stone gatherer, *68*
Stotfold, 43, 157
Stotfold Road, Hitchin, 167
Stratton, Daisy, 103
Stride, Mr. 114
Strothy, Miss, 43
Stuart Lt Wyness, 158 - 160, 162
Stuart Mill, John, 119
Suffragettes, 118-134 *(121)* 167
The Sun Hotel, Hitchin, 12, 20, 43, 47, 56, 89, 111, *116,* 123,
Sun Street, Hitchin, 42, *43, 47,* 69, 89, 90, *116, 188*
Swinburne, Algernon, 123
Sworder, Dr, 39
Sylvia, 66

Tallents, Rev E F, 165, 179
Tarbet Dr, 185
Taylor, Mrs 130
Temple Farm, Preston, 48
Terry, Ellen, 85
Thacker, William, 56
Therfield, 104
Thompson, Isaac, 19; Lucy, 58
Thornton, Thomas, 41
Thorpes Yard, Hitchin, *18, 152, 154*
Thraker, William, 56
Three Counties Asylum, 24, 28, 55, 115, 156, 167
Three Moorhens, Hitchin, 39
Thurley, Mrs, 80, 81
Tilehouse Street, Hitchin, *17,* 18, 74, 89, *108,* 119
Tilehouse Street Baptist Church, Hitchin, 183
Tilt, Rev J W, 155
Times, W O, 12, *54,* 69, 120
Titanic, 182, 183
Titmore Green, *184*
Tomlin, Annie and family, 13-18; Wilfred and Harold, 104
Tooley, Cpl W E, 25
Torr, Mr, 143
Total Abstinence Society, 100, 110
Trevor Road, Hitchin, 88
Trolley, John, 38
Tuam, Ireland, 147
Tuck, E G, 88
Turner, Nurse, 188; William, 103, 104

Underwood, Mr, 185; Tom, 103
Union Jack Working Boys' Club, 111
Union Path, Hitchin, 18
Unwin, Pc Thomas, 34, 69
Upper Stondon, 157
USA, 73, 143

Van Houten, 116
Verity, Edward, 18
Victoria, Queen, *19,* 20, 45, 61, 108, 186
Vincent, Pc, 101; Sgt, 167
Vosper Thomas, Rev Samuel and

Mabel, 32-37
Waddams, Miss, 111
Wagstaff family, 138-141
Wakes, Mar, 140
Walker, Frederica, 105; George, 104; John, 54
Walkern, 103, 104
Wallace, Bruce, 130, 183
Walsworth, 45, 116, 135
Walsworth Road, Hitchin, 39, 55, *59,* 71, *107,* 113, 157, 158, 160, 164
Walter, Phillip & Mrs, 56, 57
Ware, 34, 180
Warton, Jane, 125
Watford, 41, 42
Watson, Andrew, 116; Mrs, 17
Watton at Stone, 163
Watts, Mr B, 123
Welch, Mr, *56*
Wellbury House, 27
Welwyn, 36, 37, 49, 68, 78, 106, 128, 149, 168, 106
West Alley, Hitchin, 115, *149*
Westminster Abbey, 43, 46, 126
Weston, *49*
Westrope, Herbert, 19
Whaley, Mr, *63*
Whinbush Road, Hitchin, 122
Whiskin, Jane, 152
Whistler, 12
Whitbread, Samuel, 127, & Co, 177
White, Mr, 144
Whitwell, 25, 185
Whyley, Mr G, 166
Wilbury Hills, 160
Wild, Ernest, 95 - 97
Wildman, Henry, 20
Wilkinson, Miss, 128
Williams, Rev J, 183
Willian, 45, 118, 158-162, 176
Willoughby Osborne, Mary, 99
Wilson, John, 32, 35
Windmill Hill, Hitchin, 116
Woburn, 73, 167
Women's Realm, 65, 78, 122, 165
Wood, Arthur, 69; Henry, 179; Pc, 36; Robert, 51, Sgt, 169
Woodhouse, Simeon, 57
Woodley, Lily, 17
Woods, Annie, 47; Ed, 51; Samuel, 47
Woodside, Hitchin, 113
Workhouse, 18, 45, 47, 50, 54, 60, 92, 95, 100, 103, 104, 114, 115, 136, 148-155 *(148),* 178, 179
Workman's Hall, Hitchin, 111
Wratten Road, Hitchin, 106
Wright, J, 89; Mrs, 127
WSPU, 121, 124. 126, 127, 133, 186, 187
Wymondley,128, 162
Wymondley Road, Hitchin, 31

Yeoman, Mrs, 87
York Road, Hitchin, 146
Young, Rose, Margaret, 91-97

Zam-Buk, 87
Zeppelin, Count, 60

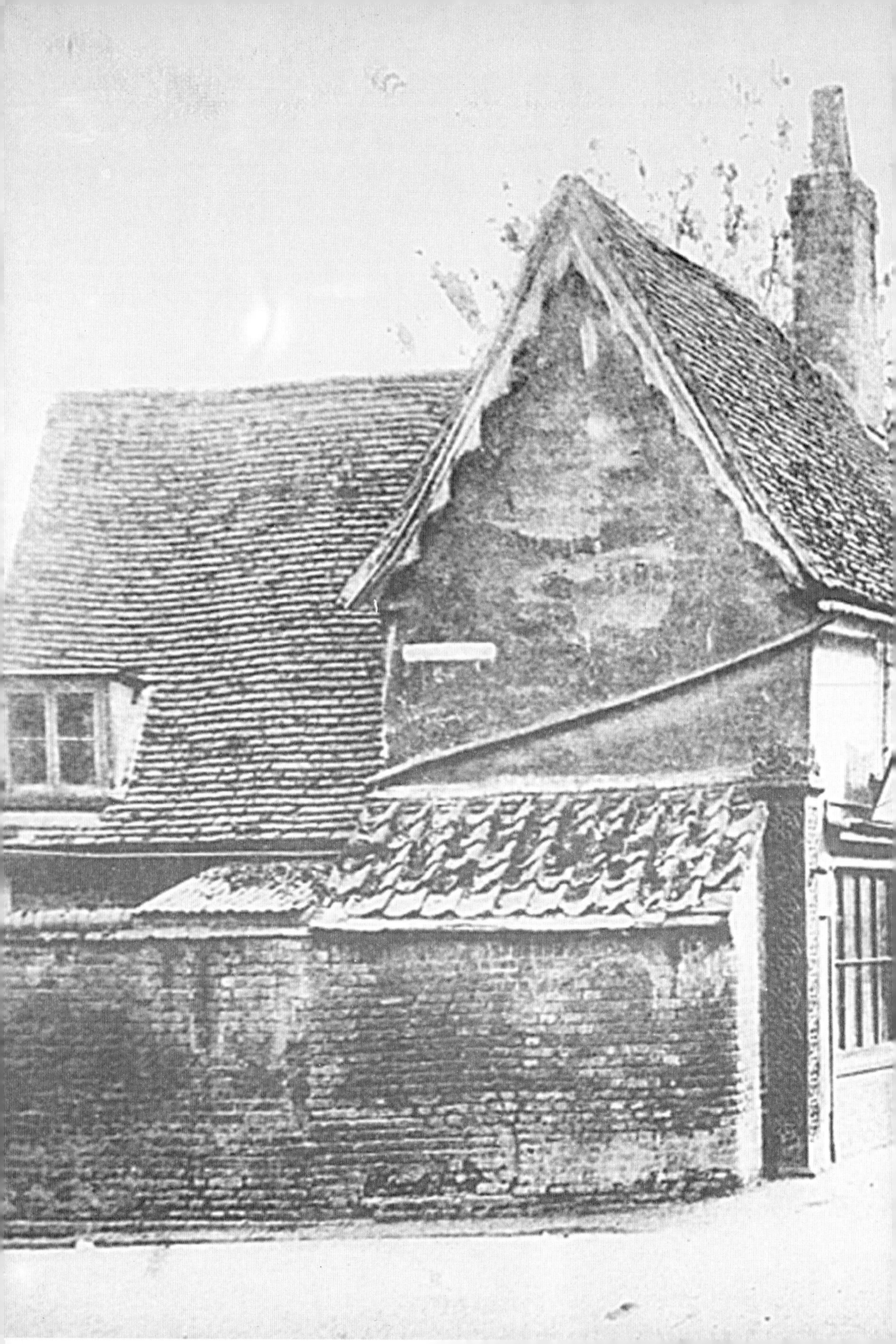